Winning Football

Bill Ramseyer

Winning Football

Bill Ramseyer

Human Kinetics

Library of Congress Cataloging-in-Publication Data

Ramseyer, Bill, 1936-
  Winning football / Bill Ramseyer.
    p. cm.
  ISBN-13: 978-0-7360-8695-0 (soft cover)
  ISBN-10: 0-7360-8695-1 (soft cover)
1. Football--Training. 2. Football--Coaching. I. Title.
  GV953.5.R36 2011
  796.33207--dc22

                              2010052858

  ISBN-10: 0-7360-8695-1 (print)
  ISBN-13: 978-0-7360-8695-0 (print)

The Web addresses cited in this text were current as of January 2011, unless otherwise noted.

Acquisitions Editor: Justin Klug; **Developmental Editor:** Cynthia McEntire; **Assistant Editor:** Elizabeth Evans; **Copyeditor:** John Wentworth; **Permission Manager:** Martha Gullo; **Graphic Designer:** Bob Reuther; **Graphic Artist:** Kim McFarland; **Cover Designer:** Keith Blomberg; **Photographer (cover):** © Human Kinetics; **Photographer (interior):** Neil Bernstein; **Photo Asset Manager:** Jason Allen; **Visual Production Assistant:** Joyce Brumfield; **Art Manager:** Kelly Hendren; **Associate Art Manager:** Alan L. Wilborn; **Illustrations:** © Human Kinetics; **Printer:** Sheridan Books

We thank Coach Bruce Wasem at the University of Virginia-Wise for assistance in providing the location for the photo shoot for this book.

Human Kinetics books are available at special discounts for bulk purchase. Special editions or book excerpts can also be created to specification. For details, contact the Special Sales Manager at Human Kinetics.

Printed in the United States of America   10 9 8 7 6 5 4 3 2 1

The paper in this book is certified under a sustainable forestry program.

Human Kinetics
Web site: www.HumanKinetics.com

United States: Human Kinetics
P.O. Box 5076
Champaign, IL 61825-5076
800-747-4457
e-mail: humank@hkusa.com

Canada: Human Kinetics
475 Devonshire Road Unit 100
Windsor, ON N8Y 2L5
800-465-7301 (in Canada only)
e-mail: info@hkcanada.com

Europe: Human Kinetics
107 Bradford Road
Stanningley
Leeds LS28 6AT, United Kingdom
+44 (0) 113 255 5665
e-mail: hk@hkeurope.com

Australia: Human Kinetics
57A Price Avenue
Lower Mitcham, South Australia 5062
08 8372 0999
e-mail: info@hkaustralia.com

New Zealand: Human Kinetics
P.O. Box 80
Torrens Park, South Australia 5062
0800 222 062
e-mail: info@hknewzealand.com

E4949

Contents

Key to Diagrams

○   Offensive player

●   Offensive player with ball

○ (dashed)   For presnap shifts, original position before motion (offense)

*○   Offensive player, possible position

//   Handoff/fake handoff

⊕   Center

⊣   Block

◐   Side of block

X or position abbreviation in dashed circle ((H))
For presnap shifts, original position before motion (defense)

——→   Run (solid line)

- - - ➤   Pass (dashed line)

∿∿∿   Presnap motion (jagged line)

↑ / ⊤   Optional routes (run and block)

QB	Quarterback	X	Defensive player
LHB	Left halfback	N	Nose tackle
RHB	Right halfback	T	Defensive tackle
FB	Fullback (R)	RT	Right defensive tackle
TB	Tailback (T)	LT	Left defensive tackle
RB	Running back	E	Defensive end
OG	Offensive guard	LE	Left defensive end
RG	Right guard	LB	Linebacker
LG	Left guard	M	Middle linebacker or Mike
OT	Offensive tackle	S	Strongside linebacker or Sam
RT	Right tackle	W	Weakside linebacker or Will
LT	Left tackle	CB	Cornerback
LE	Left end	S	Safety
RE	Right end	SS	Strong safety
Y	Tight end	FS	Free safety
R	Receiver	WS	Weakside safety
WR	Wide receiver (X, Z)	NB	Nickel back
K	Kicker	DB	Dime back
P	Punter	CO	Coach

1

Elements of Success

Success can be measured in many ways. If you are a coach, perhaps you measure success by the positive influence you have on the lives of the players you coach—the attitudes they build on and off the field, the percentage of players who graduate, the careers they enter, the relationships they develop. If you are a player, you might measure success by how hard you have worked to earn your achievements or by how much you are valued by your teammates. Many people measure coaching and playing success by the number of games or championships won or the number of winning seasons over a career. Obviously, as long as a score continues to be kept, winning will remain a vital part of success on the football field, but winning should never mean sacrificing other factors that determine achievement.

An athletic team that wants to compete consistently at the highest level must have an abundance of mental toughness. A main ingredient for producing toughness is discipline—individual discipline, team discipline, and self-discipline. In fact, the longer I coach, the more convinced I am that discipline is the most important factor in football. Yes, Xs and Os are vital, but it's the players who play the game, and you win with players who are consistent. How do you develop consistency, even under the most extreme adverse conditions? Through mental toughness. How do you develop mental toughness? Through discipline.

In discussing the importance of a disciplined team, I am not talking about rules. I am talking about the way your team responds to situations based on consistent positive habits. Discipline becomes a way of life, and that leads to success.

Discipline begins with the head coach. The head coach must be disciplined, and discipline must be an integral part of every assistant coach in order for discipline to be established in the team. If the team is expected to react with confidence, every coach must react to each situation, challenge, or crisis with confidence and positive energy. When discussing discipline, focus on what's important and factor out irrelevant distractions.

To be successful in football, you must develop the mind. In the coaching profession, we discover all kinds of equipment, books, and drills to develop and strengthen every muscle group of the body, but we do too little to train the most powerful area of the body—the mind. We should spend more time developing the mind than we do developing the biceps, hamstrings, and other major muscle groups. I firmly believe that if you can visualize something, you can achieve it; if you can see it, you can become it. I don't mean to imply that ability and personnel are not important; of course they are. But we have all seen upsets, games won by the squad with less ability. How do we explain this? The victorious underdog played better as a team, was more mentally prepared for the game, came closer to realizing its potential, or all of these.

A disciplined team plays each game with consistency and confidence. Disciplined play-ers perform in championship games as though they have been there before. They don't panic when they are behind in the final quarter. They play with poise. A disciplined team responds positively when they are the underdog, and they play with intensity when they are the overwhelming favorite. Players demonstrate consistency and confidence in their performance on the final drive of the game, when behind, or with the score tied. Simply put, a disciplined team remains focused under pressure during any given play, throughout a game, and from week to week over the course of a season. This becomes reality only when your team has attained a major dose of mental toughness, which is the ability to block out all distractions and focus only on the objective.

Philosophy

A program operates under the philosophy developed and preached by the coaching staff. This philosophy includes basic principles that guide the actions of the coaches. Each coach must completely buy into the philosophy and adhere to it.

Although there will be as many personalities as there are coaches and players, there must be only one philosophy for your football program. Your philosophy must be positive in every way. The philosophy described here has served me well in coaching and might serve as a foundation for developing your own philosophy.

1. Coaches will always totally support each other. All disagreements will occur behind closed doors and settled face to face by the coaches involved. Only regular coaching staff will attend any coaches' meeting. No coach will second guess another coach in any manner, either through words or facial expressions. Tactical ideas will always be presented in a spirit of constructive suggestion, never as a criticism of someone's else ideas. Each coach will examine his own areas for improvement rather than focusing on what he perceives to be someone else's inadequacies.

2. Coaches will be positive about and supportive of all players and promote that attitude in each player. At all times, including during games, any statements or attitudes will demonstrate confidence in all players and player groups (offense, defense, line, backs, etc.). There will be no negative statements, sarcasm, or cynicism. Coaches will not have pet players or players they are down on. Everyone will be treated fairly. Coaches evaluate players only for what they do on the practice and game field, not for any inadequacies they might otherwise have. Personnel is never discussed with other players unless the statement is positive. No statements that question commitment, guts, or the decisions of another player will be made in front of other players. Matters concerning players arriving late, violating the dress code, or committing other infractions will be handled privately by the head coach. Coaches always show poise, and they instill poise in their players. The head coach sets the pregame and halftime tone most effective for the situation, and this is the tone throughout the locker room. Coaches never lose sight of the fact that the players are the game. Each player will be treated with respect and as a team 50 to 0 and still feel respect for that opponent. We always prepare to win the game at hand. Coaches and players refrain from talking about future opponents. It's easier to focus on the current opponent and do a better job of coaching if the current opponent is the only one we talk about.

4. Coaches must be very emotional and totally enthusiastic about coaching but always in complete control of their emotions. The best coaching decisions can be made only when both feet are on the ground and the coach is thinking clearly.

5. Coaches coach the total player. We take players to their limits and saturate them with positive motivation as we work to develop total dominance on the football field. Xs and Os and technique are important, but we always strive to be the best at coaching the mind. Motivated players are successful players.

Communication and Leadership

If you are a coach, team captain, or a leader in some other respect, show your leadership by how you lead your life, through the example you set both on and off the field. If you are a head coach, you know that everyone else is watching you for indications of how to behave. If you are a team leader, you know that your attitude on the field is going to influence the rest of the team. Remember that communication and leadership are not limited to the words you speak. Your facial expressions and the way you listen also communicate and demonstrate your leadership. If you are a coach, when you say your door is always open, is it really? It might be physically open, but is the atmosphere conducive to players coming to you with questions, suggestions, and possible alternatives?

Great leaders demonstrate a strong work ethic, are approachable, enjoy what they do, and get others involved.

Demonstrate your coaching philosophy by being supportive of your players and inviting them to buy in to your system.

an individual. Correcting players will always be done in a positive manner. If a player thinks he can do it, has been told he can do it, and been reaffirmed that he can do it, he will do it. Players must be so well-schooled in fundamentals that they are free to execute at an emotional high without fear of making a mistake or being ridiculed. Inconsistent play is caused by mental, not physical, breakdowns. We constantly strive to improve our ability to coach the mental and emotional.

3. Coaches will be professional; they will be a credit to the coaching profession. There is no swearing or chewing tobacco around players. Coaches never get in verbal confrontations or say anything negative to any opposing coach or player. Coaches respect every opponent but are in awe of none. Coaches can't make statements, even among themselves, about beating

Exemplify a strong work ethic on the field and demand the same dedication from your players.

Demonstrate a Strong Work Ethic

You can't be a clock watcher and be successful. Make sure what you do is productive work, not just putting in time. But also be careful not to become a workaholic. Burnout is common in all vocations. You have to find the right mix of work and relaxation. I've seen too many coaches and athletes who thought that if working 8 hours a day, 5 days a week made them good, then working 16 hours a day, 7 days a week could make them great. Nothing is further from the truth. I've seen workaholics lose their marriages, experience breakdowns in communication with their families, and ultimately not like themselves. When on the field or in the office, work hard and efficiently, but always make time for your family and yourself.

Be Approachable

Create an environment that encourages players and coaches to come to you with problems and suggestions. Particularly if you are a coach or want to be one someday, you need to work on developing relationships in ways that make people *want* to come to you and involve you in what is going on in their lives, rather than feeling that they must go to you but don't really want to. Even if you are the head coach, remember that this is not *your* program—it is everyone's program. Make it clear that you feel you are there for your players or teammates, not that they are there for you.

Have Fun

Playing and coaching football should be fun. Players and coaches must enjoy doing what they are doing. Some people think that to have effective discipline you have to be serious 100 percent of the time and that you can never let your guard down. But the truth is, the more you let others see the human side of you, the more respect they'll have for you. Your players or teammates must know that you can have a good time and laugh, even at yourself, and not take yourself too seriously. If something funny happens during practice, feel free to laugh and kid with each other, as long as it remains positive and is never sarcastic, cynical, or malicious.

Over the years, our program has come up with many ways to keep things fun. A long day of practice makes everyone hungry, so as you might expect, much of our fun involves food. The first night players are in camp, we end the day with hot dogs, chips, and a sundae bar. Each night during summer camp, we feed them before they go to bed. We do this for several reasons: we don't want players running around town to get something to eat, we realize that some players can't afford to buy food, and we want to show them that we're going to take care of them. Each night it's something different—pizza, chicken, subs, donuts and milk, hot dogs and chips, brownies, fresh fruit, cookies—all donated from people and businesses in the community. After the final practice of summer camp, we have watermelon brought onto the practice field.

During summer camp practices, we routinely stop practice and get the squad together for some kind of team event. We might divide the squad into groups and have a trivia quiz in which all the questions are about people in the football program. We might hold a home-run derby or relay or play volleyball, softball, dodgeball, tug-of-war, crab soccer, or rugby with a big ball. We might have linemen pass to the quarterbacks and kickers, hold challenge sprints, run made-up plays with linemen in skill positions and backs on the line, pass to linemen in sprints, or chase and catch in a big circle. The objective is always to promote team unity and a positive attitude while relaxing and having fun.

By the fourth day of summer camp, players are really hurting. They ache in every muscle and are sore in places they didn't even know they had muscles. So during summer camp, usually on the fourth day of practice, we call

off evening practice and have a pool party. This is a great pick-me-up for players and coaches. Everyone is required to get in the pool, which invariably leads to all sorts of water games.

Friday night at the end of summer camp is our Talent Night. Every player must be involved in some kind of talent, either solo or as a member of a group not to exceed four players. We try to promote real talent because many players have gifts for singing, playing an instrument, acting, writing, and so on. But even without a special talent, kids enjoy this night. We have judges who rate each performance from 1 to 10. A coach acts as the master of ceremonies, and we award prizes to the top three acts. Afterward we have subs, cake, and drinks for everyone.

Following our last regular-season practice, we have Senior Day. Each senior gets three punts for distance, his last block against the underclassman of his choice, and his last tackle against an underclassman. We make this ceremony a big, emotional deal. The entire squad and coaching staff form a circle around the senior performing his block or tackle to cheer and clap for him. We finish by hoisting each senior into the air and carrying him off the field.

Get Others Involved

If I expect support for our sport from the school and community, I believe it is imperative that we support a wide variety of activities. This means encouraging athletes and coaches to cheer for the other sports and attend their games. Coaches encourage players to use all their abilities by participating in activities such as singing in the chorus, participating in musicals and plays, or running for campus government. I tell my squad that if they have abilities off the field to use them, not waste them. I want our students, staff, faculty, and administration to see our players assuming leadership roles in a variety of ways.

As a coach, I want my players to excel in the classroom. For players with unacceptable

GPAs, we hold a mandatory study hall. We also provide tutoring in any course for any player who demonstrates a need. When a player lets us know he is having trouble in a class, we immediately put him in touch with a tutor. We want to reinforce positive performance both on and off the field. Our faculty at UVA-Wise has been excellent about getting in touch with us if a player misses a class or does poorly on a test. In my 11 years here, only one player who used all four years of eligibility failed to graduate.

If you're a coach working with junior high or high school players, I suggest a mandatory study hall during the season before the start of school and, during the off-season, either before school or immediately after school. Provide tutors for those who need help, and closely monitor the study hall to ensure students are there to study.

As head coach, it is also important for me to be active in community clubs, activities, and church. At work, I take part in faculty meetings, committees, and activities, and I visit with faculty and show an interest in their expertise, projects, and demonstrations. I talk with them about their principal interests and involve as many of them as possible in our football program. There are many ways to contribute. A math teacher might help with statistics, a public-speaking teacher might be our PA announcer, a computer science instructor might run our message center, and someone in audiovisual might video our games for us.

As a team, we participate in community service. One year our entire squad helped build a special playground for an elementary school. At the end of our last spring practice, still in uniform, we pick up trash along the roads. In December we have a benefit basketball game that features our squad against members of the local media. The price of admission is the donation of canned goods, toys, or clothes to give to the shelter for abused spouses and children. As a squad, we make sure we have 100 percent participation in school clean-up days. We encourage our older players to visit area schools to talk about saying no to alcohol and drugs. My fellow coaches and I also visit local schools to discuss the tough decisions students must make in choosing their careers.

Commitment and Accountability

We expect commitment and accountability of every person involved in our football program. This begins with our school's administration. Making provisions for an experienced and committed coaching staff and granting the head coach freedom to fill his staff with coaches who share his philosophy are concrete examples of an administration's intent on excellence. Outfitting every player with the best in protective equipment is another example of a committed and accountable administration. If your team plays in a conference, all the schools in the conference should be similar in size, values, and resources. There should be a sense of mutual respect among schools along with a development of intense but friendly rivalries.

The coaching staff must commit to doing all in their power to field the most competitive team possible. They are accountable to the people who hired them. They should be involved in their community, conference, and national organizations, taking a leadership role when possible. Coaches should continue to educate themselves in the profession, whether in their first or their 41st year of coaching. By attending clinics and conventions, visiting college spring practices and professional camps, and reading books and magazines, they should stay abreast of the Xs and Os and all the innovations in the game. They should know the rule book intimately and be familiar with any rule changes so they can relay these to the rest of the team.

When players become a part of a football program, they make a commitment. There is a big difference between a decision and a commitment. A commitment includes taking responsibility. These players are now accountable to their teammates, their coaching staff, and their institution. They understand that they are under a microscope and that everything they do and say can affect the program.

Program Resources

All football programs must ensure they have the resources they require to be competitive on the field. Essential resources include staff, budget, and equipment.

Staff

All teams in a conference or league should have a similar number of assistant coaches, athletic trainers, equipment managers, and weight coaches. In junior high and some high school programs, some of these positions will be covered by coaches performing double duty. These positions are essential. The on-the-field coaching and off-the-field relationships these staff members develop with players will have a positive impact on every individual on the team and bring success to the program.

A coaching staff should surround itself with successful and loyal individuals who are knowledgeable in what they do. These individuals should be "people persons" who care deeply about the players they serve. They must understand the tremendous impact they can have on the lives of these individuals. They must understand that they are working with the total person, not only the athlete. If you are a coach, tell your staff members that you chose to surround yourself with them because you know they understand that mediocrity in the work force will yield mediocre results, and you are not interested in mediocre results.

One of the most important members of a football squad is its team trainer, who must be a certified expert in his field. I have always tried to work with trainers who work diligently at injury prevention, are cautious in their evaluation of injuries, are aggressive in their treatments, and are extremely strict in players' compliance with treatment times. Decisions on when athletes are healthy enough to return to action are medical matters, and I always let the experts handle them.

Budget

Another resource all programs must consider is their financial budget. Especially at the college level, if a program is going to be able to hire qualified coaches, they must have enough money to attract the kind of individuals they want to coach their team. Very few programs at any level can provide a budget that allows coaches to purchase everything they need, but the budget must always permit a team to put each player in high-quality protective gear. Coaches need to be able to tell the parents of players that their sons will be outfitted in the best helmets and shoulder pads available. These items should never be skimped on. If a program can't afford to safely equip their players, they can't afford to field a football team. There must also be enough in the budget to outfit every player in the program. Having players stand around, waiting for gear while others are practicing, even for one day, does not reflect positively on a program.

For game jerseys and pants, I have always kept the same design from year to year. In doing so I avoid the major expense of buying new jerseys and pants for the entire team. Each year I buy two dozen new, which gives us a complete cycle every four years, avoiding a gigantic expense all at one time.

Equipment

Teams must have up-to-date field equipment, including sleds and dummies and punting, passing, and kicking machines that permit coaches to train athletes at a level competitive with opponents. An option for programs with limited funds is to visit universities or professional teams and ask for used field equipment they are planning to replace.

Other expensive but very important equipment includes the components required for video breakdown. Current video technology enables teams to instantly recall plays on a monitor or to compile a DVD of hundreds of offensive plays or defensive stunts, extremely helpful both for self-scouting and for scouting opponents. Teams can see their own tendencies that must be broken or tendencies of an opponent that will help in preparing their game plan. Video equipment is expensive but should not be considered a frill. This equipment is essential for teams to compete each week. In a pinch, teams with small budgets might ask someone with an interest in video to film their practices and games using a home video camera. This will require more time to break down tendencies but can be done at little to no expense.

The primary principles discussed in this chapter are being positive and having discipline. The two go hand in hand. As a coach, absolutely nothing will prevent me from being positive. Because I am disciplined, I adhere to the philosophy of completely controlling everything I have the ability to control and not wasting time or energy worrying about things beyond my control. I set this example for everyone around me and teach them through my speech and actions to do the same.

2

Personnel and Position Assignments

Evaluating the abilities of coaches and players and assessing how their skills will best fit a team is a challenge for all football programs, but these decisions are among the most important a head coach will make. They might be the difference between a successful season and a disappointing season. Part of the decision-making process is determining who the positive leaders are and who might become leaders, and then putting these individuals in positions to maximize their skills both on and off the field. The head coach needs to determine who has the self-discipline to put his team on his back and carry it through the difficult and demanding times that occur in every season. The coaching staff works with these individuals and gives them responsibilities of leadership, understanding that they will lead as their personalities dictate—some vocally and others through their actions.

Coaching Staff Essentials

On a coaching staff, there is no substitute for loyalty. You must have two-directional loyalty throughout your staff. Loyalty is more important than any other trait. When looking to fill a coaching vacancy, many head coaches think mainly of the candidate's knowledge of the Xs and Os in the area of his expertise. Although knowledge and expertise are extremely important, they are teachable. It's much harder, and maybe impossible in some cases, to teach loyalty, character, professionalism, and integrity. But these are essential ingredients if your program is going to pass the test of time and succeed long term.

Lack of loyalty can quickly tear a staff, and ultimately a program, apart. Disloyalty can be detected in several ways. It might not show itself in negative talk. It might be seen in what is left unsaid or in the look on someone's face. When a head coach suspects a staff member of disloyalty, he should communicate with him as quickly as he can. He should pull him aside and make sure they understand each other. Sometimes what appears to be disloyalty is simply miscommunication. Head coaches should be fair, but also trust their instincts. Disloyalty must be dealt with immediately, before it infects a team.

When I say that loyalty is of prime importance to a coaching staff, I do not mean to minimize the value of one's knowledge of the game. That said, I remember that Bo Schembechler at Michigan used to routinely change staff members' on-the-field coaching duties every few years because he felt it was good to learn something new and that this would invigorate the coaches, who in turn would get players excited about a new coach at their position.

Regardless of the title given to each coach, there must be a well-delineated hierarchy of responsibility. Table 2.1 shows an example of how duties can be assigned to assistant coaches. This is fairly easily done in the areas of offense and defense but much more difficult for special teams.

To take advantage of coaching expertise, consider having most, if not all, coaches participate in teaching each special team. Whether there is one special-teams coordinator or a different coach in charge of each special team, break down every unit so that each coach is in charge of a small number of players. Don't have players standing around watching while a special-team unit is practicing. Because offensive linemen are not usually involved in many kicking game practices, keep these players together with their offensive line coach to practice offensive line drills while the rest of the team works on special teams. The same can be said for quarterbacks and many wide receivers. Keep them busy with meaningful drills. To emphasize to their squads how vital it is to have good special-teams play, some head coaches assume responsibility for their special teams and include Special-Teams Coordinator as part of their title. Game-day responsibility should include having each kicking team gather at the 50-yard line around the coordinator with each coach responsible for substitution just as he is for offensive or defensive group substitution.

On game day, coaches should be selected to view the game from the press box. These coaches must have the ability to analyze Xs and Os as well as individual performance. They must be able to inform sideline coaches, who have the worst vantage point in the stadium, when players employ the wrong technique or fall short of expectations and ways to counter the defensive and offensive looks being used by the opponent. If a team has few assistants, the best assistant should be in the press box. If there's only one assistant, he shouldn't be on the sideline; he needs to be where he can see alignments and spacings. He is the eyes of the head coach, and it is vital that he communicates well. The head coach should spend considerable time with this assistant prior to game day, describing exactly what information he wants from him and teaching him where to train his eyes when the ball is snapped. The assistant should be supplied with forms to complete so that at halftime the head coach can get the information he needs to make adjustments for the second half.

All coaches have to deal with a variety of people in public, so they need to have engaging personalities. They must be motivators and be able to relate to the players they coach. Although the head coach makes final disciplinary decisions, each coach must himself be a disciplinarian and accept nothing less than constant improvement and striving for perfection in how the player plays his position. An exceptional coach will not be a clock watcher. He will work tirelessly to prepare his players and get the best execution possible out of each player under his care.

Coaches must be effective recruiters. For high school coaches, this means recruiting potential athletes out of the hallway or

TABLE 2.1 Primary Responsibilities for Assistant Coaches

Assistant coach	Primary duties
Offensive line coach	1. Coordinate the interior offensive line. 2. Work with special teams: extra point/field goal interior offensive line, shotgun punt interior offensive line. 3. Prepare offensive 9 vs. 7 practice scripts. 4. Break down opponent video. 5. Work with equipment manager.
Receivers coach	1. Coordinate the wide receivers. 2. Work with special teams: extra point/field goal holder and kicker, hands team (LE, LH, RH, RE), shotgun punt punter, semispread punt punter, spread punt punter. 3. Prepare offensive 7 vs. 7 practice scripts. 4. Break down opponent video. 5. Break down own team's offensive tendencies.
Running backs coach	1. Coordinate the offensive backs. 2. Work with special teams: kickoff reception (LH, RH, FB, S), kickoff coverage (5, 6, 7), hands team (FB, S). 3. Break down opponent video 4. Record helmet awards for offense and special teams. 5. Work with athletic trainer. 6. Break down opponent's defensive tendencies.
Secondary coach	1. Coordinate the defensive backs. 2. Work with special teams: kickoff coverage (H, S, K), hands team (LT, LG, C, RG, RT), Oskie (K, S, H), extra point/field goal defense (LC, RC, free, SS), punt coverage (gunners and wings for spread; ends for semispread; wide receivers for shotgun). 3. Prepare defensive 7 vs. 7 practice scripts. 4. Break down opponent video. 5. Break down own team's defensive tendencies.
Defensive line coach	1. Coordinate the defensive line. 2. Work with special teams: kickoff coverage (2, 3, 4), kickoff return (LT, LG, C, RG, RT), Oskie (5, 6, 7, 8), extra point/field goal defense (LT, LE, RT, RE), punt defense defensive line, punt coverage for spread. 3. Prepare defensive 9 vs. 7 practice scripts. 4. Break down opponent video. 5. Break down opponent's offensive tendencies.
Linebacker coach	1. Coordinate the inside and outside linebackers. 2. Work with special teams: kickoff coverage (1, 8), kickoff return (LE, RE), Oskie (1, 2, 3, 4), extra point/field goal defense (S, M, W), punt defense (S, M, W), punt coverage (interior five for spread and semispread, TE for shotgun). 3. Break down opponent video. 4. Record helmet awards for defense and special teams.

convincing junior high players to continue their football endeavors. For college coaches, this means evaluating talent, getting to know those who have displayed the talent, and, after concluding the players have the right ingredients, convincing those selected to join the program.

Position-Specific Attributes

Regardless of the position being played, there's no such thing as having too much speed and quickness on your team. The phrase "speed kills" is absolutely true when it comes to modern football, no matter at what level. Up to a point, speed and quickness can neutralize size. Size doesn't help much if you don't get there first. However, size and strength are important when you reach the point of attack and need to deactivate the opponent.

These are the qualities that coaches look for in each position:

The **quarterback** is a leader, one who inspires teammates and instills confidence. He must have passing skills, running ability, or both. Ideally, he's tall enough to look over his offensive line and find open receivers. This is someone who makes good decisions, possesses self-confidence, and immediately dismisses bad plays and comes back with big plays.

The **running back** has quickness, agility, and flexibility and is big enough to be a blocker. He is a hard runner, determined not to let one tackler bring him down. The smaller he is, the quicker and faster he better be.

The **tight end** has size, strength, and flexibility and can catch passes. He can become a consistent and dominating blocker. Quickness is a plus but not a necessity.

The **offensive lineman** has size, strength (especially bench press strength), and flexibility. He must require no ego stroking and be able to live with no fame.

The **defensive lineman** has enough size to complement his quickness, strength, and flexibility.

The **linebacker** has enough size and strength to be a vicious tackler. He is able to immediately terminate the positive momentum of the ballcarrier. He has the necessary quickness, speed, and flexibility to cover pass receivers.

The **defensive back** has the quickness to break on the ball and play the ball in the air, the speed to cover the fastest offensive receivers, and the ability to run backward and change direction without losing a step. He is an excellent tackler.

In addition, coaches always look for players who can make outstanding contributions in special-teams play. Even at the professional level, players often get a coach's attention and make the squad because of their play on special teams. If a player is quick, hard-nosed, disciplined, and consistent, coaches will find a place for him.

Player Evaluations

Coaches should remind players that they are being evaluated every single day, not just on game days. They evaluate first-hand everything that players do in practice as well as games. Players need to know this so that they never become complacent in their performance. They also must know that they are being assessed as teammates and will conform to a certain standard of behavior if they expect to play.

We tell our players that just because they started last week, there's no assurance they'll start this week. A first-teamer from the previous year is not guaranteed the same spot this year. Players need to know they can't stand still; they must always strive to improve. You either get better or you get worse—you don't stay the same. We want to put the best players on the field every week, and that means the best *current* players. No one owns a position, and as head coach, I don't owe anyone anything. Part of the constant evaluation involves who works best with the team and is totally a team player. We might not have the most

Evaluate players every day to make sure you field the best team on game day.

talented 11 on the field but the 11 who work best as a team. I think Knute Rockne said it best: "The secret is to work less as individuals and more as a team. As a coach, I play not my 11 best, but my best 11."

Even when a player makes a crucial mistake, the coach should look for something the player did well. Players should be taught that when they make a mistake, no matter how big, they need to turn it into a positive, which takes tremendous effort. For example, if a quarterback throws an interception but then makes the tackle, the coach, and the player, should focus on the tackle. Players need to be reminded that an important part of their evaluation has to do with the energy they are expending when they are not at the point of attack, as in these examples:

Backside offensive lineman

- Experiment with various horizontal and vertical splits when the split does not have an impact on the play.
- Never let a defensive player cross your face no matter how far you are from the point of attack.

Wide receiver

- Stay with your block—even when the ballcarrier is on the opposite side of the field.
- Run your pattern with all the effort you would give if you were sure the ball was coming to you.
- Sell misdirection on all your patterns.
- Confuse the defense with your motion.

Offensive back

- Carry out your fake to help the ballcarrier.
- Take pride in being a consistent blocker.

Linebacker and defensive back

- Take the proper pursuit course no matter how far away the ball is.
- Sprint to the ball when the ball is in the air.

Backside defensive lineman

- Get to heel depth of the offensive line and find the ball.
- When the ball goes away, get to ball depth and check counter or reverse.

The closest scrutiny certainly comes with video assessment of performance, both in practice and in games. It is essential that players see themselves on video and share in that assessment. Coaches view the video first and make written comments on every play.

I have never been a proponent of detailed performance checklists. To me it boils down to he got the job done or he didn't. That doesn't mean I won't correct something if I feel it will make a player more consistent and better. But if he can make plays, regardless of the position he plays, that is what it's all about.

When the player views his tape, his position coach is beside him to give him positive reinforcement on plays executed correctly and, for other plays, to point out his mistakes and how to correct them. Each player should hear some comment on his performance on every single play. Regardless of what a video evaluation shows, I believe a positive approach is preferable and produces better long-term results than berating and humiliating a player does. I want all players to be positive in all aspects, and that is difficult if the coach is negative and constantly tears players down. Also, we must remember that some players are gamers—they don't stand out in practice but make their presence felt once the whistle blows.

Depth Chart and Substitutions

Football is a tough game full of violent collisions. The season is long, and injuries will occur. The goal is to have enough backup players who can contribute when first-team players go down so there is not a significant drop in performance. The players coming off the bench must be able to come in, make plays, and make a difference. But probably no team in the world feels it has sufficient depth. Consider the following needs.

On offense, the personnel packages are based on the type of offense used—power game, pure passing offense, or a balance of the two—and the game situation, including down and distance, field position, score, time remaining, and time-outs remaining. There might be a call for zero, one, two or three tight ends (wing and double tight end); zero, one, two, three, four, or five wide receivers; zero, one, two, or three running backs; and five offensive linemen.

Defensive depth depends on the same game situation and the front, secondary coverage, and personnel package required. One might have three, four, five, or six defensive linemen; one, two, three, four, or five linebackers; and three, four, five, or six defensive backs.

Based on the maximum number of each of these positions—16 offensive players and 17 defensive players—you are already up to 33 players, and this doesn't include any backups. Add backup players to give starters periodic rest time, special-teams players such as a long snapper, punter, kicker, holder, punt returner, and kick returner, and the number quickly exceeds 50.

Substitutions are required to cover injuries and disciplinary decisions and for tactical reasons. For all substitution situations, the coach should have a plan that has been communicated to the squad.

▨ Rotation of players with similar abilities. If you have three offensive guards of similar ability, rotate them every series, every quarter, or every so many plays. This gives all three sufficient rest, a sense of involvement, and a feeling they are contributing.

▨ Injury replacements. Tell your squad to anticipate the situation. If a player goes down with an injury, in most situations the squad knows who will be his replacement. That player must be up and ready to enter the game even before the coach calls for him. If the injured player is either a quarterback or center, that replacement, without being told, must be up and taking practice snaps as soon as the injury takes place.

▨ Long run or interception return. Following a long run, the coach might choose to replace a running back or receiver for a play or two. The same could be true for a long interception return if that player normally goes both ways and would stay on the field at an offensive position. Again, the next in line must anticipate the situation and be ready to go.

▪ Experience next to inexperience. If, for example, an offensive lineman goes down and the next at his position is a rookie with very little experience, the coach might want to shift personnel to put an experienced player beside the newcomer. This will increase the rookie's confidence and performance because the veteran can help him with assignments and calls.

▪ Best unit rather than next in line. If an offensive right tackle goes down, and the depth chart second-team player at right tackle is not as good as the second-team left tackle, bring in the left tackle and play him at right tackle or keep him at left tackle and move the first-team left tackle to right tackle.

▪ Special teams. Have all special-teams personnel anticipate the situation. If you are on defense, and it is third and long, all punt-defense personnel must be ready to go on the field on fourth down. If you have the ball and are within field goal distance, all field goal personnel must be ready to go on fourth down.

A coach must ensure that all players can execute the Xs and Os they are asking them to learn, given their age, experience, and contact hours with the team and the size of the coaching staff. Coaches must give players a package they are capable of learning. For example, if the offense is jumping offside or repeatedly turning over the ball, it might be that they are trying too hard to learn the system and can't concentrate on the physical execution required. In such cases, the coach should cut back on what he is asking them to learn and do well with a smaller package. It's better to add later, a little at a time, than to overwhelm players with a system that is too complex.

I can't overstate the importance of placing each player at the position that maximizes his abilities, best complements his teammates' skills, and results in the greatest possible team strength. Achieving success on the field might sometimes mean placing a player at his second-best individual position to create a more competitive unit, and that is what it is all about. Positioning becomes a case of putting all the pieces of a puzzle together in the right spaces to finish the project.

Making player decisions is not a one-time job. It's an ongoing, never-ending, and very important aspect of a coach's mission. A coach must consider much more than simple football ability. It is crucial that each player fits into the role of a team player and that his goals and aspirations are compatible with team goals. In every way, he must be a *we* player, not a *me* player. This too is something the coach must always be watching for and evaluating. When coaching high school ball, I had to remove the best athlete we had from our squad because he would not put his individual aspirations second to the team's goals. To field a successful team, the coach must make some difficult decisions.

3

Football Conditioning

Rigorous conditioning in the off-season is extremely important. In most areas where football is played, preseason practice begins in hot and often humid conditions. If the athlete has not conditioned his body during the off-season, weather conditions can pose a dangerous threat. Further, because football is a full-contact sport, weight training is an important part of conditioning. Of course the most comprehensive year-round conditioning program will not guarantee escape from all injuries, but developing strength and endurance significantly reduces the risk of many types of injuries, and in some cases diminishes the severity of injuries. A comprehensive off-season program also enhances the development of speed, quickness, and agility and permits athletes to improve the skills necessary for high-quality performance.

This is not meant as an endorsement for players becoming one-sport athletes and concentrating all their attention on football. I firmly believe that junior high, high school, and possibly even college are times to enjoy all sports for which athletes have the ability to play and contribute. Participating in more than one sport (including following the conditioning program the coach of that sport demands during the season) will certainly keep athletes fit. Encouraging athletes to participate in other sports instead of insisting they make a choice between sports also facilitates relationships among coaches.

The conditioning year is divided into these seasons:

- Winter: Winter conditioning begins in January when classes resume and lasts for 10 weeks.
- Spring: Four weeks are devoted to spring conditioning and practice. This period begins after the 10-week winter program. For high schools and middle schools, this period begins when the state association permits the beginning of spring ball. For colleges, this period begins when the national association permits it.
- Summer: Summer practice lasts 8 weeks, leading up to summer camp.

■ In-season: The in-season begins the first week of summer camp and lasts through the end of the season.

Institutions not permitted to have year-round conditioning must tailor their conditioning programs to comply with the local, state, or national rules and regulations under which they operate.

The emphasis of the conditioning program changes depending on the season, but the program culminates in the athlete being in his strongest and most competitive physical condition possible for the football season. When the season ends after the final playoff game, players should have a few weeks off without a required program.

Winter Conditioning

The emphasis for winter conditioning is to develop bulk and strength, so the prescription is heavy resistance, few repetitions, and several sets. Along with increasing strength, we want to improve quickness and coordination, so we spend a lot of time drilling that as well. Upper-body lifting is done every other day; lower-body lifting is done on the alternate days.

Warm-Up Stretching

Each practice, game, and off-season workout begins with deep-stretching exercises. Each stretch is held for 20 seconds. These are gradual, deep-stretching exercises with no jerky or ballistic movements.

NECK ROLL

Slowly move the head clockwise, bending the neck as far as possible. Repeat counterclockwise.

ARM ROLL

Slowly move the outstretched arms clockwise in small circles, gradually increasing the size of the circles. Repeat counterclockwise.

CROSSING FEET

Cross the right foot in front of the left foot. Keeping the knees locked, bend over and touch the ground. Don't bounce; this is a slow, deep stretch. After 20 seconds, cross the left foot in front of the right and repeat.

SQUAT PUSH-OUT ON THE KNEES

From a squatting position, clasp your hands and use your elbows to put steady pressure against the insides of your knees.

GRAB ANKLES AND LOCK KNEES

From a standing position, bend over and grab your ankles, locking your knees.

SITTING TRUNK TWIST

From a sitting position, turn the trunk to the left as far as possible and hold for 20 seconds. Repeat, turning to the right.

SOLE TO SOLE

Sit and grab the feet, placing them sole to sole as close to the crotch as possible. Use the elbows to put pressure on the insides of the knees.

LEGS IN A V

Begin in a seated position. Extend the legs in a V. Lean the upper body over the right knee, working to lower the face to the right knee. Hold for 20 seconds. Switch to the left knee and hold 20 seconds. Finish by stretching between your legs, lowering the face in the middle.

HEEL TO BUTTOCKS

Sit with the left leg extended. Bend the right leg and place the right heel against the right buttock. From this position, lower the nose to the left knee. Hold for 20 seconds, and then lie back with the shoulders flat on the ground and the right knee firmly on the ground. Hold for 20 seconds, and then rise out of the position. Repeat with the right leg extended and the left heel to the left buttock.

FOOT TO OPPOSITE HAND

Lie flat on the ground. Extend arms straight out to the sides. Without raising the shoulders, raise the right leg and touch it to the left hand. Hold the deep stretch for 20 seconds. Repeat on the other side, bringing the left foot to the right hand.

THIGH TO FACE

Lie on your back. Grab the right thigh and bring the right leg toward your face. Hold the stretch for 20 seconds. Repeat with the left leg.

KNEES, ANKLES, HIPS

Kneel on both knees. Reach back and grab hold of each ankle. Thrust the hips up and out; hold the stretch for 20 seconds.

ACHILLES STRETCH

Stand with feet shoulder-width apart. Place the right foot forward as far as comfortable while keeping the left heel flat on the ground. Lean the upper body forward to stretch the left Achilles. Hold for 20 seconds. Switch legs, bringing the left foot forward and keeping the right heel flat on the ground; repeat the stretch.

GROIN STRETCH

Place the right foot forward farther than was done for the Achilles stretch. Lean forward toward the right foot far enough that the left heel can no longer stay in contact with the ground. Hold the stretch for 20 seconds. Switch legs, placing the left foot forward, and stretch for 20 seconds. Finally, stand with feet parallel and spread wide. Lean the upper body far to the right until you feel a stretch in the groin on the left side. Repeat, leaning to the left to stretch the groin on the right side.

PARTNER HAMSTRINGS

Face a partner. Lift your right leg to 90 degrees and place your right heel in the cupped hands of your partner. Bend your upper body forward, bringing your nose toward your right knee. Hold the stretch. Without switching legs, lift your upper body, turn your torso to the left, bend over, and bring your nose toward your left knee. Hold the stretch. Switch legs, lifting your left leg to 90 degrees with your left heel in the cupped hands of your partner. Repeat the stretch to the left knee, lift the torso, and, without switching legs, stretch to the right knee. Change roles with your partner.

BULL NECK

In this exercise for the neck, the partner applying the pressure must not provide so much resistance as to actually move the head. This is a static exercise with no movement involved.

Get on your hands and knees. Your partner puts his hands on the back of your head. Try to raise your head as your partner applies steady pressure. Next, your partner cups his hands under your chin and applies pressure as you attempt to lower your chin. Next, your partner applies pressure to the right side of your head as you attempt to bend your neck to the right. Finally, your partner applies pressure to the left side of your head as you attempt to bend your neck to the left. Change roles with your partner.

Cardiovascular Warm-Up

We begin off-season cardiovascular workouts with these form-running drills. If weather permits, these drills are done on the football field; otherwise they can be done inside. When done outside, the drills are run for 30 yards. If inside, they are shorter, depending on the size of the facility.

Critically evaluate each athlete in every drill. When conducting running drills, many coaches just let players run. But the art of running involves many components. Because running is fundamental to almost everything done in football, it is essential that every part of the skill of running is taught and retaught.

Let players know when they do things correctly, and teach them to correct what they do wrong. Critique them constantly, reinforcing correct technique. Never accept less than 100 percent effort in each drill. If a drill is at full speed, do not accept less from players or they'll know that you don't mean what you said—a fatal mistake. If you mark a finish line and an athlete slows down one stride before that line, immediately let him know that's not acceptable and won't be tolerated. If you don't respond in this manner, you will lose them. Mark a start and finish line for every drill, and stress to players that not adhering to these lines is as critical as lining up offside in a game, jumping before the start command, or stopping or slowing down 6 inches before the goal line. Off-season, players do each of these drills daily. In-season, they do a few of them, alternating drills each day. Multisport athletes who are conditioning for or playing their second sport are expected to follow the guidelines established for them during the season.

HALF-SPEED

Run at half-speed while concentrating on techniques that aid running skill. Keep the head up, facing straight ahead. Bend elbows and keep them close to the chest. Arms pump in rhythm in opposition to stride (right arm moves forward as left foot strides; left arm moves forward as right foot strides) with toes pointed in slightly. The body leans slightly forward with weight in front of the feet. Run on the balls of the feet.

THREE-QUARTER SPEED

Run at three-quarter speed with the same attention to running mechanics as in the half-speed drill.

HIGH KNEES

Hold your arms straight out in front, palms down. Lift knees high enough to hit palms. Perform the drill for 30 yards, focusing on correct form, not speed.

CROSSOVER

Imagine a vertical line in front of you. Each time you step with the right foot, plant the right foot to the left of that line. Each time you step with the left foot, plant the left foot to the right of that line. Perform the drill for 30 yards, focusing on correct form, not speed.

BACKWARD RUN

While running backward, focus on the mechanics that make for an optimal backward run. Keep weight forward over the front of your feet, toes pointed in slightly. Hold elbows to the sides of your chest. Arms pump in opposition to the strides of your feet. Keep your head up and your body in a slight crouch with your knees bent.

CARIOCA

Turn to the side and assume a crouched position with feet parallel. To go to the right, step with the left foot in front of the right foot; then step to the right with the right foot. Step with the left foot behind the right foot; then step to the right with the right foot. Repeat the sequence for 30 yards. Reverse and go to the left, moving the right foot either behind or in front of the left foot.

TAPIOCA

Use the same action as in the carioca, except take ministeps only, barely clearing the other foot. Use quick steps.

VERTICAL BOUNCE

Each stride is a vertical bouncing stride. Swing the opposite arm as high as possible, as if twisting the lights in the ceiling. Although the drill covers 30 yards, the emphasis is on the vertical jump. Both feet will be momentarily off the ground. Alternate feet while performing the vertical jump.

LEAPING, BOUNDING, HORIZONTAL STRIDE

Each stride is a leaping, bounding, horizontal stride, similar to the step portion of the triple jump. Reach out as far as possible with the lead foot while thrusting the opposite arm forward vigorously. Alternate the leaping foot. The coach sets a goal of a certain number of strides to reach the 30-yard finish line.

45-DEGREE CUT EACH WAY

When a coach says "go," sprint straight ahead. On the coach's command of "left" or "right," make a 45-degree cut in the direction called. Plant the outside foot and make a quick, sharp 45-degree cutting step with the near foot.

45-DEGREE TURN WHILE RUNNING BACKWARD

When a coach says "go," sprint backward. On the coach's command of "left" or "right," turn in the direction called and continue moving straight back. Emphasize opening the hips to the right or left to stay with a receiver making a cut.

45-DEGREE CUT WHILE RUNNING BACKWARD

When a coach says "go," sprint backward. On the coach's command of "left" or "right," turn in the direction called and, using crossover steps, sprint backward at a 45-degree angle. Open the hips to accommodate the cut without losing distance with an imaginary receiver. Keep your eyes on the coach as you cut. Continue to run the drill, increasing the number of cuts to the left and right.

SHUFFLE AND PIVOT

Turn to the side and assume a crouched position. Take two shuffle strides and then reverse pivot. Repeat the sequence.

ACCELERATION

Run at three-quarter speed for 15 yards, and then accelerate to full speed. Make a definite, noticeable, instant acceleration.

BACKWARD AND FORWARD SPRINT

When a coach says "go," sprint backward. On the coach's second "go," turn 180 degrees and sprint forward. Emphasize ripping the near arm to help you make a quick turn.

FULL TURN

When a coach says "go," sprint forward. On the coach's second "go," turn clockwise 360 degrees and continue sprinting. Emphasize ripping the near arm to help you make a quick turn. This drill is to simulate losing, and then quickly regaining, your orientation during a football play.

When a coach says "go," sprint forward. On the coach's second "go," turn counterclockwise 360 degrees and continue sprinting. Emphasize ripping the far arm to help you make a quick turn. This drill is to simulate losing, and quickly regaining, your orientation during a football play.

SPRINT FROM STATIONARY RUN

Many times during a game, a player must adjust his movement and change direction as quickly as possible without losing a step. These drills assist in quickly making that adjustment.

Turn to the side. Run in place. When a coach says "go," turn 90 degrees and sprint. Emphasize ripping the near arm to help you make a quick turn.

Turn to the side. Run in place. When a coach says "go," turn 270 degrees and sprint forward. Emphasize ripping the far arm to help you make a quick turn, as if recovering after losing your physical orientation during a football play.

STATIONARY SPRINT TO BELLY FLOP

When a coach says "go," turn to the side and sprint in place. On the coach's second "go," belly flop to the ground then immediately get up and sprint toward the 30-yard finish line. This drill simulates being out of control, regaining your equilibrium, and getting to the point of attack.

GROUND TO SPRINT

Lie flat on your abdomen. When a coach says "go," get to your feet and sprint to the finish line. Again, this drill simulates being out of control, regaining your equilibrium, and getting to the point of attack.

Lie flat on your back. When a coach says "go," get to your feet and sprint forward to the finish line. This drill simulates losing control, regaining equilibrium, and getting to the point of attack.

EXPLOSIVE STARTS

This race is only 5 yards because the focus is on the start. Emphasize exploding out of the start with perfect form. Use a sprinter's start with both hands on the ground and much of your weight forward on your hands. Place feet in a slightly staggered narrow stance. At the start, roll your body weight forward over the hands, and, rather than lifting your hands, thrust them back as you bolt out of your stance. As you run, make sure every movement of each part of the body is going straight ahead—no wasted motion. Repeatedly practice coming out of a start.

This drill improves 40-yard-dash time. Most players coming out of high school think that their 40-yard-dash time is two or three 10ths faster than it really is. Improving 40-yard-dash times not only creates better players but also boosts their confidence.

Circuit Drills

After form running, divide the group into four smaller groups. Each group performs drills picked from the plyometric, rope maze, jump rope, speed rope ladder, dot drills, and stair drills described in this section. Groups rotate to new drills every 10 minutes.

To be included in the battery of drills, a drill must satisfy and enhance at least one of these goals: increased static and dynamic strength, endurance, agility, coordination, or explosive power.

PLYOMETRIC DRILLS

Use a set of boxes from a low of 18 inches to a high of 48 inches. Each player competes alone. That is, he uses boxes at the height at which he can safely perform the drill, always striving to improve his performance. Choose from any of the following drills. Do as many repetitions as possible in 15 seconds.

- Bound up from the floor, landing with both feet flat on top of the box. Jump down. Repeat.
- Bound completely over the box and land on both feet. Repeat.
- Stand between two boxes of different heights. Bound on top of one, jump back to the floor, and bound on top of the other box, always landing on both feet. Repeat.
- Face to the side. Bound on top of a box, landing on both feet, and jump down on the other side, again landing on both feet. Repeat. Face the same direction throughout the drill.
- Bound on top of a box, jump down, and immediately bound back onto the box. When you jump down, just hit the floor and recoil right back up without catching yourself and setting your feet.
- Bound up on the box and jump down to the floor on your right foot only. After bounding for 15 seconds on your right foot, switch to your left foot and repeat.

ROPE MAZE

A rope maze attached to an aluminum frame can be found at most sporting goods stores. If you don't have a rope maze, secure the rope about 12 inches above the floor. Choose from any of the following drills, focusing on form rather than speed.

- Run through the maze hitting every opening with the right foot in squares on the right and the left foot in squares on the left.
- Run through the maze using crossover steps to hit every opening with the right foot in squares on the left and the left foot in squares on the right.
- Run through the maze. On every other square, step with the right foot in squares on the right and the left foot in squares on the left; then, using crossover steps, step with the left foot in squares on the right and the right foot in squares on the left.

- Hop through the maze with feet together. Hit every square.
- Hop through the maze with feet together. Hit every other square.
- Bound through the maze with feet coming down parallel to each other and at the same time but in separate squares. Bound up and turn 180 degrees, coming down facing the opposite direction with feet in separate squares. Continue through the maze.

JUMP ROPE

You can use regular or heavy jump ropes, employing a number of drills. Choose from the following drills, or have players create a jump rope routine.

- Jump quickly with feet together, counting the number of successful jumps in 30 seconds.
- Jump quickly, alternating feet. Count the number of successful jumps in 30 seconds.
- Jump continuously for a set time to build endurance.
- Jump and move forward, alternating feet.
- Jump and move forward with feet together.
- Turn the rope backward and jump, alternating feet.
- Turn the rope backward and jump with feet together.
- Do double jumps (the rope goes around twice per jump).
- Jump on the right foot only.
- Jump on the left foot only.
- Jump while twisting the rope. Begin with a normal jump, alternating feet. Then, without breaking the rhythm, place one hand over the other to cross the rope and continue jumping. Then go back to holding the rope normally.

Repeat, moving back and forth from holding the rope normally and crossing the rope. Next, do the same thing with feet together.

- Jump three times on the right foot, three times on the left foot, and then three times with feet together.
- Alternating feet, jump while running the perimeter of the gym floor or a similar distance outside. The rhythm is to jump with the right foot, step with the left foot, step with the right foot, then jump with the left foot. Continue around the gym floor.

SPEED ROPE LADDER

This is a series of quick footwork drills. The coach may choose which drills the players should do. Set up the rope ladder as shown in figure 3.1.

- Move through the ladder, stepping with each foot in every opening. Both the right and left foot go into each opening.
- Alternate feet, with one foot in each opening.
- Step with the right foot in the first opening, then skip an opening. Step with the left foot in the next opening, then skip an opening.
- Step with the right foot in the first opening, then skip two openings. Step with the left foot in the next opening, then skip two openings.
- Step with the right foot in an opening, and then the left foot in the same opening. Moving up a row, step with the right foot outside the ladder and the left foot in an opening one row forward. Step with the right foot in the same opening. Moving up a row, step with the left foot outside the ladder and the right foot in an opening one row forward. Continue this sequence through the ladder.

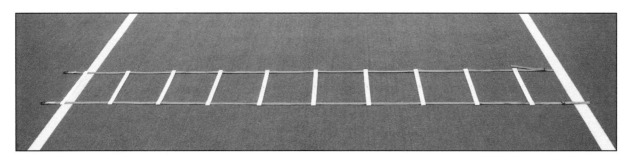

Figure 3.1 Setup for rope ladder drills.

■ Step outside to the right of the ladder with feet together. Moving up a row, step outside the ladder to the left with feet together. Moving up a row, step outside the ladder to the right with feet together. This sequence can also be done with the right foot only or the left foot only.

■ Sprint 5 yards to the ladder, and then move through the ladder, stepping with each foot in every opening. Both the right foot and the left foot go into every opening.

■ Step with feet together in the first opening, then straddle the ladder, landing with feet apart and outside the ladder. Step with feet together in the second opening, then feet apart and outside the ladder.

■ Face the ladder from the right side. Step into the ladder with the right foot, then the left foot. Step out of the ladder with the right foot, then the left foot. Move up to the next opening and repeat. Continue down the ladder.

■ Face the ladder from the left side. Step into the ladder with the left foot, then the right foot. Step out of the ladder with the left foot, then the right foot. Move up to the next opening and repeat. Continue down the ladder.

Include position-oriented drills as part of the speed rope ladder drills. For example, offensive linemen include the post foot and jab with the hands to simulate pass protection. See the position-specific training drills for ideas.

DOT DRILLS

Dot drills develop quickness and reaction as well as strength and endurance. The dots form the shape of five spots on a domino (figure 3.2). Dots are 18 inches apart. Athletes do one drill for 15 seconds. Put eight sets of dots side by side so that eight athletes can drill at the same time. If there are more than eight athletes, after the first group finishes the first drill, the second group of eight does the same drill while the first group rests; then the first group of eight does the next drill, and so on. If the group size is eight players or fewer, there is no time for rest between drills. In fact I tell them the next drill as they finish the current one. The variation of drills is limited only by your imagination. Choose from a variety of drills, doing some every day and changing the remainder from day to day to keep things fresh.

■ Begin with your feet on the bottom two dots. Hop to the middle dot, landing with both feet

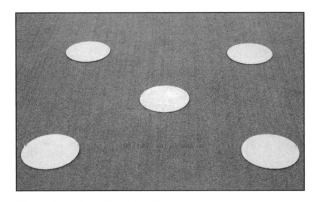

Figure 3.2 Setup for dot drills.

on the middle dot. Hop to the top two dots, one foot on each dot. Without turning, hop backward to the middle dot and back to the start position.

■ Begin with your feet on the bottom two dots. Hop to the middle dot, landing with both feet on the middle dot. Hop to the top two dots, one foot on each dot. After hitting the top two dots, turn 180 degrees. Hop back to the middle dot and back to the bottom two dots. Turn and hop through the sequence again. Emphasize quickness and correct form in hitting the dots, not just coming close.

■ Start with your right foot on the bottom right dot. Hop to the middle dot, the top right dot, the top left dot, the middle dot, and the bottom left dot, all on your right foot. Options: Do the drill while hopping on your left foot (begin on the bottom left dot) or while hopping on both feet (begin on the bottom right dot).

■ Begin with your feet on the bottom two dots. Hop and place your right foot on the middle dot and your left foot on the bottom right dot. Hop back to the start position.

■ Begin with your feet on the bottom two dots. Hop and place your left foot on the middle dot and your right foot on the bottom left dot. Hop back to the start position.

■ Combine the previous two drills. First alternate with each hop for 20 seconds, and then hop 15 seconds on one side and 15 seconds on the other side.

■ Begin with your right foot on the bottom right dot. Hop to the middle dot on your right foot, and then to the top left dot. Place your left foot on the bottom left dot. Hop to the middle dot on your left foot, and then to the top right dot.

■ Begin with your right foot on the bottom right dot. Hop to the middle dot on your right foot, and then to the top right dot. Place your left foot on the top left dot. Hop to the middle dot on your left foot, and then to the bottom left dot.

■ Begin with your left foot on the bottom right dot. Hop to the middle dot on your left foot, and then to the top right dot. Place your right foot on the top left dot. Hop to the middle dot on your right foot, and then to the bottom left dot.

■ Begin with your feet on the bottom two dots. With both feet, hop to the middle dot and back as fast as you can for 5 seconds. Make your feet go faster than you thought possible.

■ Begin with your right foot on the bottom right dot. Hop to the middle dot on your right foot, and then to the bottom left dot. On your left foot, hop to the middle dot, the top right dot, and the top left dot.

■ Begin with your feet on the bottom two dots. With both feet, hop to the middle dot. Hop, cross feet, and land on the top two dots with your right foot on the top left dot and your left foot on the top right dot. Turn and hop to the middle dot, landing on both feet. Hop, cross feet, and land on the bottom two dots. Turn and repeat.

For the last two minutes, players go to one end of the sets of dots, turn to face all eight sets of dots, and do a series of drills in which they move through all eight sets, one athlete at a time, before sprinting back to the start point. Players move single file through all eight sets of dots, one right after the next, until they have all completed one drill. They then move to the next drill. The coach picks the drills.

■ Begin with your feet on the bottom two dots. With feet together, hop to the middle dot. With feet apart, hop to the top two dots. Continue through each set of dots.

■ Begin with your feet on the bottom two dots. With feet together, hop to the middle dot. With feet apart, hop to the top two dots. Turn 180 degrees to hop backward to the next set. Move backward through the second set with the same footwork. Turn 180 degrees and hop forward through the third set. Continue through each set of dots.

■ Begin with your right foot on the bottom right dot. On your right foot, hop to the top right dot. Place your left foot on the bottom left dot of the second set. On your left foot, hop to the top left dot of the second set. Continue through each set of dots.

■ Begin with your left foot on the bottom right dot. On your left foot, hop to the top right dot. Using a crossover step, land with the right foot on the bottom left dot of the second set. This will require a slight hop. Continue through each set of dots.

■ Begin with your left foot on the bottom right dot. Using a crossover step, place your right foot on the top left dot of the first set, facing the remaining set of dots. Hop and use a crossover step to place your left foot on the bottom right dot of the second set. Use a crossover with your right foot to step to the top left dot of the second set.

■ Begin with your left foot on the bottom right dot. Use a crossover with your right foot to step to the bottom left dot of the first set. Use a crossover with your left foot to step to the top right dot of the first set. Take another crossover step with your right foot, landing on the top left dot of the first set. Move to the second set and continue.

■ Begin with your right foot on the bottom right dot. On your right foot, hop to the middle dot and then to the top right dot. Place your left foot on the bottom left dot of the second set. On your left foot, hop to the middle dot and then to the top left dot of the second set. Continue through each set. Repeat, switching feet.

■ Begin with your feet on the bottom two dots. Leap to the bottom two dots of the second set. Continue through each set.

■ Begin with your right foot on the bottom right dot. On your right foot, hop to the middle dot and then to the top left dot. Hop with your left foot to the bottom left dot of the second set. On your left foot, hop to the middle dot and then to the top right dot of the second set. Continue through each set.

STAIRS

In stair drills, the emphasis is on building endurance while stressing form and quickness. The drills are done by one player at a time. The next player in line begins as soon as the player ahead of him gets to the top of the stairs. The stairs should be concrete, not wood. Make sure that there is no moisture on the steps or on the soles of the players' shoes. Players should go full speed to the top of the steps, but they are not given a time limit. For all drills, 12 to 15 steps is fine. Vary the drills from day to day.

For most drills, the player ascends the stairs and then walks back down. There are limitless ways to perform stair drills. Use your imagination to think of new sequences.

- Step with the right foot on the first step, the left foot on the second step, and so on.
- Step with the right foot on the first step and then the left foot on the first step. Step with the right foot on the second step and then the left foot on the second step, and so on.
- Alternate feet on every third step. Begin with the right foot on the floor. With the left foot, step on the third step. With the right foot, step on the sixth step. Continue this pattern up the stairs.
- Take two steps at a time, alternating feet.
- Jumping with feet together, hit every step.
- Jumping with feet together, hit every other step.
- Jumping with feet together, hit every third step.
- Hop on the right foot, hitting the first step and the second step; then switch to the left foot for the third and fourth steps.
- Walk backward up the steps.
- Face to the right or left and carioca up the stairs (see p. 20).
- With feet together, hop to the top of the stairs in as few hops as possible. The focus is on hopping up as many stairs at a time as possible.
- While alternating feet, get to the top of the stairs in as few strides as possible. The focus is on striding up as many stairs at a time as possible.
- With feet together, get to the top of the stairs as quickly as possible. The focus is on speed as you hop up the stairs.
- While alternating feet, get to the top of the stairs as quickly as possible. The focus is on speed as you stride up the stairs.
- While alternating feet, complete as many round trips in 30 seconds as possible.
- With feet together, complete as many round trips in 30 seconds as possible.
- With feet together, hop up two steps and then down one step, and so on.
- Hopping on the right foot only, hop up one step at a time halfway up. Switch to the left foot and hop the rest of the way.
- Hop on the right foot only one step at a time to the top.
- Hop on the left foot only one step at a time to the top.

Running

Although some running drills can be incorporated into the circuit drills, they are usually done separately for cardiovascular conditioning.

RUNNING DRILLS

- Distance running. Develop endurance by running a set number of laps around a track, football field, or gym.
- Parachute running. Sprint with a parachute harnessed to your chest. This strengthens the legs and develops power.
- Resistance running. Use rubber ropes and harnesses. Sprint with resistance holding you back. You can adjust the amount of resistance. This strengthens the legs and develops power by placing an extra load on the runner.
- Hill sprints. Sprint up a hill and walk down to strengthen the legs and develop power. Sprint down the hill and walk up. This forces you to overstride to maintain balance, improving your quickness and speed. Use whatever hills are available, striving for a distance of 30 to 50 yards.
- Towed running. Use rubber ropes and harnesses to force you to overstride to maintain balance, improving your quickness and speed.

Position-Specific Training Drills

Although most training drills are done by all players regardless of their positions, some drills are specific to football positions. These drills develop speed and quickness. On certain days, one or more workout stations are replaced with position-specific drills.

WIDE RECEIVER

Through these drills, wide receivers develop concentration, coordination, timing, the vertical jump, and all the components of running patterns; they also practice stalking the defender.

■ Misdirection. Run full speed, selling the misdirection needed to perform each and every pattern in your pass offense. Make the defender believe you're running a pattern that you're not. Sell him on the pattern that you're faking so that you create separation when you finish the pattern called.

■ Long-ball drill. Run down a long pass thrown by the quarterback or coach. This drill requires full-speed acceleration to catch up to a long ball in flight.

■ Stalk block. This is a downfield block that wide receivers often have to make. Stay between the defender and the ball. Break down and bend at the hips and knees as you approach the defender. Mimic his movements. This drill can be done against air or as a full-speed drill with a ballcarrier and against a defender.

■ One-hand drill. To assist with concentration on the ball, practice catching increasingly difficult passes with one hand while running at full speed. Passes are thrown by a coach or quarterback.

■ Ball machine drill. Face away from the ball machine. On the coach's signal, turn and catch the ball. Complete a rapid-fire sequence of five catches. On the final catch, secure the ball, turn, and sprint 40 yards into the end zone.

■ Crossfield blocking drill. Sprint across the field and throw a stand-up block into a dummy.

■ Hail Mary drill. Sprint 40 yards into the end zone. Time your jump to come down with the ball to win the game. Practice reacting to a tipped ball, which is usually what will happen on a Hail Mary pass in a game. First do this drill with only one defender. Then progress to using several defenders and receivers sprinting to the area to try to tip the ball.

■ Tap tap drill. Catch a pass while dragging a foot inbounds before crossing the boundary. Because of the importance of exact timing and accuracy, this drill works best when a quarterback throws the pass.

RUNNING BACK

In doing these position-specific drills, the running back develops balance, concentration, coordination, stamina, and proper body lean.

■ Pop-up balance drill. Run upfield with the ball. Lean forward to throw yourself out of balance.

For as long as you can, keep from falling down by popping yourself back up with one hand.

■ Sideline drill. Several defenders with shields station 3 yards inside the boundary. Head upfield between the shields and the boundary. The defenders jolt you with the shields in an attempt to knock you out of bounds. As you gain confidence, anticipate the contact and deliver directly into the shields, administering punishment to the defenders rather than receiving punishment.

■ Piggyback ride. Holding a football, carry a partner piggyback to simulate a tackler hanging on and trying to bring you down. Have your partner shake and twist as you sprint 25 yards.

■ Stiff-arm drill. Begin on the 35-yard-line hash mark. The first standup dummy is on the 30-yard-line numbers with other dummies placed at the 25-yard hash mark, the 20-yard-line numbers, the 15-yard-line hash mark, and the 10-yard-line numbers. As you round the first dummy, place the ball in your outside hand and deliver a stiff arm to the dummy (figure 3.3). Weave back and forth through the rest of the dummies, each time placing the ball in your outside hand and delivering a stiff arm with your inside arm. Finish the drill by sprinting the final 10 yards across the goal line.

■ Over-the-head drill. As you sprint downfield, the quarterback or coach lofts the ball over your head. You must find the ball, adjust to it, and bring it in.

Figure 3.3 Running back stiff-arm drill.

- Check flare drill. Start from a backfield position. Set up as if to check for a rusher to block; then flare and catch the pass.
- Check alley drill. Start from a tight slot position. Set up as if to check for a rusher to block; then run the alley pattern and catch the pass.

OFFENSIVE LINEMAN

The position-specific drills for offensive linemen develop the optimal stance, acceleration out of that stance, and balance; they also improve each lineman's ability to quickly get to the point of attack.

- Stance and take-off. Practice the perfect stance, both right- and left-handed. Explode out of your stance for 10 yards.
- Long-pull drill. Place standup dummies at various linebacker positions for you to react to. As you round the corner and turn downfield, dip your inside shoulder to enable you to make the turn more quickly and get into position to look back to the inside for someone in pursuit.
- Crossfield blocking drill. From a three-point stance, jam a standup dummy with the outside hand to simulate keeping the defensive man from crossing your face. Sprint crossfield and block a standup dummy.

DEFENSIVE BACK

In doing these drills, defensive backs increase their coverage range and speed in the backpedal and improve their ability to play the ball in the air, their timing, their vertical jump, and their balance. They also get practice in catching the football.

- Long-ball drill. Use the same drill as used for the wide receivers (p. 27).
- Horizontal coverage drill. Backs execute at full speed, reacting to the ball in flight. Increase the horizontal coverage distance. The coach throws the ball (never have a quarterback throw a ball that is meant to be intercepted).
- Hail Mary drill. Use the same drill as used for the wide receivers (p. 27).
- Backpedal drill. Practice sprinting backward using proper mechanics.
- Come to drill. Line up 20 yards in front of the coach. At the coach's signal, start forward at full speed. The coach passes the ball to you.

Catch the ball and sprint to the coach. Most of the time, the coach will throw the ball high, so you must judge the height of the ball. Sometimes, however, the ball will be thrown slightly to your right or left.

- Tap tap drill. Use the same drill as used for the wide receivers (p. 27). Backs learn to sense where they are in relation to the sideline, intercept the ball, and drag one foot inbounds before crossing the boundary.

LINEBACKER

In their position-specific drills, linebackers develop balance and agility, improve their backpedaling abilities, and practice catching the ball.

- Shuffle and footwork drill. Lay three planks vertically side by side, spaced 2 yards apart. A ballcarrier sweeps right or left. As the ballcarrier moves, shuffle laterally, lifting your feet over the planks and staying level (figure 3.4). Maintain leverage on the ballcarrier. After clearing the last plank, meet the ballcarrier with a form tackle.
- Drop drill. Two receivers stand 12 yards deep and 7 yards apart. Begin in normal starting position; then quickly drop between the two receivers as the quarterback begins his drop. Without faking, the quarterback throws to one of the receivers. Make the interception and return it at full speed.
- Retreating drill. Linebackers must be able to move quickly and keep their eyes on the passer as they move to their assigned pass-defense area. To accomplish this, move to the hook area using a crossover step. Get 10 to 12 yards deep by the time the quarterback's arm starts forward. If you have not reached that depth, level off so you'll be in a balanced position, ready to move to either side to intercept the pass. The passer throws the ball to your right or left. Get to the ball, make the interception, and return it at full speed.
- Hook area coverage. The wide receiver runs directly along the hash marks and then breaks into a pattern. Retreat quickly to the hook area; then play the receiver and break up the pattern.
- Interception challenge drill. With a partner, stand 7 yards apart and 15 yards in front of a coach. The coach throws the ball directly

Figure 3.4 Linebacker shuffle and footwork drill.

between you and your partner, and you both go after it. Play the ball; the best man comes down with it. Try to intercept the ball at its highest point.

DEFENSIVE LINEMAN

In doing these position-specific drills defensive linemen improve their lateral movement, coordination, quickness, and the ability to quickly change directions.

- Step-over drill. Face a coach. To your left are several dummies lying on the ground with 2 yards between each dummy. Move back and forth over the dummies with your knees pumping high, following the coach's hand signals. Continue through the final dummy. Keep your eyes on the coach and keep your shoulders parallel. As soon as you are over the final dummy, sprint 5 yards to a held standup dummy and apply a form tackle.
- Direction drill. Face a coach with your shoulders square. Move right or left at the coach's command. Use a crossover step to change direction. After several changes of direction, the coach will point up. Reach up to deflect the pass. When the coach points down, fall to

your hands and knees and pop back up. The drill ends with a 5-yard sprint, forward roll, and form tackle into a standup dummy.
- Pursuit drill. Explode into a dummy or shield, and then sprint to the ballcarrier 30 yards to your right or left at a depth consistent with where the ballcarrier would be when the defensive lineman arrives.

Motivating Challenges

To lift spirits and motivate players, several times during the off-season we finish the day with fun competitions such as team hand ball, artillery ball, or king of the hill. We do these activities on the gym floor, or, if weather permits, on the artificial turf game field.

In our version of team hand ball, we use a volleyball and have each team defend a goal. The goal is the mat on the wall underneath the basket, or an indoor soccer goal, or a marked-off area of similar size. The team with the ball passes the ball from player to player; the player with the ball can take only two steps unless he's rolling or dribbling the ball. The other team can use almost any method to take the ball away; this game gets very physical. The only way to score is to throw the ball at the goal from outside the three-point arc.

For artillery ball, we use as many volleyballs as we can find. Players throw the balls at their opponents. If a ball hits a player, he's out of the game. If a player catches the ball, the thrower is out. The game ends when all players on one team are eliminated.

King of the hill is a challenge competition between two players in a small, confined circle, such as the center circle of a basketball court. The two contestants lock up. Each attempts to get his opponent down on a knee or shove him out of the circle. When either occurs, the winner is declared, and he meets the next challenger.

Testing and Evaluation

After 10 weeks of winter workouts, we devote several days to testing. We measure each player's height and weight, vertical jump, and times in the 20-yard dash, 40-yard dash, 20-yard backward sprint, 5-yard shuffle run, 5-yard shuttle run, and 20-yard box run.

For the 5-yard shuffle run, players face straight ahead in the middle of the 5-yard space. They shuffle to the right and touch the line with a hand. They shuffle 5 yards to the left and touch that line with a hand. They shuffle back to the right through the start position.

For the 5-yard shuttle run, players face straight ahead in the middle of the 5-yard space. They sprint to the right and touch the line with a hand. They sprint 5 yards to the left and touch that line with a hand. They sprint back to the right through the start position.

For the 20-yard box run, use tape to mark a box on the gym floor. Players start from the left bottom corner of the square. They shuffle to the right through one leg of the box, sprint backward through the second leg, shuffle to the left through the third leg, and finish the square by sprinting forward to the start position.

We also evaluate players in the bench press, both for maximum weight and for the number of reps they can do with 225 pounds.

Prior to the bench press maximum test, each player must warm up thoroughly. Then each player gets a recorded lift. We don't want players to attempt a maximum lift if there's a chance for failure. We want them to complete and record a lift and then proceed to their maximum weight.

As with the bench press maximum, for the bench press reps at 225 pounds, we strictly enforce correct lifting form. We do not count an attempt that does not include a total lockout of the elbows. Feet must be flat on the floor with the back flat on the bench through the total range of motion.

Iron Man Team and Individual Contests

We conclude the winter workouts of our conditioning program with team and individual contests. Whenever the offense and the defense get to compete against each other in anything, players get excited about it. We change events from year to year, so they'll always confront something new and challenging for which they're not prepared. Small prizes, such as something from the campus bookstore, are awarded to winners.

TEAM EVENTS

- Corn sack relay. Players divide into four-man relay teams. The first player bear hugs a 100-pound sack of corn and runs 30 yards, circles a cone, and runs back 30 yards to the start position, handing the bag to the next player.
- Sprint medley. Four players make up a relay team. This race consists of an 800-meter leg and 100-, 200-, and 400-meter legs. One player on the relay team runs each leg.
- Tug of war. One four-man team tries to pull the other team across a marked line.
- Gator pull. Tie a rope to the front of a gator, small pickup truck, or golf cart. A four-man team pulls the gator 60 yards up a slight incline. The team with the best time wins.

INDIVIDUAL EVENTS

■ Pickup truck push. Push a pickup truck 60 yards.

■ Tractor tire flip. Flip a tractor tire over repeatedly for 20 yards.

■ Discus tire throw. Throw a car tire for distance, as in a discus throw.

■ Stair lift. Place four 45-pound weight plates in a wooden box with a rope handle. Lift the box up the stairs one step at a time for 12 steps.

■ Sled pull. Using a hand-over-hand method, pull a sled loaded with four 45-pound weight plates for 30 yards up a hill.

■ Iron cross lift. Hold one 10-pound weight plate in each hand at 90-degree angles to the sides. Keep the weight to your sides for as long as possible above a marked spot on the wall that corresponds to 90 degrees.

■ Sledge hammer lift. Hold a sledge hammer in both hands extended 90 degrees in front of you. When the hammer begins to lower, the stopwatch is stopped.

■ Hill sprint. Wearing boots, sprint up a significant hill for 30 yards.

Spring Practice

During spring practice, the weight-lifting load is lightened so players can concentrate on strength maintenance. We continue form running drills, incorporating them into the practice schedule.

Summer

Unlike at larger universities, most of our players at UVA-Wise go home for the summer. So our summer workouts are strongly encouraged but voluntary. Every player receives a booklet that describes exactly what to do on each day of the 8-week program. The program is designed in hopes that players will arrive at camp strong and in tiptop shape. If you are at a high school or middle school level, you won't have to worry about players leaving town. If you are at the college level, it will be up to the head coach to make workouts mandatory or not. We strongly encourage all players to complete the 8-week summer program to prepare them for summer camp.

Heavy lifting and an increase in cardiovascular conditioning is prescribed during the weeks leading up to summer camp. Regardless of whether your players stay in town or not, they are all on the same program, although players not on campus are responsible for their own workouts.

Agility and Quickness Drills

Agility and quickness are mandatory in the sport of football, and both can be improved through daily drills. Begin by instructing the correct way to move the body. Eliminate any body positioning that does not contribute to quick acceleration and the fastest movement. Will these drills ensure the development of an Olympic sprinter? Of course not, but each player will move closer to his biological limits of quickness and agility. Obviously, size and strength are important in football, but if the player does not get to the point of attack in time, he is of little value to the team. Football features obstructed movement and constant changes of direction. These drills develop the ability to accelerate, change direction, maintain balance, recover quickly, and reduce fatigue. These abilities along with the increased muscular strength gained through systematic weight lifting promote a player's ability to play football competitively.

20-YARD SHUTTLE RUN

Mark three lines, each 5 yards from the other. The lines can be marked with tape on a gym floor, with cones, or you can use the yard markings on a football field. The middle line serves as the start and finish line. Straddle the start and finish line. Break to your left. With your hand, touch the line 5 yards to your left. Do not leap to touch the line. Turn and sprint past the start and finish line to the far line 10 yards away. Touch that line with your hand. Turn and sprint through the start and finish line. Run through the start and finish line. As you run, move in a straight path. Keep movements as efficient as possible. Do not rotate your body when you change directions. Use your feet to prepare to change direction. Pump your arms and legs as you run, keeping you abdominal muscles relaxed. Repeat, but this time break to your right first. This counts as one repetition. Do three repetitions.

FOUR-CORNER DRILL

Mark a square 10 yards by 10 yards. Start in a three-point stance outside the square. Sprint forward to cone 1. Carioca to cone 2, keeping your back to the square (see p. 20). Sprint backward to cone 3. Carioca to cone 4 while facing the square (figure 3.5). One complete trip around the square counts as one repetition. Do three repetitions.

DIAGONAL FOUR-CORNER DRILL

Mark a square 10 yards by 10 yards—as was used in the four-corner drill, except the cones are numbered differently. Start in a three-point stance outside the square. Sprint diagonally to cone 1 and touch it with your hand. Sprint to cone 2 and touch it. Sprint diagonally to cone 3 and touch it. Sprint

to cone 4 and touch it. One complete trip to touch all four cones counts as one repetition. Do three repetitions.

DIAGONAL FOUR-CORNER DRILL FOR DEFENSIVE BACKS

Use the same square and cones as for the diagonal four-corner drill. Start in a two-point stance outside the square. Sprint diagonally to cone 1 and touch it with your hand. Sprint backward to cone 2 and touch it. Sprint diagonally to cone 3 and touch it. Sprint backward to cone 4 and touch it. One complete trip to all four cones counts as one repetition. Do three repetitions.

Eight-Week Summer Conditioning Program

Much of the eight-week conditioning program (figure 3.6) is progressive. Each week is set up to increase cardiovascular fitness, strength, and agility from the previous week. The last week eases off slightly so players are rested going into the beginning of camp.

Figure 3.5 Action for four-corner drill.

Eight-Week Conditioning Program

Notes

- When a time is designated for sets of sprints, that time should be the average time for that set.
- For weight lifting, use whatever weight resources are available: Nautilus, Hammer, similar machines, or free weights.

WEEK 1

Weight Lifting

Do three times per week, working both the upper and lower body.

Stretching and Conditioning

Do four times per week.

- Stretching exercises from the winter conditioning program (p. 18)
- 30 push-ups
- 30 bent-leg sit-ups
- 30 step-ups on each leg (60 total) on a step 12 or 13 inches high
- 4 pull-ups or chin-ups

Running

Run four times per week.

First and second days

- Perform form running drills: half-speed, three-quarter speed, high knees, crossover, and backward run (beginning on p. 26).
- Run 1-1/2 miles in 12 minutes.
- Run 40 yards up a 25- to 30-degree slope for one set of five reps, resting between each rep by walking for 30 seconds.

Third day

Same as the first and second days, but run 1-1/2 miles in 11 minutes.

Fourth day

Same as the first and second days, but run 1-1/2 miles in 10 minutes.

(continued)

Figure 3.6 Sample eight-week conditioning program.

Eight-Week Conditioning Program (continued)

WEEK 2

Weight Lifting
Do three times per week, working both the upper and lower body.

Stretching and Conditioning
Do four times per week.
- Stretching exercises from the winter conditioning program (p. 18)
- 30 push-ups
- 30 bent-leg sit-ups
- 30 step-ups on each leg (60 total) on a step 12 or 13 inches high
- 4 pull-ups or chin-ups

Running
Run four times per week.

First, second, and third days
- Perform form running drills: carioca; tapioca; vertical bounce; leaping, bounding, horizontal stride, and 45-degree cut each way.
- Run 2 miles in 13-1/2 minutes.
- Run 40 yards down a 25- to 30-degree slope for one set of five reps, resting between each by walking for 30 seconds.

Fourth day
Same as the first, second, and third days, but run 2 miles in 13 minutes.

WEEK 3

Weight Lifting

Do three times per week, working both the upper and lower body.

Stretching and Conditioning

Do four times per week.

- Stretching exercises from the winter conditioning program (p. 18)
- 50 push-ups
- 50 bent-leg sit-ups
- 50 step-ups on each leg (100 total) on a step 12 or 13 inches high
- 8 pull-ups or chin-ups

Running

Run four times per week.

First day

- Run 200 meters for two sets of three reps, resting between each by walking for 60 seconds. Backs, linebackers, and receivers should complete each rep within 30 seconds, linemen within 32.5 seconds.
- Run 100 meters for one set of four reps, resting between each by walking for 30 seconds. Backs, linebackers, and receivers should complete each rep within 12 seconds, linemen within 12.7 seconds.

Second day

- Run 2 miles. Backs, linebackers, and receivers should complete the 2 miles within 13 minutes, linemen within 14 minutes.
- Do the 20-yard shuttle run (p. 31).

Third day

- Run 400 meters for one set of three reps, resting between each by walking for 90 seconds. Backs, linebackers, and receivers should complete each rep within 85 seconds, linemen within 90 seconds.
- Run 100 meters for one set of four reps, resting between each by walking for 30 seconds. Backs, linebackers, and receivers should complete each rep within 12 seconds, linemen within 12.7 seconds.

Fourth day

- Run 200 meters for two sets of three reps, resting between each rep by walking for 30 seconds. Backs, linebackers, and receivers should complete each rep within 30 seconds, linemen within 32.5 seconds.
- Run 100 meters for one set of four repetitions, resting between each by walking for 30 seconds. Backs, linebackers, and receivers should complete each rep within 12 seconds, linemen within 12.7 seconds.

(continued)

WEEK 4

Weight Lifting

Perform three times per week, working both the upper and lower body.

Stretching and Conditioning

Do four times per week.

- Stretching exercises from the winter conditioning program (p. 18)
- 50 push-ups
- 50 bent-leg sit-ups
- 50 step-ups each leg (100 total) on a step 12 or 13 inches high
- 8 pull-ups or chin-ups

Running

Run four times per week.

First day

- Run 100 meters for one set of five reps, resting between each by walking for 30 seconds. Backs, linebackers, and receivers should complete each rep within 12 seconds, linemen within 12.7 seconds.
- Sprint 55 yards for one set of 10 reps, resting between each by walking for 30 seconds. Backs, linebackers, and receivers should complete each rep within 6.5 seconds, linemen within 6.9 seconds.
- Do any 15 of the stair drills (p. 25).

Second day

- Run a 2-mile Fartlek run, alternating among sprinting, jogging, and walking each 200 yards. Backs, linebackers, and receivers should complete the run within 16 minutes, linemen within 17 minutes.

Third day

- Run 200 meters for two sets of four reps, resting between each rep by walking for 60 seconds. Backs, linebackers, and receivers should complete each rep within 30 seconds, linemen within 32.5 seconds.
- Do hill sprints (p. 26). If no hill is available, sprint for 55 yards for one set of 10 reps, resting between each by walking for 30 seconds. Backs, linebackers, and receivers should complete each rep within 6.5 seconds, linemen within 6.9 seconds.

Fourth day

- Run 1 mile, then rest by walking for 15 minutes. Backs, linebackers, and receivers should complete the run within 6-1/2 minutes, linemen within 7 minutes.
- Do any 10 jump rope drills (p. 23).

WEEK 5

Weight Lifting

Do three times per week, working both the upper and lower body.

Stretching and Conditioning

Do four times per week.

- Stretching exercises from the winter conditioning program (p. 18)
- 75 push-ups
- 75 bent-leg sit-ups
- 75 step-ups each leg (150 total) on a step 12 or 13 inches high
- 12 pull-ups or chin-ups

Running

Run four times per week.

First day

- Run 200 meters for two sets of four reps, resting between each rep by walking for 60 seconds. Backs, linebackers, and receivers should complete each rep within 30 seconds, linemen within 32.5 seconds.
- Run 40 yards down a 25- to 30-degree slope for one set of five reps, resting between each by walking for 30 seconds.
- Do dot drills (p. 24).

Second day

- Sprint 55 yards for two sets of six reps, resting between each rep by jogging for 30 seconds. Backs, linebackers, and receivers should complete each rep within 6.5 seconds, linemen within 6.9 seconds.
- Run 100 meters for one set of five reps, resting between each by walking for 30 seconds. Backs, linebackers, and receivers should complete each rep within 11.5 seconds, linemen within 12.2 seconds.
- Do any 15 of the stair drills (p. 25).

Third day

- Run a 2-mile Fartlek run, alternating sprinting, jogging, and walking each 200 yards. Backs, linebackers, and receivers should complete the run within 16 minutes, linemen within 17 minutes.
- Do hill sprints (p. 26). If no hill is available, sprint for 55 yards for one set of 10 reps, resting between each by walking for 30 seconds. Backs, linebackers, and receivers should complete each rep within 6.5 seconds, linemen within 6.9 seconds.
- Do the four-corner drill (p. 32).

Fourth day

- Run 40 yards for two sets of five reps, resting between each rep by walking for 30 seconds. Backs, linebackers, and receivers should complete each rep within 4.9 seconds, linemen within 5.2 seconds.
- Run 400 meters for one set of two reps, resting between each by jogging for 90 seconds. Backs, linebackers, and receivers should complete each rep within 60 seconds, linemen within 65 seconds.

(continued)

Eight-Week Conditioning Program *(continued)*

WEEK 6

Weight Lifting
Do three times per week, working both the upper and lower body.

Stretching and Conditioning
Do four times per week.
- Stretching exercises from the winter conditioning program (p. 18)
- 75 push-ups
- 75 bent-leg sit-ups
- 75 step-ups each leg (150 total) on a step 12 or 13 inches high
- 12 pull-ups or chin-ups

Running
Run four times per week.

First day
- Run 1 mile, then rest by jogging for 14 minutes. Backs, linebackers, and receivers should complete the run within 6-1/2 minutes, linemen within 7 minutes.
- Run 200 meters for one set of two reps, resting between each by jogging for 60 seconds. Backs, linebackers, and receivers should complete each rep within 28 seconds, linemen within 30.5 seconds.
- Run 40 yards up a 25- to 30-degree slope for two sets of five reps, resting between each rep by walking for 30 seconds.
- Do any 15 of the stair drills (p. 25).

Second day
- Run 40 yards for two sets of five reps, resting between each rep by jogging for 30 seconds. Backs, linebackers, and receivers should complete each rep within 4.9 seconds, linemen within 5.2 seconds.
- Run 100 meters for one set of four reps, resting between each by jogging for 30 seconds. Backs, linebackers, and receivers should complete each rep within 11.5 seconds, linemen within 12.2 seconds.
- Do the 20-yard shuttle run (p. 31).
- Do the four-corner drill (p. 32).
- Do the diagonal four-corner drill (p. 32) or, for defensive backs, the diagonal four-corner drill for defensive backs (p. 32).

Third day

- Run 400 meters for one set of four reps, resting between each by walking for 85 seconds. Backs, linebackers, and receivers should complete each rep within 75 seconds, linemen within 80 seconds.

- Do hill sprints (p. 26). If no hill is available, sprint for 55 yards for one set of 10 reps, resting between each by walking for 30 seconds. Backs, linebackers, and receivers should complete each rep within 6.5 seconds, linemen within 6.9 seconds.

Fourth day

- Do the form running drills: half-speed, three-quarter speed, high knees, crossover, backward run, tapioca, and leaping, bounding, horizontal stride (beginning on p. 20).

- Run 200 meters for one set of three reps, resting between each by jogging for 60 seconds. Backs, linebackers, and receivers should complete each rep within 28 seconds, linemen within 30.5 seconds.

- Run 100 meters for one set of four reps, resting between each by jogging for 30 seconds. Backs, linebackers, and receivers should complete each rep within 11.5 seconds, linemen within 12.2 seconds.

- Do any 10 of the jump rope drills (p. 23).

(continued)

WEEK 7

Weight Lifting

Do three times per week, working both the upper and lower body.

Stretching and Conditioning

Do four times per week.

- Stretching exercises from the winter conditioning program (p. 18)
- 100 push-ups
- 100 bent-leg sit-ups
- 100 step-ups each leg (200 total) on a step 12 or 13 inches high
- 16 pull-ups or chin-ups

Running

Run four times per week.

First day

- Run 40 yards for two sets of five reps, resting between each rep by jogging for 30 seconds. Backs, linebackers, and receivers should complete each rep within 4.9 seconds, linemen within 5.2 seconds.
- Run 100 meters for one set of four reps, resting between each by jogging for 30 seconds. Backs, linebackers, and receivers should complete each rep within 11.5 seconds, linemen within 12.2 seconds.
- Do dot drills (p. 24).
- Do the 20-yard shuttle run (p. 32).
- Do the four-corner drill (p. 32).
- Do the diagonal four-corner drill (p. 32) or, for defensive backs, the diagonal four-corner drill for defensive backs (p. 32).

Second day

- Run a 1-mile Fartlek run, alternating sprinting, jogging, and walking each 200 yards. Backs, linebackers, and receivers should complete the run within 7-1/2 minutes, linemen within 8 minutes.
- Do hill sprints (p. 26). If no hill is available, sprint for 55 yards for one set of 10 reps, resting between each by walking for 30 seconds. Backs, linebackers, and receivers should complete each rep within 6.5 seconds, linemen within 6.9 seconds.

Third day

- Run 55 yards for one set of eight reps, resting between each by jogging for 30 seconds. Backs, linebackers, and receivers should complete each rep within 6.2 seconds, linemen within 6.6 seconds.
- Run 200 meters for one set of two reps, resting between each by jogging for 60 seconds. Backs, linebackers, and receivers should complete each rep within 27 seconds, linemen within 29.5 seconds.
- Do the form running drills: carioca, tapioca, vertical bounce, leaping, bounding, horizontal stride, and 45-degree cut each way.

Fourth day

- Run 40 yards for three sets of five reps, resting between each rep by jogging for 30 seconds. Backs, linebackers, and receivers should complete each rep within 4.9 seconds, linemen within 5.2 seconds.
- Do any 15 of the stair drills (p. 25).

WEEK 8

Weight Lifting

Do three times per week, working both the upper and lower body.

Stretching and Conditioning

Do four times per week.

- Stretching exercises from the winter conditioning program (p. 18)
- 100 push-ups
- 100 bent-leg sit-ups
- 100 step-ups each leg (200 total) on a step 12 or 13 inches high
- 16 pull-ups or chin-ups with palms away from the body

Running

Run three times per week.

First day

- Run 55 yards for two sets of eight reps, resting between each rep by walking for 30 seconds. Backs, linebackers, and receivers should complete each rep within 6.2 seconds, linemen within 6.6 seconds.
- For all players except offensive linemen, run 40 yards for two sets of five reps down a 25- to 30-degree slope, resting between each rep by walking for 30 seconds. Then run 40 yards for one set of five reps up a 25- to 30-degree slope, resting between each by walking for 30 seconds.
- Offensive linemen do the reverse. Run two sets uphill and one set downhill.

Second day

- Run 200 meters for one set of three reps, resting between each by jogging for 60 seconds. Backs, linebackers, and receivers should complete each rep within 26.5 seconds, linemen within 29 seconds.
- Run 100 meters for one set of two reps, resting between each by jogging for 30 seconds. Backs, linebackers, and receivers should complete each rep within 11.5 seconds, linemen within 12.2 seconds.
- Do the 20-yard shuttle run (p. 31).
- Do the four-corner drill (p. 32).
- Do the diagonal four-corner drill (p. 32) or, for defensive backs, the diagonal four-corner drill for defensive backs (p. 32).

Third day

- Run 40 yards for three sets of five reps, resting between each rep by walking for 30 seconds. Backs, linebackers, and receivers should complete each rep within 4.9 seconds, linemen within 5.2 seconds.
- Do dot drills (p. 24).

In-Season

During the season, required lifting is limited to Mondays and Thursdays, with an emphasis on strength maintenance (lighter resistance and more repetitions). At the first week of preseason camp, players participate in a weight-lifting clinic, where they are introduced to the acceptable lifting technique for each lift that is part of the routine. Many young players have not been taught the correct form for lifting heavy weights. Teaching the correct form will not only enhance their lifting capability but also minimize the risk of injury. Older players might need this training, too, because bad habits sometimes creep into technique.

The middle practice in summer camp three-a-days is devoted entirely to special teams, agility, and conditioning.

My philosophy has always been that players must report to camp in great physical condition. Practice keeps players in shape but does not get them in shape. The purpose of preseason camp is not conditioning. This time is needed for coaches to teach players to improve their playing skills and learn the system. Players should be conditioned when they arrive.

4

Individual Offensive Skills and Drills

In this chapter we break down each offensive position, explain the skills needed to play the position, and present several drills designed to improve the player's effectiveness. The art of successfully passing the football, catching the ball, running patterns, receiving a handoff, performing a multitude of run and pass protection blocks, carrying the football, shedding would-be tacklers, employing effective vertical and horizontal splits, and using the proper stance are some of the individual skills that we'll cover here. Improving skills position by position goes a long way toward building a highly effective offense. The emphasis here is on individual offensive play; team offense is covered in chapter 6.

Quarterback

At the high school level and after, only the head coach should have contact with the quarterback regarding football unless the head coach delegates the responsibility to a quarterbacks coach. In everything the coach says and does in front of the team and the rest of the coaching staff, he must display total confidence in his quarterback. This does not mean that he never corrects the quarterback, but when he does, he does it quietly and away from other players and coaches. When the quarterback makes the wrong decision on a play, instead of ridiculing him, the coach asks the quarterback what he saw and lets him explain what caused him to make the decision he did.

The head coach should spend a tremendous amount of time with his quarterback leading up to game day. As soon as the coaching staff develops the offensive game plan, the head coach meets with the quarterback and details the game plan to him. He reviews the plan with him every day of game week, getting him to the point where he can explain the game plan and the rationale for it himself. He looks at each of the opponent's defenses and coverages. He tells the coach which plays he will automatic out of and the options he can choose from when he automatics. The coach has him reveal the plays on which he will railroad (run to the opposite direction) or when the receiver should be open because of the coverage being employed. The coach uses diagrammed cards, video, and PowerPoint presentations as appropriate.

If the defense stems (moves from one alignment to another during the quarterback's cadence), the quarterback will know that the cadence must be either very quick or very long—quick so that he can snap the ball before the defense stems or long enough after the defense changes fronts to give the offensive line enough time to recognize the new front and make the proper blocking adjustments. When running the two-minute offense, the quarterback knows the automatic personnel package, the automatic formation for the week, and the short list of plays to run in each situation. The team is already in the automatic formation, and the snap count is predetermined, so the only call the quarterback must make is the play. There's no need to spike the ball and deprive his team of an opportunity to move the football. He just waits for the referee to put the ball in play.

If you are the head coach, remember that it's not what *you* know but what your quarterback knows that is most important. The quarterback is the offensive coach on the field.

Running Plays

On running plays, it is the quarterback's responsibility to get the ball to the running back. The running back must be at the right place at the right time with his hands in the proper position to receive the ball, but the exchange is the responsibility of the quarterback. (See the handoff drill and figure 4.1.) If the quarterback feels the timing is off and there is even the slightest possibility that he cannot secure the exchange, the quarterback pulls the ball back in and follows the running back into the hole.

Figure 4.1 Handoff drill: *(a)* ballcarrier is ready to receive the ball; *(b)* quarterback presses the ball into the ballcarrier's abdomen; *(c)* ballcarrier clamps down on the ball to secure it.

The quarterback must make a handoff and a fake handoff look exactly the same. He uses his body to hide the ball. He must be a magician and take great pride in his ability to deceive the defense. He should carry out his fakes even longer than he thinks necessary. Causing even one defensive player to lose one step might be the difference between an average run and a big gain.

HANDOFF DRILL

The handoff drill (figure 4.1) is performed by the quarterback and the ballcarrier. Emphasize the ballcarrier employing the proper technique to receive the ball—near elbow up with thumb down, far elbow 4 to 6 inches from the body—and the quarterback pressing the ball into the ballcarrier's abdomen as the ballcarrier clamps down on the ball to keep it secure.

Pass Drops

In the passing game, the quarterback's drop must be consistent. He must drop quickly and sprint. The faster the quarterback gets to his drop, the more time he has to read the coverage and find the open receiver. On a three-step drop, the quarterback should get at least 5 yards deep. On a five-step drop, he gets at least 7-1/2 yards deep, and on a seven-step drop he gets at least 10 yards deep.

A three-step drop demonstrates the three key steps of all drops. On all drops, the first step is a separation step as the quarterback breaks away from the center. As the right-handed quarterback rides his hands forward for the snap, he reaches back with the right foot. The second step is a deep step to provide as much depth as possible. The final step is a balance step. The quarterback puts minimal weight on the back foot because he needs to transfer his weight to the front foot again in order to pass.

In a five-step drop, after the first separation step, the second, third, and fourth steps are big, sprinting steps to gain depth. The quarterback holds the ball near his ear, not his waist, because he will need the ball at ear height for delivery (figure 4.2). The feet point east and

Figure 4.2 On a five-step drop, the quarterback holds the ball near his ear, preparing to pass the ball.

west (toes point toward the sideline), and the feet chop. Chopping the feet allows the quarterback to be ready to move quickly in any direction to avoid sudden pressure from the pass rush. The quarterback leads with the elbow, drives the ball forward, and follows through with the arm and shoulder all the way past his waist (figure 4.3 on page 46). He delivers the ball over the front foot, stepping into the pass and using his hips to follow through.

The quarterback controls the linebackers and secondary with his eyes. As he drops, he does not look in the direction he intends to pass. Instead he views the intended receiver with his peripheral vision. He stands tall, stepping in the direction of the pass and throwing over his front foot.

When stepping toward the target, the quarterback must not take too big a step. If he does, the pass will tend to be low and he will not involve his hips in his follow-through. When a right-handed quarterback is throwing to the left, he must make sure he does not open up too far. Instead, he steps directly toward his target, keeping his front foot in the middle of his body. Opening up too far forces him to throw only with his arm, thereby losing velocity because the shoulder and hips aren't involved.

Figure 4.3 Quarterback throwing sequence: *(a)* lead with the elbow; *(b)* drive the ball forward; *(c)* follow through with the arm and shoulder.

Coverage Reads

Prior to the snap of a passing play, the quarterback takes a presnap read to assess the defensive coverage. He also takes a postsnap read to confirm his observation or change his mind based on the actual pass coverage.

If the secondary's presnap alignment is three deep with a strong safety in a walk, or 3 to 5 yards off and 3 to 5 yards outside the tight end or slot, the quarterback could assume that the coverage will be a three-deep and four-under zone. If the free safety moves over to a head-up position on the number two receiver, this tells the quarterback to look for pure man-for-man coverage with the distinct possibility that the strong safety will blitz. When the strong safety moves to a head-up position on the number two receiver, it appears that man-free safety coverage will be used. (This means that all receivers are covered with defenders playing man-to-man coverage while the safety is free to help inside-out on patterns breaking to the inside.) If the strong safety is in a head-up position on the number two receiver and the free safety starts to move toward one of the cornerbacks, it's likely that man coverage with a corner blitz will be used. If there are two deep safeties with two corners and three linebackers in their normal run alignment underneath, the presnap assumption is a two-deep and five-under zone. If the same coverage is shown except the linebackers are head-up on eligible receivers, the assumption is a two-deep zone and five-under man. If the corners line up slightly inside the wide receivers with their bodies turned toward those receivers, the coverage is a two-deep zone and five-under man again but with the trail technique.

If there are four deep defensive backs, the postsnap read is even more essential because of the many options: four-deep zone, combo coverage (1/4, 1/4, 1/2), invert, corner roll, three-deep zone, or man, with either a corner or safety blitz. Well-disguised coverages are common as defenses squirm from one alignment and coverage to another on the snap, making postsnap reads tougher to accomplish but essential to conduct with accuracy.

Blitz Reads

Being able to read the blitz is essential for both the receiver and the quarterback. Let's start with the linebacker blitz. Assume the quarterback has called a pass play from a formation in which the offensive back is in a position that prevents him from blocking the blitz. Both the offensive back and quarterback must recognize this. On the snap, as the offensive back sees the linebacker leave, he occupies the space vacated by the linebacker, and the quarterback delivers the pass to the back. With the wide receivers, tight ends, fullback, and running back, go through all plays from a number of formations until they become automatic for both the receiver and the quarterback.

Move from the linebacker blitz to corner blitzes and free- and strong-safety blitzes. Again involve all receivers, using multiple formations, shifts, and motion. Understand that instead of a linebacker blitz, the linebacker might be replaced with a defensive tackle or end. The point is to rehearse regularly so that all involved feel comfortable, confident, and ready to take advantage of all potential blitzes rather than fall victim to them.

Passing Drills

Leading up to summer camp, the quarterback must pass the ball at least 250 times each day. Every pass has a purpose. Just as an archer aims precisely for the bulls-eye and not just the target, each time the quarterback passes the ball, he has a bulls-eye in mind, such as the receiver's left ear, belt buckle, or right elbow. The smaller the bulls-eye, the better. As the quarterback warms up for practice, the coach tells him the location of the desired bulls-eye.

QUARTERBACK WARM-UP

A quarterback and receiver stand 10 yards from another quarterback and receiver. Both quarterbacks kneel next to their receivers. The ball is passed to a receiver, who hands the ball to the quarterback kneeling beside him. The quarterback passes to the receiver 10 yards away, who hands the ball to the quarterback kneeling beside him. Continue for 5 minutes.

For the second part of the warm-up, the receivers and quarterbacks remain in the same spacing, but now both quarterbacks stand with their feet parallel. They run through the same sequence: the receiver hands the ball to the quarterback next to him, and the quarterback throws to the receiver 10 yards away. The quarterback does not move his feet. Instead he throws with his upper body. Continue for 5 minutes.

In part three, the receivers move back 5 yards so they are 15 yards from the opposite quarterback. The quarterbacks step into the pass. Continue for 5 minutes.

Conclude the warm-up by bringing in a center to execute the snap. The quarterback passes from a three-step and five-step drop, sprint out, and play action. Move the receiver deeper for these passes. Continue for 5 minutes.

COACH RUSH

To help the quarterback get accustomed to staying in the pocket, a coach rushes from the outside. After taking a five-step drop, the quarterback steps up into the pocket and delivers the pass.

OFF-BALANCE PASS

Sometimes it's impossible to take a pass drop by the book. For example, if a linebacker blitz is not picked up, the pass must be executed off-balance. This can still lead to a successful play if the quarterback rehearses it often so that when it happens in a game he reacts on instinct.

A coach rushes, and the quarterback makes the pass from an off-balance position, with something on the ball. The quarterback must consciously attempt to throw hard because this pass does not have his body behind it, only his arm. The receiver should be only a short distance away at first. Gradually increase the distance.

SCRAMBLE

Sometimes the only way to make a play is to scramble. Here again, there must be a plan, and the plan must be rehearsed regularly. Have a coach rush and force the quarterback to break the pocket. The receivers know to level off at whatever depth they are when the scramble begins. They then go in the same direction as the scramble, waving their arms so the quarterback finds them, and the pass is delivered. When the receiver is within 5 yards of the sideline, he turns and runs upfield.

READ DRILL

This read drill involves reading whoever is responsible for the curl area. The quarterback is on the near hash with a receiver 7 yards from the sideline and 7 yards deep. This represents a player who has run a 10-yard curl and come back tight to 7 yards. Another receiver is 15 yards from the sideline and 8 to 10 yards deep, representing a receiver who has run a 10-yard curl, read the linebacker drop as being more wide than deep, and so rounded his curl behind the linebacker's drop. The read of the linebacker's drop affects where the quarterback will pass the ball. If the linebacker's drop is more deep than wide, the quarterback passes to the outside receiver. If the drop is more wide than deep, the quarterback passes to the inside receiver.

An extension of this drill is to have a receiver actually run a complete curl route and read the linebacker's drop. Run the drill daily so that the quarterback and wide receiver are consistently on the same page, reading the drop and arriving at the same point. This way the quarterback always knows what path the receiver will take, and the wide receiver always knows where the ball will be thrown.

INDIVIDUAL ROUTES AGAINST AIR

With the receivers, run all individual routes against air. Receivers run through all the routes that they use in the offense without any defensive players involved.

Wide Receiver

Wide receivers must possess a variety of skills to be effective on the field. Solid, dependable hands for catching the ball are key, but so are the ability to get open and the willingness to block downfield. An effective wide receiver is quick and athletic, able to use his footwork to shake off defenders and get open. He must have good timing and solid coordination with the quarterback. His field and ball awareness need to be top notch. The wide receiver is one of the most athletic players on the field.

Stance

In every position except tight, the wide receiver takes a two-point stance with arms flexed (figure 4.4a). In a tight formation (figure 4.5), the wide receiver takes a three-point stance (figure 4.4b). In a two-point stance, the wide receiver's inside foot is back so he can look inside and see when the ball is snapped. There is no excuse for a wide

Figure 4.4 Wide receiver's stance: *(a)* two-point stance for any formation except a tight formation; *(b)* three-point stance for a tight formation.

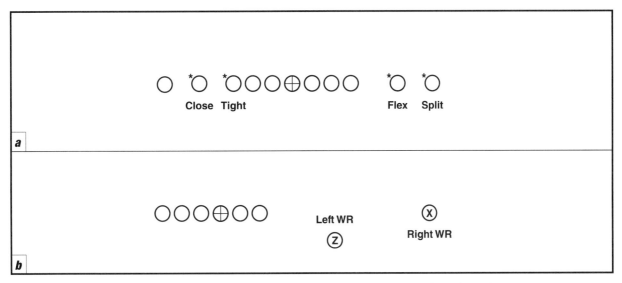

Figure 4.5 *(a)* Close, tight, flex, and split positions for wide receivers; *(b)* two formation for wide receivers.

receiver to move before the snap and be guilty of an illegal procedure penalty.

Split

Splits (see figures 4.6 and 4.7) are extremely important for wide receivers, and it is essential that they use splits to their advantage. If running a pattern that breaks outside, the wide receiver takes a minimum split to allow room to complete the pattern inbounds. The wide receiver must have control of the ball with one foot inbounds to complete a legal catch. On a pattern such as a diagonal, the wide receiver employs a wide split to give room for the break inside before he gets to the outside linebacker coverage. On plays for which the width of the split has no effect on the play, such as a running play to the opposite side, the wide receiver changes the split from play to play to confuse the opponent.

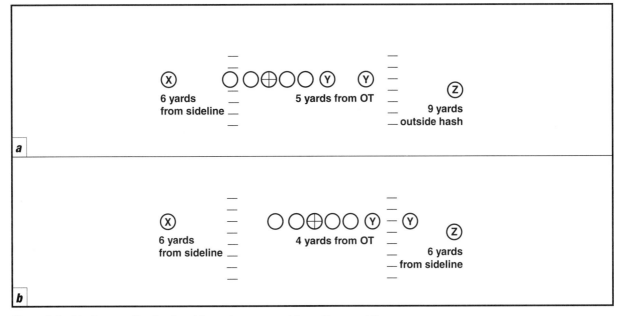

Figure 4.6 Maximum split rules for wide receivers, pro set formations, and flex.

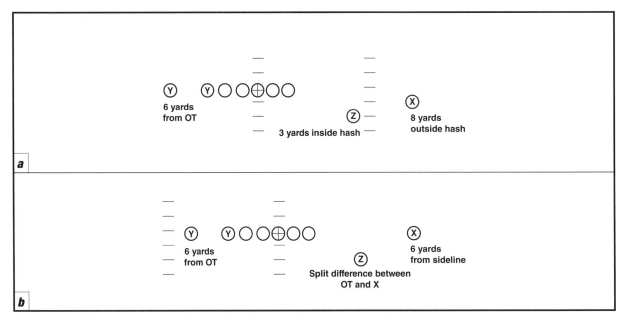

Figure 4.7 Maximum split rules for wide receivers, twins formations, and flex.

Release

Wide receivers can use several releases when a defender is pressuring. For the head and shoulders fake (figure 4.8*a*), on the snap of the ball, the wide receiver quickly moves his head and shoulders inside as he releases outside, or vice versa. For the rip (figure 4.8*b*), the wide receiver forcefully takes his near arm up through his opponent's armpit and rips him off. For the swim (figure 4.8*c*), the wide receiver grabs the opponent's near elbow with his far hand as he swings his near arm over the opponent, removing the target from him. Against a press, the wide receiver steps back momentarily (figure 4.8*d*), causing the defensive back to lunge and lose his balance; then the wide receiver swims.

Approach

This is the initial break, how the receiver attacks the defender, the positioning that he wants to attain, whether inside or outside, relative to the alignment of the defender.

Move

This is the main phase of the pattern, the movement made as the receiver attains the correct depth and positioning. The receiver is now stretching the coverage, preparing to sell the defender on misdirection.

Misdirection

On every pattern, the receiver must make his defender think that he is running something that he is not. Sometimes that means selling one misdirection, sometimes two. This must be done while running full speed. The receiver can't free himself by slowing down to change direction. He might sell the defender that he is going deep, then make his cut outside, or fake an inside break and run a corner pattern.

Burst

This is the finish, the final phase of the pattern. The burst is the final cut, occurring as the receiver gets his head around to locate the ball.

Figure 4.8 Wide receiver releases: *(a)* head and shoulders fake; *(b)* rip; *(c)* swim; *(d)* step back against a press.

Shift and Motion

The shift and motion are two ways to change formations at the last moment, causing the defense to adjust. Assurance must be made that before and after a receiver shift, all receivers are eligible and no one is covered up. The offense must be motionless one full second after completion of the shift and before initiating motion. Receivers and running backs must learn when to start moving, how fast to move, and how to change gears to hide the destination and reverse motion. In general, when using motion, go close to full speed. Force the defense to react in as little time as possible.

Wide receivers must know that if the quarterback says "motion," they can initially align in any formation the team uses and motion from there to the formation called. If a final destination for motion is called, wide receivers begin in the formation called and motion to the designated final position. Sometimes they motion to the center of the formation and then reverse the motion back to where they began. This forces the secondary to adjust to a new formation and then have to quickly react to another formation. Ideally you can catch them in a situation in which some of the defensive players adjusted but some did not.

Pass Reception

When receiving a forward pass (figure 4.9), the receiver keeps his eyes on the ball. He focuses on the front tip of the ball coming at him, especially for the last 6 inches of the pass. He catches the ball with his fingertips. He catches the ball with both hands and avoids catching it with his chest. His first responsibility is to catch the ball. Then he secures the ball and runs.

After receiving a short or intermediate pass, the receiver tucks the ball and lowers his upfield shoulder. He gets his pads down to drive upfield in a north–south direction. This technique gives the receiver a better way of attaining additional yardage by splitting defenders as they converge on the throw. Sideline tackles are usually high, so the receiver should drop his inside shoulder and helmet. The yards after the catch are extremely important.

Receiver Blocks

Receivers hold the key not only to a successful passing game but, with practice and a total commitment to blocking, a successful running game as well. Receivers must learn to sprint to the defender until they are close enough to reach out and almost touch him, then break down and put themselves in a position between the defender and the ballcarrier. The defender, by his movement, will tell the blocker where the ballcarrier is. The receiver must learn that he doesn't have to knock the defender down. In fact, in some cases there need be no contact at all for a totally effective block. The receiver can make a great block without ever touching the defender. The defining objective is to stay between the defender and the ballcarrier. The receiver moves in the direction that the defender moves.

To practice the crackback block (figure 4.10), begin with a walk-through and then progress to a full-speed block in front of the defender and above his waist. Use the wide receivers, outside linebackers, running back, and quarterback. The quarterback pitches the ball to the running back. The outside linebacker reacts to the ball to make the block more realistic.

Figure 4.9 Receiving a forward pass: (a) catch the ball, (b) secure the ball, (c) run.

Figure 4.10 Receiver performing a crackback block.

Blitz Recognition and Reaction

Receivers must know who to read on each play from each formation and how to respond if that defender blitzes. The receiver yells "blitz!" as he replaces the defender, looking for the ball.

Receiver Drills

Receivers should work with the quarterback on several drills, including the Quarterback Warm-Up, Scramble, and Individual Routes Against Air. These drills are described with the quarterback drills, beginning on page 47.

KISS THE BALL

This drill reminds receivers not to take their eyes off the ball before catching the pass. When the receiver makes the catch, he kisses the ball. Alternatively, paint a number on the ball and have the receiver call out the number as he catches the pass. This shows that his eyes have followed the ball all the way into his body. This is a variation of common quarterback and receiver drills. For most receivers, the drill is an eye-opener, making them realize they have not been following the pass all the way into their hands.

LONG BALL

Sprint 40 to 50 yards. The quarterback throws the ball with some air under it. The receiver makes the correct adjustment to the ball. Add a linebacker or defensive back to work against.

TENNIS BALL DRILL

Use a tennis ball machine. Receivers practice quick repetitions, concentrating on the tennis ball coming hard at them from different locations. They catch the ball emphasizing concentration and eye–hand coordination.

DISTRACTION DRILL

A linebacker stands between the receiver and the quarterback. The linebacker waves his arms in front of the receiver as the ball approaches or might even try to slightly deflect the pass. This prepares the receiver to react to the distractions that occur in a game and forces him to concentrate only on the ball.

COME TO THE BALL

Receivers must learn that the longer the ball is in the air, the more time the defense has to react to it. Thus receivers must develop the knack of coming back to the ball once it is released, especially on a hitch route.

Begin the drill with the receiver at the end point of the pattern. The pattern can be a hook, curl, or hitch. As the ball is released, the receiver comes back to the ball, shortening his distance to the pass. The coach should emphasize to the receiver that failing to come back to the ball gives the defender time to knock down the pass or intercept it. The receiver must reduce the amount of time the ball is in the air.

TAP DRILL

In college football, the receiver needs to get only one foot on the ground inbounds after the catch. The receiver breaks toward the sideline. The passer times the pass so that the receiver has to work hard to get one foot down. This develops his ability to concentrate on catching the ball while staying aware of his relation to the sideline.

PATTERNS

Run all individual routes against air. This drill allows one quarterback and one receiver at a time to work together on all passing routes. The quarterback works on his drop and timing his release of the ball. The receiver works on all elements of the pattern, concentrating on the ball and the catch. The drill doesn't end with the catch. On completion of the catch, the receiver makes a move and accelerates downfield.

Offensive Lineman

Offensive linemen must be football smart. They must know how to exploit and take advantage of the defensive man's alignment. Teach offensive linemen to use the defender's alignment to become more efficient, effective, and consistent blockers. Strength is important, but technique is more important. In great detail, teach linemen the correct technique for executing every block.

Horizontal and Vertical Line Splits

If used wisely, splits can create an advantage for the offensive lineman for whatever job he is being asked to perform. Adjust splits to facilitate blocking. If the defense moves with the split, the offense can dictate the defensive alignment. If the defense doesn't move, you will have created superior blocking angles.

Horizontal Splits

Horizontal splits (figure 4.11) are used to move a blocker closer to his target, create larger areas for the defense to defend, or to deceive the defense when the play is going in the other direction.

The play-side guard or tackle who is assigned to slip block the lineman outside of him should take a maximum split to gain an advantage. The play-side tackle or slot who is assigned to slip block the lineman on him or shading him should take a minimum split to reduce the reach area of the inside blocker, with whom the lineman is slipping. The backside guard or tackle who is pulling to trap or lead takes a minimum split so that he can get there more quickly. The play-side guard who is covered by a lineman who is to be trapped takes a maximum split to make the lineman more vulnerable.

If the play is being run inside, the offensive linemen take maximum splits to create better running lanes and to give the defender more area to defend. If the play is being run outside,

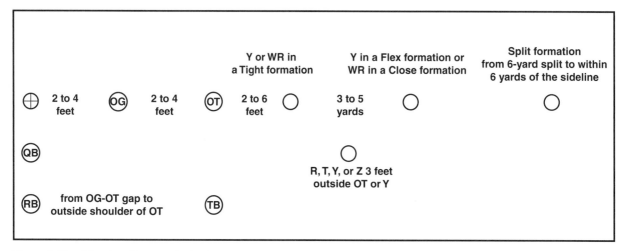

Figure 4.11 Offensive alignment for horizontal splits: tight, flex, close, and split.

the offensive linemen take minimum splits so the ballcarrier can get to the corner more quickly.

The backside linemen play around with their splits because the width of their splits has no bearing on the play. This keeps the defense guessing and prevents them from predicting your offense when the play is to one side.

In general, the whole line will tighten on drop-back passing plays. If the tight end is blocking outside or releasing, he doesn't have to tighten.

Vertical Splits

Vertical splits (figure 4.12) are every bit as vital to the success of a play as horizontal splits are. By rule, the head of any lineman outside the center must break the plane of the center's hips. This means that the vertical split could be as much as 2-1/2 to 3 feet.

The offensive line crowds the ball with a minimum vertical split on quarterback sneaks and power plays. They take a maximum vertical split on drop-back passes. This makes the defense move farther before making contact. The defensive lineman must commit and give the blocker more time to read the direction of his charge. Getting off the ball allows time for the blocker to read and react to twist stunts and other types of defensive maneuvers.

As in horizontal splits, to keep the defense guessing, the offensive line should play with

various vertical splits when using them does not affect the assignment.

Run Blocks

The first two steps of a block involve technique; after that, blocking is all attitude. The cardinal rule of blocking is an offensive lineman should never let a defensive player cross his face. The lineman must block him.

Drive Block

The drive block (figure 4.13) is used when the offensive lineman is blocking a man head up or in a shade on him. The offensive lineman steps to the middle of the defender's body, with his back arched and head up. The offensive lineman explodes into the defender, hands to the breastplate, and drives him off the ball. The offensive lineman dominates the defender and finishes the block by turning the defender so that the lineman's body is between the defender and the ball.

Reach or Hook Block

The reach block (or hook block; figure 4.14) is used when the defender has an alignment advantage and is closer to the point of attack than the offensive lineman. The defender might be in an inside shade, head up, or outside shade of a lineman to the offensive blocker's outside. The offensive lineman steps directly to the middle of the defender's body with his

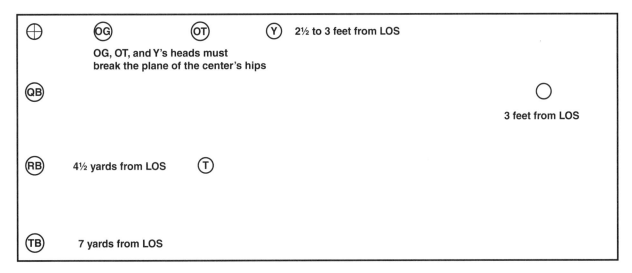

Figure 4.12 Offensive alignment for vertical splits.

Figure 4.13 Drive block.

Figure 4.14 Reach (or hook) block.

outside foot. He jams the defender's sternum with his inside hand and controls the defender with his outside hand on the defender's shoulder pad. The offensive lineman works his body around as he drives the defender off the line of scrimmage, eventually sealing the defender with his tail in the hole.

Horn Block

The horn block is used when the inside blocker is covered or shaded to the outside. The outside blocker blocks down, and the covered blocker horn blocks outside off his tail up on the linebacker. The covered blocker does not wait for the outside blocker to make his block. Instead, the covered blocker simply takes immediate quick steps in a path to avoid contacting his partner.

Fold Block

The outside blocker is covered or shaded to the inside. The inside blocker blocks out, whereas the covered blocker fold blocks inside off his tail up on the linebacker. The covered blocker does not wait for the inside blocker to make his block. He takes immediate quick steps in a path to avoid contacting his partner.

Short Trap

When executing the short trap, the offensive lineman must expect the defender to come straight across the line of scrimmage or attack the trapper. The offensive lineman takes the first step and replaces the center's foot with his near foot, which is pointed slightly upfield, aimed at the most difficult block to make. He brings his feet up under himself so the back does not trip. If the defender shoots across the line of scrimmage, the offensive lineman lets him go and turns upfield to block the second level.

Long Trap

The offensive lineman takes a minimum horizontal split and a maximum vertical split. He takes a shallow course down the line of scrimmage. When he makes contact, he brings his feet up under himself so the back does not trip. If the defender comes across the line of scrimmage, the offensive lineman kicks him out. If the defender veers down inside, the offensive lineman hooks him and swings his hips around to log him in. If the defender sits in the hole, the offensive lineman goes in to root him out.

Long Pull

If the offensive lineman is to pull and a linebacker steps up in the line, the offensive lineman stays in to block the linebacker if it is impossible for a teammate to block him. The offensive lineman takes a minimum horizontal split and a maximum vertical split. Down the line of scrimmage, he takes a course that is shallow yet deep enough to avoid the feet of any offensive linemen. As he rounds the corner and turns downfield, the offensive lineman dips his inside shoulder so he can make his turn more quickly and be in position to look back to the inside for someone in pursuit. The offensive lineman does not pass up anyone. If a linebacker blitzes, the offensive lineman blocks him.

Slip Power Block

The slip power block enables the offense to get more people to the point of attack than the defense. Two adjacent offensive linemen block a defensive lineman, with the inside blocker reaching. For example, an offensive guard and tackle block a defender in a 4 or 5 technique. The outside blocker jams his inside hand to the outside breastplate of the defender, stopping his momentum, so the inside blocker can replace him. The inside blocker jams the sternum with his inside hand, with his outside hand on the shoulder pad, so he can control the defender. If the linebacker doesn't come, both blockers take linemen upfield and finish. If the linebacker comes outside, the outside blocker comes off the slip block and finishes the linebacker, and the inside blocker reaches, controls, and finishes the lineman. If the linebacker comes inside, the inside blocker comes off and goes to the second level to finish the linebacker, and the outside blocker finishes the lineman.

Power Slip Block

The outside blocker has an alignment advantage on the defensive lineman. Both blockers attack the defensive lineman, with the inside blocker using the drive block technique (p. 55). When the inside blocker feels the contact by the outside blocker, he turns the axis of his body so that both blockers are working at parallel lines of force. Together they drive the defender down inside and off the line of scrimmage, with one of them coming off to block the pursuing linebacker.

Cross Shoulder Block

This block is used when the player assigned to the offensive lineman is well inside the offensive lineman and the ball is going outside. The defender's penetration into the backfield must be stopped, and he has the physical advantage by his alignment. The offensive lineman steps with the inside foot aimed at where the defender will be when the offensive lineman gets there, not where he is at the snap. The offensive lineman hits the defender where he bends, with his head in front to stop the defender's forward movement. The offensive lineman drives the defender down the line of scrimmage into the pile.

Scoop Block

The offensive lineman aims for the near shoulder of the defensive lineman one man removed from himself (backside guard versus a 0 technique or call-side guard versus a 4 technique). If the defender slants to the offensive lineman, he takes him. If not, the offensive lineman is on a good course to pick up a linebacker.

Crossfield Block

This block is 95 percent determination and desire and 5 percent technique and ability. The offensive lineman releases at the outside leg of the first lineman to his inside. If the offensive lineman is to release and there is a man in his area, the offensive lineman crosses his face. If the adjacent lineman's rule calls for him to block a defender to the inside, the offensive lineman releases underneath that block. The offensive lineman sprints across the field ahead of the play, aiming for a spot where he can stay between the defender and the ball. The offensive lineman does not leave his feet to make the block. He gets in front of the defender and blocks above the waist. In fact, the offensive lineman can make an effective block without touching the defender by simply keeping his body between the defender and the ball. The defender's movement tells the offensive lineman how he must adjust.

Draw Block

The offensive lineman immediately shows pocket pass protection to initiate a pass rush from the defender. As the defender gets into his rush, the offensive lineman aggressively attacks the defender by taking an approach that puts himself between the rusher and the ballcarrier. The offensive lineman turns and seals the defender, using the defender's momentum against him.

Pass Protection

When protecting the pocket (figure 4.15), the offensive lineman bends at the hips and knees as if sitting down and arches his back with

Figure 4.15 Offensive lineman protecting the pocket: *(a)* ready stance; *(b)* offensive lineman jams the defender.

his head up. The offensive lineman assumes a staggered stance with the inside foot up, while maintaining a crouched sitting position with his upper body weight over his feet. He keeps his open hands out in front of his chest and close together, thumbs almost touching, and his elbows in tight and close to his sides. He maintains this position throughout the block. The offensive lineman moves with the count and pushes backward with the bridge of his fingers as he takes the proper step. The offensive lineman jams the defender with his hands to the breast plate, then gets separation and repeats the jam until the ball is released. He must not extend his arms and lock his elbows. If he does, the defender will grab his arms and pull him through, causing him to lose balance and giving the defender the opportunity to beat the offensive lineman.

The position of the post foot, the offensive lineman's up foot, is the most important aspect of pocket pass protection. (The rear foot is the set or kick foot.) As long as the inside foot is up, it will be extremely difficult for the defender to cross the face of the offensive lineman and beat him to the inside. Inside is where the defender wants to go because it's a straight line and the shortest distance to the quarterback. In the offensive lineman's presnap stance, his inside foot is up. Usually his first step will be with the outside foot as he gets separation from the line of scrimmage. This is followed quickly by the post foot. However, if the defender is crowding the line of scrimmage and veering to the inside gap, the offensive lineman steps back slightly off the line with his inside foot followed quickly by his outside foot so that he retains a staggered stance with his inside foot up. Stepping first with the inside foot permits the offensive lineman to take away a hard slanting charge to the inside. He must deny the inside move. The first step can be back and to the inside to counter such a move, but it must be followed immediately by a step with the outside foot. The post foot (the inside foot) must be up throughout the play. Nothing should cause the offensive lineman to drop that foot behind the outside foot. When a defensive pass rusher beats the blocker, it's almost always because the blocker dropped his post foot and gave the defender an opportunity to cross his face. The center may get help if he is covered and the inside linebacker does not rush. In this case, the center's post foot is the foot opposite from where he anticipates help is coming.

When blocking a man head on, the offensive lineman crowds the ball in his stance so he can immediately get his hands on the defender. If blocking a man outside of himself, the offensive lineman must be deeper from the ball in his stance so he can intersect the defender and keep him from getting to the quarterback.

Throughout the play, as the offensive lineman mirrors the defender's charge, he must remember where his quarterback is, keeping in mind that his job is to stay between the defender and the quarterback. He must put himself in a position so the only route available to the defender is to the outside. If the defender goes outside, the quarterback can step up in the pocket and avoid the rush. The offensive lineman keeps his post foot in position and works the defender up to the outside so that he ends up going past the quarterback. Every time he jams the defender's chest with his hands, the offensive lineman gets separation again by retreating a step with both feet. The offensive lineman gives ground grudgingly, but if he doesn't get separation, he gives the defender an opportunity to match his weight and strength with his own. The offensive lineman must remember that the defender knows where he is going, so he will have to mirror the defender and react to every movement he makes.

Pass Protection Techniques

As he approaches the defender, the offensive lineman bulls his neck (snaps his head up and straightens his neck) with his arms and hands up. He bulls his neck so he is under control and cocked. His knees should be slightly bent, his feet staggered as they were in the stance, and his tail low (figure 4.16a). His arms are poised to uncoil, elbows close to his body.

Figure 4.16 Pass protection: offensive lineman *(a)* approaches the defender, *(b)* makes contact, and *(c)* follows through.

His feet must be constantly ready to move. The offensive lineman picks his aiming spot—the inside top corner of the defender's number—and focuses on it. The aiming spot's movement controls the offensive lineman's foot movement. He must have eye–foot coordination.

At contact (figure 4.16b), the offensive lineman is in position to block. If the defender is head up, he can go three ways. The offensive lineman denies the defender those ways by staying balanced. If the defender is inside, the offensive lineman post steps him to the inside and drives him into the pile. If the defender is outside, the offensive lineman kick steps and slides to take half a man away from him. This protects the inside rush lane. The offensive lineman keeps his shoulders square to the line of scrimmage at all times so he doesn't give the rusher a lane to the quarterback. When the defender is close enough to reach for the offensive lineman, he explodes his hands and arms into the defender's numbers and bench presses him away (figure 4.16c). He must keep his tail low and head back when doing this. If the defender bounces away, the offensive lineman sets up for him again. If the defender stays in contact with the offensive lineman, he either post steps the defender to the inside or kick steps and slides (rides the defender) to the outside past the quarterback. If the defense crosses, offensive blockers are released to new charges when the two blockers contact each other.

The offensive lineman must always move his feet and maintain his position between the defender and passer. He must expect the defender to try to break arm contact and get around him. He must know the favorite moves of his opponent and how to counter them. He rides the defender when the defender goes to the outside. He throws his head in the direction his opponent is moving if he feels the defender slipping away. If the rusher uses an arm-over move, the offensive lineman drives his head across the defender's chest and rivets his cross shoulder into the defender's armpit to hook him when his rib cage is exposed. The offensive

lineman then drives the defender away from the quarterback.

The concept in pocket pass protection is to block areas. If the defense runs twist stunts or linebacker blitzes, bump off and maintain the pocket rather than staying with a particular man and risk having offensive linemen run into each other. Stay with a particular man if a back's assignment is a stunting linebacker. Because he is off the line and has a clear picture of the stunting linebacker, the back will take the defender wherever he goes, and the offensive lineman will stay with the defensive lineman.

Cut Protection

This technique cannot be used in high school in accordance with current rules.

The cut block is used when the quarterback is taking a three-step drop. The purpose of this technique is to get the defender's hands down to protect his knees. If he is permitted to rush with his arms in the air, he will knock down the pass (because in a three-step drop the quarterback is very close to the line of scrimmage).

The offensive lineman takes the same first step used in pocket protection and raises up, feigning protection for the drop-back pass. He wants the defender to recognize pocket protection and rush very hard. The harder and quicker the rush, the more vulnerable the defender is to the cut block. If a lineman is not covered, he helps the adjacent blocker.

The offensive lineman lets the rusher come to him, then lowers his shoulders, keeping his back parallel to the field, and aggressively shoots his inside shoulder at the rusher's outside knee. This causes the rusher to drop his hands and arms to protect his knee. You want him on the ground. The offensive lineman cannot lunge at air; he must wait until the rusher is within arm's length. The offensive lineman shoots the shoulder through the knee, not to the knee. This is a very aggressive block. Though it sounds potentially dangerous, this technique is not designed to injure an opponent; when executed correctly, there's very little chance of an injury.

When using this technique, offensive backs sprint to the line of scrimmage and cut the outside knee of the first charger past the tackle's block, or the slot's block if using eight-man front blocking.

Play-Action Pass Protection

When faking a running play and then passing, the objective is to make the defense react to the fake run. Making this happen requires more than just a good fake by the quarterback and running back. The blocking must also fake the run. The offensive lineman attacks the defender aggressively, keeping his body between the defender and the spot where the quarterback will set up for the pass. Although maintaining contact while driving a defender downfield is legal, doing so creates a gap in line blocking. So keep the contact at the line of scrimmage. The offensive lineman must not permit the defender to turn him. He keeps his shoulders parallel to the line of scrimmage.

For the drop-back screen, the offensive lineman's movements must convince the rusher that he is attacking a drop-back pass. Depending on the philosophy of the play itself, the offensive lineman may pass protect the rusher for one, two, or three seconds. Whatever the required time of contact, to make the play successful, the offensive lineman must make the rusher feel that he is defeating the block. The offensive lineman uses the position of his body to give the defender only one lane in which to take his rush, that being away from the direction of the pass.

For the play-action screen, the offensive lineman attacks the defender as he would on the play-action pass being simulated. Play-action screens usually require the blocks to be held for three seconds. The offensive lineman convinces the rusher he has beaten the block, and then gives the defender only one lane in which to continue his rush. The lane given the defender is the lane away from the destination of the screen pass. Forcing the defender to take the lane given him is essential to the success of the play.

Running Back

Ball security is a major focus of the running back. Even so, because a fumble, interception, blocked kick, or onside kick can put any player in possession of the ball, every player, regardless of position, must practice ball security. To be absolutely sure that the ball is secure, it must be covered with both hands. This should be the case when the running back receives a handoff or is going through heavy traffic. The near elbow and forearm come down on top of the ball while the opposite elbow, 3 or 4 inches from the belly, cradles the bottom of the ball (figure 4.17). The palms of each hand are cupped around the tips of the ball.

Figure 4.17 Running back securing the ball.

If the running back is running outside, and if moving the ball from one hand to the other will not jeopardize ball control, he should have the ball in the hand away from the defender. If shifting the ball from hand to hand might make him lose control of the ball, he must not take that chance. When the ball is in the running back's far hand, not only must the defender go through the running back's body to get to the ball, but the running back can also use his near arm to stiff-arm the defender. Drill all players, not just running backs, on how to protect the ball and prevent having it stripped.

NO-FUMBLE DRILL FOR RUNNING BACKS

Players with shields stand at both sides of the quarterback to running back exchange. As the exchange is made, the players use their shields to slap at the ball, attempting to jar the ball loose. The ballcarrier must cover the ball with both hands. So the running back can't anticipate the contact, change it up sometimes by having the players swing at his legs with the shields. The players with shields can use every conceivable method to attempt to strip the ball.

5

Individual Defensive Skills and Drills

In this chapter we look at individual skills needed to play effectively on the defensive side of the football. The skills are categorized by defensive line, linebackers, and defensive backs.

Tackling

Just as any discussion of offense begins with blocking, so it is with tackling when talking about defense. To be sound on defense, a team must tackle with great consistency. Many drills address the proper art of tackling and help the tackler gain confidence in his ability to get it right.

It's very important to begin where the player is and gradually progress to more competitive and aggressive tackling drills. If he starts too advanced, he might shy away from full contact.

The first thing to instill is confidence. A tackler should begin by getting the feel of a proper tackle, simply walking through the correct form and technique.

FORM TACKLING

Stress perfect stance and form—knees bent, back erect, neck bulled, and upper body out in front over the feet (figure 5.1a). There's no full contact here; this drill is all about form. Players must get the feel of correct tackling technique. A group of defensive players in a horizontal line do the drill simultaneously, or in rapid fire succession. Each tackler is across the line from a ballcarrier. If drilling many players at a time, use an imaginary ball instead of a real ball. The ballcarrier carries the ball in his right hand. The tackler steps across the line in proper tackling form and puts his face mask on the ball in a lifting motion with arms outstretched to the side. The tackler hits and lifts with the face mask.

Figure 5.1 Form tackling drill: *(a)* tackling stance; *(b)* contact; *(c)* tackle.

The second time through, the tackler hits, lifts, and rips his hands up through the ballcarrier's armpits to jar the ball loose, wrapping his arms around the ballcarrier's waist (figure 5.1*b*).

The third time through, the tackler hits, lifts, wraps his arms around the ballcarrier, locks his wrists, pulls the ballcarrier to himself, and picks up the ballcarrier, following through for three steps (figure 5.1*c*). The entire action should be one continuous motion. The tackler starts low and works up through the ballcarrier, disrupting his momentum and dislodging his contact with the playing surface.

Repeat the drill with the ballcarrier holding the ball in his left hand. Finally, flip roles. The ballcarriers become the tacklers and repeat the drill.

ACROSS-THE-BOW TACKLING

Use the same mechanics as in form tackling to teach players to make perfect tackles from the side. Each tackler is across the line from a ballcarrier, who is also 2 yards in front of the tackler. The ballcarrier carries an imaginary ball in his far hand. At the signal, the ballcarrier moves forward on a diagonal, and the tackler moves down the line, driving his shoulder into the ballcarrier's chest with his head in front and arms stretched out to the side. Again, there's no full contact here. The tackler hits and pinches with his head, neck, and shoulders, using a lifting motion with the shoulder.

The second time through, the tackler hits and pinches with the head, neck, and shoulders and lifts the ballcarrier, ripping his hands up through the ballcarrier's armpits to jar the ball loose and then wrapping his arms around the ballcarrier's waist.

The third time through, the tackler hits, lifts, wraps his arms, locks his wrists, pulls the ballcarrier toward him, picks him up, and follows through for three steps. The entire action should be one continuous motion, starting low and working up through the ballcarrier, disrupting his momentum and dislodging his contact with the playing surface.

Repeat the drill with the ballcarrier holding the ball in his left hand, moving diagonally in the opposite direction. Finally, flip roles. The ballcarriers become the tacklers; repeat the drill.

Once players master these two drills, progress to more competitive tackling drills. Even then, keep drills in a limited area so the tackle is made within two or three steps. Don't make players sprint full speed for 10 or 20 yards directly into each other. No player, no matter how experienced, wants to do that, and no player should be asked to demonstrate his toughness in such a way.

BUMP AND TACKLE

At the signal, the ballcarrier moves sideways and toward the line of scrimmage. The tackler moves laterally with him and bumps him at the line of scrimmage. The ballcarrier gets hit, bounces back, gets hit, bounces back, and so on. The tackler bumps, sets himself, bumps, sets himself, and on the third hit tackles the ballcarrier. The tackler must hit from the inside out rather than head on. This denies the ballcarrier the option of cutting either way. Hitting from the inside does not allow the cutback. When hitting the ballcarrier, the tackler aims his head at the ball.

FORWARD ROLL TACKLING

The tackler and ballcarrier face each other 4 yards apart. At the signal, the tackler does a forward roll, gets up quickly, breaks down, and drives into the ballcarrier, accounting for all of the momentum.

GOAL-LINE TACKLING

The tackler stands at the goal line with his back to the ballcarrier, who is on the 3-yard line. The coach tosses the ball to the ballcarrier and hollers "ball!" The tackler whirls around, stays level, and keeps his leg drive. The ballcarrier must not score.

LEVERAGE TACKLING

This drill can be used for every defensive group and in several sequences. It might start with one defensive player against a ballcarrier, progress to one defensive player against one blocker and a ballcarrier, and, finally, to two defensive players (one takes on the blocker and turns the ballcarrier back inside, and the other goes in the hole to clean up) against a blocker and a ballcarrier.

Place four cones in a line with 5 feet between each cone to represent the line of scrimmage. This spacing gives the ballcarrier three holes to choose from. He will turn into one of the holes and attempt to run over the tackler. He runs just as a normal ballcarrier would, complete with fakes and changes of pace. For the defense, the idea is to meet the ballcarrier in the hole and not permit him to cross the line of scrimmage. The drill demonstrates to the defense what is meant by *leverage* and how to maintain leverage by staying slightly laterally behind the ballcarrier and using the sideline as another defensive player.

When using two defensive players, the lead defensive man attempts to do it all—turn the play in, shed the blocker, and make the tackle. At the least, he must turn the play in and take on the blocker.

RUSH DRILL

Two blockers station opposite the tackler and 7 yards in front of the passer. The tackler must get through the blockers to the passer and tackle him high so he cannot throw. The tackler attacks one of the blockers, or one and then the other—any way to get to the passer.

Blocking Alignments and Techniques

The various alignments with their accompanying applied techniques are described according to the position of the defensive lineman or linebacker in relation to each offensive lineman. Those positions are either head on, inside shoulder, or outside shoulder (figure 5.2).

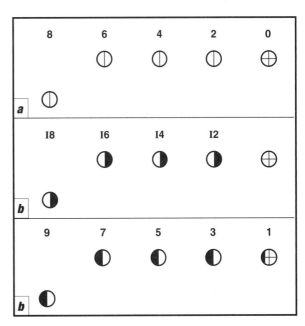

Figure 5.2 Blocking alignments: *(a)* head on; *(b)* inside shoulder; *(c)* outside shoulder.

Lineman Techniques

Each defensive lineman has his own list of techniques for defeating offensive blocks. These techniques differ slightly depending on the alignment of the defensive lineman.

0 Technique

The 0 technique is used head on across from the offensive center. The lineman uses a three-point stance with feet slightly staggered (figure 5.3). His feet are no wider than shoulder-width apart. He balances on the grounded hand on his fingertips, not his knuckles. His feet are extended back, putting a lot of weight on his grounded hand. His free hand is shoulder high, ready to jam the offensive lineman. He aligns across from the nose of the center from the line of scrimmage to 18 inches deep.

The defensive lineman keys through the center to the ball. If the center attacks him, the lineman attacks the center and maintains a head-up position on him. If the center pass blocks, the lineman checks draw and goes. If double-teamed, the lineman attacks the power man.

The lineman's first responsibility is the A gap to either side. He cannot be hooked either way. He should be able to cover either side and make the play head on by the time the ball gets there. He must take everything inside. If pass shows, the lineman rushes in a controlled manner, checking the draw and middle screen,

and then turns it on to get to the passer. He rushes to the side of his original orientation, either tight or split.

To execute his responsibilities, the lineman must move on the ball and deliver a blow. He hits up with a hand shiver and locks his elbows. He must get his hand under the blocker's pads. If the center attacks, the lineman attacks him back and finds the ball. If he's overpowered, the lineman gives ground grudgingly in the direction from which he came. If double-teamed, the lineman must hold his point right there. He turns and fights the power block. Putting his nose in the ground, he does anything to make the hump right there. He must not get moved back past the line of scrimmage.

1 Technique

For the 1 technique, the lineman uses a three-point stance with feet staggered and his gap hand up (figure 5.4). His feet are shoulder-width apart or narrower. He balances on the fingertips rather than knuckles of the grounded hand. His gap hand is shoulder high and ready to jam the offensive lineman. He aligns with his inside eye on the offensive center's outside ear, 6 to 12 inches off the line of scrimmage.

The defensive lineman keys through the center and near guard. If the center attacks, the lineman attacks him back. If the center pass blocks, the lineman checks the screen and

Figure 5.3 Lineman's initial position in the 0 technique.

Figure 5.4 Lineman's initial position in the 1 technique.

makes a move through his A gap. If the center tries to leave him or attacks only with his inside arm, the lineman keeps the center on the line and moves with him to keep from getting reached by the guard. If double-teamed, the lineman attacks the power man. If the offensive guard pulls behind the center, the lineman fights across the center's head, checking for the ballcarrier on a quick trap, then works into a pursuit course while checking for a cutback. If the offensive guard pulls outside and the center tries to reach the lineman, he fights down the line for the cutback. If the offensive guard pulls outside and the center does not try to reach the lineman, he checks for a trap before flowing down the line, looking for a cutback. If the offensive guard blocks down on the lineman, he immediately works to cross his face, staying on the line of scrimmage.

The lineman is responsible for the A gap. He must not be hooked by the center, nor driven off the line of scrimmage by the guard. If pass shows, the lineman checks for a draw or middle screen, then rushes the inside alley on the split side.

To execute his responsibilities, the lineman moves on the ball and immediately attacks the center. He hits up with his inside forehand, bringing the hand clear up and locking his elbow. If he doesn't bring the forehand clear up, the blocker will get to his body. He must get his pads under the blocker's pads. If the center attacks, the lineman attacks him back, reading the center's head to find the ball. If overpowered, the lineman gives ground grudgingly in the direction he came from. If double-teamed, he must be able to hold his point right there and then turn and fight the power block. He puts his nose in the ground and does anything to make the hump there.

Inside 2 Technique

For the inside 2 technique, the lineman uses a three-point stance with feet staggered and his gap hand up (figure 5.5). His feet are shoulder-width apart or narrower. He balances on his fingertips rather, not his knuckles. His gap hand is shoulder high and ready to jam the offensive lineman. He aligns with his outside eye on the offensive guard's inside ear 18 inches off the line of scrimmage.

The lineman keys through the guard to the ball. If the guard attacks, the lineman attacks him back. If the guard pass blocks, the lineman checks for a screen and then makes a move through the A gap or pinched B gap. If the guard hooks him, the lineman checks his gap until the ball is gone, then fights across the guard's face down the line of scrimmage, looking for a cutback and deepening the wider he goes. If the guard pulls across the center, the lineman closes down, looks to the inside, and finds the ball. He attacks the center's block, keeping his outside arm free. If double-teamed, the lineman attacks the power man. If the

Figure 5.5 Lineman's initial position in the inside 2 technique.

guard pulls outside, the lineman steps to the center's head, checking for a false-key trap, then works back down the line to the offensive tackle and fights across his face, getting pursuit course depth if the back is outside him. If the center blocks out and the guard folds inside, the lineman fights across the center's face, or, at least, fills the A gap with the center's body.

The lineman is responsible for the A gap. He must not be trapped or driven inside. If pass shows, the lineman checks for a draw or middle screen and then rushes his inside lane.

To execute his responsibilities, the lineman moves on the ball and immediately attacks the offensive guard. He hits up with his outside forehand, bringing his hand clear up and locking his elbow. If he doesn't bring the forehand clear up, the blocker will get to his body. He must get his pads under the blocker's pads. If the offensive guard attacks, the lineman attacks him back and finds the ball. If overpowered, the lineman gives ground grudgingly in the direction he came from. If double-teamed, the lineman must hold his point right there and then turn and fight the power block. He puts his nose in the ground and does anything to make the hump there.

2 Technique

For the 2 technique, the lineman uses a three-point stance with feet slightly staggered (figure 5.6). His feet are shoulder-width apart or narrower.

He balances on his fingertips, not his knuckles. His free hand ready to jam the offensive lineman. He aligns nose on to the offensive guard with his outside eye to the offensive guard's nose so he can't be hooked. He sets up 18 inches off the line of scrimmage.

He keys through the guard to the ball. If the guard attacks, the lineman attacks him back. If the guard pass blocks, the lineman checks for a screen and makes a move through the A gap or pinched B gap. If the guard hooks, the lineman checks his gap until the ball is gone, then fights across the guard's face down the line of scrimmage, looking for a cutback and deepening the wider he goes. If the guard pulls across the center, the lineman closes down, looking to the inside to find the ball. He attacks the center's block, keeping his outside arm free. If double-teamed, the lineman attacks the power man. If the guard pulls outside, the lineman steps to the head of the center, checking for a false-key trap, then works back down the line to the offensive tackle and fights across his face, getting pursuit course depth if the back is outside of him. If the center blocks out and the guard folds inside, the lineman fights across the center's face or, at least, fills the A gaps with the center's body.

First the lineman is responsible for the B gap. He must never be hooked. If pass shows, the lineman checks for a draw or middle screen, then rushes his inside lane.

Figure 5.6 Lineman's initial position in the 2 technique.

To execute his responsibilities, the lineman moves on the ball and immediately attacks the offensive guard. He hits up with his inside forehand, bringing it clear up and locking the elbow. If he doesn't bring the forehand clear up, the blocker will get to his body. He must get his pads under the blocker's pads. If the offensive guard attacks, the lineman attacks him back and finds the ball. If overpowered, the lineman gives ground grudgingly in the direction he came from. If double-teamed, the lineman must be able to hold his point right there then turn and fight the power block. He puts his nose in the ground and does anything to make the hump there.

3 Technique

For the 3 technique, the lineman uses a three-point stance with his feet staggered and his gap hand up (figure 5.7). His feet are shoulder width or narrower. He balances on his fingertips rather than his knuckles. His gap hand is ready to jam the offensive lineman. He aligns with his inside eye to the offensive guard's outside ear 18 inches off the line of scrimmage.

He keys through the guard to the ball. If the guard attacks, the lineman attacks him back. If the guard pass blocks, the lineman checks for a screen and makes a move through the B gap or wide A gap. If the guard blocks inside, the lineman stays low and close to the guard's block, looking for a trapping guard or isolating back. If the guard pulls across the center, the lineman closes down, looks to the inside, and finds the ball. He attacks the center's block, keeping his outside arm free. If double-teamed, the lineman attacks the power man. If the guard pulls outside, the lineman steps to the center's head, checking for a false-key trap. Then he works back down the line to the offensive tackle and fights across his face, getting pursuit course depth if the back is outside of him.

His first responsibility is the B gap. He must never be hooked. If pass shows, the lineman checks for a draw or middle screen, then rushes his inside lane.

To execute his responsibilities, the lineman moves on the ball and immediately attacks the offensive guard. He hits up with his inside forehand, bringing it clear up and locking his elbow. If he doesn't bring the forehand clear up, the blocker will get to his body. He must get his pads under the blocker's pads. If the offensive guard attacks, the lineman attacks him and finds the ball. If overpowered, the lineman gives ground grudgingly in the direction he came from. If double-teamed, the lineman must be able to hold his point right there then turn and fight the power block. He puts his nose in the ground and does anything to make the hump there.

Figure 5.7 Lineman's initial position in the 3 technique.

Inside 4 Technique

For the inside 4 technique, the lineman uses a three-point stance with his feet staggered and his gap hand up (figure 5.8). His feet are shoulder width or narrower. He balances on his fingertips rather than his knuckles. His gap hand is shoulder high and ready to jam the offensive lineman. He aligns with his outside eye on the offensive tackle's inside ear 18 inches off the line of scrimmage.

He keys through the tackle to the guard then to the ball. If the tackle attacks, the lineman attacks him back and checks the guard. If the tackle pass blocks, the lineman steps to the guard, checks for a screen, and makes a move through the pinched B gap or A gap. If the tackle hooks, the lineman checks the guard, holding his gap until the ball is gone, then fights across the tackle's face down the line of scrimmage, looking for a cutback and deepening the wider he goes. If the tackle pulls across the center, the lineman jams him, closes down, and looks inside to find the ball. He attacks the guard's or center's block, keeping his outside arm free. If double-teamed, the lineman attacks the power man. If the tackle pulls outside, the lineman steps inside to the guard's head, checking for a false key. If the guard blocks him out, the lineman squeezes the A gap and finds the ball. If the guard tries to reach the lineman, he jams him, finds the

ball, and takes a proper pursuit course down the line of scrimmage as the ball passes.

The lineman's first responsibility is protecting the B gap, squeezing the A gap, and supporting the C gap. He must not be trapped or driven inside. If pass shows, the lineman checks for a draw or middle screen and then rushes his inside lane.

To execute his responsibilities, the lineman moves on the ball and immediately attacks the offensive tackle. He hits up with the outside forehand, bringing the hand clear up and locking his elbow. If he doesn't bring the forehand clear up, the blocker will get to his body. He must get his pads under the blocker's pads. If the offensive tackle attacks, the lineman attacks him back and finds the ball. If overpowered, the lineman gives ground grudgingly in the direction he came from. If double-teamed, the lineman must hold his point right there and then turn and fight the power block. He puts his nose in the ground and does anything to make the hump there. If the offensive guard attacks, the lineman attacks him back and finds the ball.

4 Technique

For the 4 technique, the lineman uses a three-point stance with feet slightly staggered (figure 5.9). His feet are shoulder-width apart or narrower. He balances on his fingertips, not his

Figure 5.8 Lineman's initial position in the inside 4 technique.

knuckles. His free hand is shoulder high, ready to jam the offensive lineman. He aligns nose on offensive tackle's nose to outside eye so he can't be hooked. He sets up 18 inches off the line of scrimmage.

He keys the tackle's block and the near back. If the tackle attacks, the lineman attacks him back. He must be sure the tackle does not block him in. He keeps his outside arm free. If the tackle releases inside, the lineman squeezes the blocker down and keeps him off the inside linebacker. He keeps his shoulders square to the line of scrimmage and looks for a guard trap or tight end down block. If the play is away and he is the widest lineman, the lineman pursues through the backfield at ball depth. If he is not the widest lineman, he pursues down the line to the center and gets to the ball. Against pass protection, if he is the outside rusher, the lineman has the primary responsibility for the outside screen. He checks for a running back slipping to the outside late and then uses an outside contain pass rush.

The lineman's first responsibility is the C gap. He keeps the tackle off the inside linebacker and closes the off-tackle play to his inside. He must never be blocked in. Against option, the end is responsible for the quarterback, and the tackle is responsible for the dive. If responsible for the sweep, the lineman strings it out and turns it in, keeping it squeezed as tight as possible without getting hooked so the back can't cut inside easily. Against flow away, the end squeezes to the B gap and then trails through the backfield at ball depth until the ball crosses the line of scrimmage. The tackle squeezes to the center and takes the proper pursuit course.

To execute his responsibilities, the lineman short jabs with his inside foot and hits with his inside forehand. He brings the forehand clear up and locks his elbow. If the back attacks, the lineman attacks him back by meeting him as deep as possible with his inside foot and inside shoulder. The lineman gets his pad under the back's and then strings it out by keeping his outside foot free. As he sheds each blocker and strings out the play to the sideline, the lineman tries to meet each blocker deeper. If not attacked by the back, the lineman finds the action. He looks for the first man that could block him. He looks immediately for a pulling guard. The lineman keeps his shoulders parallel with the goal post and looks in rather than turns in. He steps into the charge of the guard, keeping his shoulders parallel to the line of scrimmage, and uses his inside forearm to get under the guard's pads and raise his charge.

Figure 5.9 Lineman's initial position in the 4 technique.

5 Technique

For the 5 technique, the lineman uses a three-point stance with feet staggered and his gap hand up (figure 5.10). His feet are shoulder-width apart or narrower. He balances on his fingertips, not his knuckles. His gap hand is shoulder high, ready to jam the offensive lineman. He aligns with his inside eye on the offensive tackle's outside ear, 18 inches off the line of scrimmage.

The lineman keys the tackle's block and the near back. If the tackle attacks, the lineman attacks him back. He must be sure the tackle does not block him in. He keeps his outside arm free. If the tackle releases inside, the lineman squeezes the blocker down and keeps him off the inside linebacker. He keeps his shoulders square to the line of scrimmage and looks for a guard trap or tight end down block. If the play is away and he is the widest lineman, the lineman pursues through the backfield at ball depth. If he's not the widest lineman, the lineman pursues down the line to the center and gets to the ball. Against pass protection, if he's the outside rusher, the lineman has primary responsibility for the outside screen. He checks for a running back slipping late to the outside and then uses an outside contain pass rush.

His first responsibility is the C gap. He keeps the tackle off the inside linebacker. He closes the off-tackle play to his inside. The lineman must never be blocked in. Against option, the end is responsible for the quarterback, and the tackle is responsible for the dive. If responsible for the sweep, the lineman strings it out and turns it in, keeping it squeezed as tight as possible without getting hooked so the back can't cut inside easily. Against flow away, the end squeezes to the B gap and then trails through the backfield at ball depth until the ball crosses the line of scrimmage. The tackle squeezes to the center and takes the proper pursuit course.

To execute his responsibilities, the lineman short jabs with his inside foot and hits with his inside forehand. He brings the forehand clear up and locks his elbow. If the back attacks, the lineman attacks him back by meeting him as deep as possible with his inside foot and inside shoulder. He gets his pad under the back's and then strings it out by keeping his outside foot free. As he sheds each blocker and strings out the play to the sideline, the lineman tries to meet each blocker deeper. If not attacked by the back, the lineman finds the action by looking for the first man who can block him. He looks immediately for a pulling guard. He keeps his shoulders parallel with the goal post and looks in rather than turns in. He steps into his charge, keeping his shoulders parallel to the line of scrimmage, and uses his inside forearm to get under the guard's pads and raise his charge.

Figure 5.10 Lineman's initial position in the 5 technique.

Inside 6 Technique

For the inside 6 technique, the lineman uses a three-point stance with feet slightly staggered (figure 5.11) or a two-point stance with feet balanced. His feet are shoulder-width apart or narrower. He balances on his fingertips, not his knuckles. His gap hand is shoulder high, ready to jam the offensive lineman. His alignment depends on the player opposite him. Against a tight end, the lineman aligns his outside eye on the tight end's inside eye. Against a slot, the lineman aligns his outside eye on the offensive player's inside eye. Against no third offensive player, the lineman moves to a 5 technique. He aligns on the line of scrimmage.

The lineman feels the tight end and keys the offensive tackle to the backfield. On a run toward him against the option, the lineman has the dive or quarterback based on the outside linebacker's "you-me" call. Against the power or sweep, the lineman attacks through interference with an inside-out relationship. On a run away from him, he squeezes to the B gap, trails through the backfield at ball depth until the ball crosses the line of scrimmage, and then takes the proper pursuit course.

The lineman's first responsibility is the C gap, keeping his inside arm free. He must slow the tight end's release and never be blocked out. Against option, the lineman has the dive or quarterback based on the outside linebacker's "you-me" call. Against pass, the lineman checks the outside screen and rushes with a contain course.

To execute his responsibilities, the lineman drives through the tight end's shoulder. He gets to heel depth, squares up, and plays ball.

6 Technique

For the 6 technique, the lineman uses a three-point stance with feet slightly staggered (figure 5.12). His feet are shoulder-width apart or narrower. He balances on his fingertips, not his knuckles. His gap hand is shoulder high, ready to jam the offensive lineman. He aligns nose on tight end's nose to outside eye so he can't be hooked. He sets up 18 inches off the line of scrimmage.

The lineman keys through the tight end to the ball. He reads the tight end's movement first. If the tight end blocks him, the lineman fights the tight end to keep him from getting position on the lineman. If the tight end tries to hook, the lineman works to stay head up on the tight end while driving him off the line of scrimmage. If the tight end tries to move inside, the lineman rides him in, keeping him off the linebacker and maintaining leverage on the play. The lineman looks for a back or guard to come to kick him out. If the tight end releases outside, the lineman jams him and mirrors his steps, then steps back inside

Figure 5.11   Lineman's initial position in the inside 6 technique, three-point stance.

Figure 5.12 Lineman's initial position in the 6 technique, three-point stance.

and keeps his shoulders square, checking for option or pass. If the tight end pass blocks, the lineman checks for a screen or draw and then rushes with outside contain.

The lineman's first responsibility is the D gap. Against the running game, the lineman is responsible for containing the outside play and helping to squeeze the off-tackle play. Against the option, the lineman has the pitch. Against the pass, the lineman has contain rush.

To execute his responsibilities, the lineman reads the tight end's head while getting into him by jamming his hands and helmet into the tight end's numbers. If the tight end goes in, the lineman rides him in, keeping him off the linebackers. He looks for a trapping guard or back. The lineman must not let the tight end block him out. He keeps the tight end from

getting into position. He must help squeeze the off-tackle play. The lineman must not let the tight end hook him. He must work upfield through the tight end's outside shoulder, turning wide plays back into pursuit. Against the pass, the lineman holds the tight end on the line of scrimmage as long as possible. He checks for the wide screen and then rushes the quarterback, keeping him contained. Against flow away, the lineman checks for the counter, squeezes through the C gap, and then pursues through the backfield, staying as deep as the ball and watching for the reverse.

7 Technique

For the 7 technique, the lineman uses a three-point stance with feet slightly staggered (figure 5.13). His feet are shoulder-width apart or

Figure 5.13 Lineman's initial position in the 7 technique, three-point stance.

narrower. He balances on his fingertips, not his knuckles. His gap hand is shoulder high, ready to jam the offensive lineman. He aligns with his inside eye on the tight end's outside ear, 18 inches off the line of scrimmage.

The lineman keys through the tight end to the ball. First, he reads the tight end's movement. If the tight end blocks the lineman, he fights the tight end to keep him from getting position. If the tight end tries to hook, the lineman works to stay head up on the tight end while driving him off the line of scrimmage. If the tight end tries to move inside, the lineman rides him in, keeping him off the linebacker and keeping leverage on the play. He looks for a back or guard to come to kick him out. If the tight end releases outside, the lineman jams him and mirrors his steps, then steps back inside and, keeping his shoulders square, checks for option or pass. If the tight end pass blocks, the lineman checks for a screen or draw and then rushes with outside contain.

The lineman's first responsibility is the D gap. Against the running game, he contains the outside play and helps squeeze the off-tackle play. Against the option, the lineman has the pitch. Against pass, the lineman has contain rush.

To execute his responsibility, the lineman reads the tight end's head while getting into him by jamming his hands and helmet into the tight end's numbers. If the tight end goes in, the lineman rides him in, keeping him off the linebackers. He looks for a trapping guard or back. The lineman must not let the tight end block him out. He must keep the tight end from getting into position and help squeeze the off-tackle play. He must not let the tight end hook him. He must work upfield through the tight end's outside shoulder, turning wide plays back into pursuit. Against the pass, the lineman holds the tight end on the line of scrimmage as long as possible. He checks for the wide screen and then rushes the quarterback, keeping him contained. Against flow away, the lineman checks for the counter, squeezes through the C gap, and then pursues through

the backfield, staying as deep as the ball and watching for the reverse.

8 Technique

For the 8 technique, the lineman uses a three-point stance with feet staggered and the outside foot back. He is angled inside toward the near back in a sprinter's stance. He aligns over the ghost outside the tight end or tight slot. If there's not a tight end or tight slot, he switches to a loose 5 technique. He aligns on the line of scrimmage, looking inside to be sure he is onside.

The lineman moves on the movement of the ball. He keys the near back. If the near back attacks, the lineman attacks him back, driving him back and forcing the sweep deep. If the near back disappears inside, the lineman continues inside, adjusting to attack the next back (running back or fullback) that comes. If the near back swings to the outside, the lineman finds the next back, whether a pitch man or pass blocker, removing the next back if he is the pitch man or attacking and containing the quarterback if it's a pass play. If the near back goes across the formation, the lineman trails at ball depth through the backfield.

The lineman's first responsibility is the D gap. Against the running game, the lineman's duties are to force the off-tackle by squeezing it, stop sweeps by attacking the lead blocker and forcing it deep, and stop reverses. Against the passing game, the lineman attacks the quarterback, maintaining his outside contain.

To execute his responsibilities, the lineman attacks hard off the tight end's butt to a point 4-1/2 yards deep in the offensive backfield behind the B gap, keying the near back and turning everything back inside. If the near back attacks, the lineman attacks him hard, keeping his outside arm free and forcing all action deep so that all can flow to it. The lineman has pitch on the option, so he must not allow the lead back to pin him inside to allow the pitch man outside. If the near back disappears inside, the lineman adjusts his course to the next back and looks immediately down the line of scrimmage to see if the quarterback is on (option) or off (run or pass) the line of scrimmage. Against option, the lineman has the pitch and should take the pitch man out of the play. Against the pass, the lineman has contain rush and gets to the quarterback. If the near back swings to the outside, the lineman finds the next back, be it pitch man or pass blocker, removing him if he is the pitch man or attacking and containing the quarterback if it is a pass play. If the near back goes across the formation, the lineman continues into the backfield at ball depth, checking for counters, reverses, and bootlegs.

Inside Linebacker Techniques

Let's move to linebacker techniques, including stance, alignment, depth, keys, responsibilities, and execution. First we'll deal with techniques normally employed by inside linebackers and then move to those usually assigned to outside linebackers.

0 Technique

For the 0 technique, the linebacker uses a two-point stance with his feet parallel and his weight on the balls of his feet (figure 5.14). He is in a relaxed semicrouch with his arms in front. He aligns with his nose on the offensive center's nose, 4 to 5 yards deep.

The linebacker keys the backfield set, aware of the blocking scheme and the quarterback. Against a full backfield flow to the tight-end side, the linebacker checks his A gap and then flows down the line of scrimmage, playing inside-out on the ball and ready to take on blockers. He keeps his outside arm free and his shoulders parallel. When the ballcarrier turns up, the linebacker attacks up into the ballcarrier, playing inside-out. Against a full backfield flow to the split side, the linebacker flows and steps up to the B gap, ready to take on the lead blocker head up. He keeps his outside arm free and his shoulders parallel. If the guard or tackle tries to block him, the linebacker drives the guard or tackle back into the gap. If the ball flows outside, the linebacker flows down the line, playing inside-out and looking for the

Figure 5.14 Linebacker's initial position in the 0 technique.

cutback. When the backs split, the linebacker hangs back and finds the ball, unless his A gap is attacked immediately. If it is, he steps up hard and jams all action back into the backfield.

When used with slide, the linebacker's responsibility is the C gap to the tight side and the B gap to the split side. When used in 70 defenses, the linebacker's responsibility is the A gap to the tight side and the B gap to the split side.

To execute his responsibility, the linebacker takes a short step in the direction of the flow with the foot away from the flow to keep from being overextended and flowing too quickly. If flow is to the tight side, he checks his A gap and continues to flow laterally, keeping an inside-out position on the ball. If the flow is to the split side, he flows up to his B gap while finding the ball and then continues to flow laterally, keeping an inside-out position on the ball. The linebacker must keep the ball in front of him. He must not overrun the ball and must be ready for a cutback.

1 Technique

For the 1 technique, the linebacker uses a two-point stance with his feet parallel and his weight on the balls of his feet (see figure 5.14). He is in a relaxed semicrouch with his arms hanging in front so his hands hang below his knees. He aligns nose on to the tight-side ear of the offensive center, 4 to 5 yards deep.

The linebacker keys the backfield set and is aware of blocking schemes and the quarterback. Against a full backfield flow to the tight-end side, the linebacker checks his A gap and then flows down the line of scrimmage, playing inside-out on the ball, ready to take on blockers. He keeps his outside arm free and his shoulders parallel. When the ballcarrier turns up, the linebacker attacks up into him, playing inside-out. Against a full backfield flow to the split side, he flows and steps up to the B gap, ready to take on the lead blocker head up. He keeps his outside arm free and his shoulders parallel. If the guard or tackle tries to block him, the linebacker drives the guard or tackle back into the gap. If the ball flows outside, he flows down the line, playing inside-out and looking for the cutback. When the backs split, the linebacker hangs back and finds the ball, unless his A gap is attacked immediately. If it is, he steps up hard and jams all action back into the backfield.

The linebacker's first responsibility is the A gap to the tight side and the B gap to the split side.

To execute his responsibility, the linebacker takes a short step in the direction of flow with the foot away from the flow to keep from being overextended and flowing too quickly. If flow is to the tight side, he checks his A gap and continues to flow laterally, keeping an inside-out position on the ball. If flow is to the split side, he flows up to his B gap while finding the ball and then continues to flow laterally, keeping an inside-out position on the ball. He must keep the ball in front of him. He must not overrun the ball and must be ready for a cutback.

2 Technique

The linebacker uses a two-point stance with feet parallel and weight on the balls of his feet (see figure 5.14). He is in a relaxed semicrouch with arms hanging in front so his hands hang below his knees. He aligns nose on to the nose of the offensive guard, 4 to 5 yards deep.

The linebacker keys the backfield set and is aware of the blocking scheme and quarterback. He keys from near back to far back to ball. Against a full backfield flow to his outside, the linebacker flows down the line of scrimmage, inside-out on the ball, ready to take on blockers. He keeps his outside arm free and his shoulders parallel. Once the ballcarrier turns up, the linebacker attacks up at him, playing inside-out. When all backs go away from him, the linebacker steps to the center and flows down the line of scrimmage, staying inside-out on the ball. He flows only if all backs go wide. If a back comes inside, he plugs into the center's head, reading a possible trap or cutback by the second back. When backs cross or one back comes straight at him, the linebacker doesn't plug or scrape. He hangs there and is prepared to jam straight ahead, protecting his A gap if the near back gets the ball or pursuing if the ball goes wider. If both backs come straight ahead (isolation), the linebacker attacks the first blocker with his outside forehand and inside arm free.

The linebacker's responsibility is the A gap to his side and then the ball.

To execute his responsibility, the linebacker takes a short step in the direction of flow with the foot away from the flow to keep from being overextended and flowing too quickly. If the flow is to him and past the A gap, he continues to flow laterally, keeping an inside-out position on the ball. He must keep the ball in front of him. He must not overrun the ball and must be ready for the cutback. If flow is away from him, he checks both A gaps for counters and cutbacks and then flows slowly to the ball, checking for cutbacks.

3 Technique

For the 3 technique, the linebacker uses a two-point stance with feet parallel and weight on the balls of his feet (see figure 5.14). He's in a relaxed semicrouch with arms hanging in front so his hands hang below his knees. He aligns nose on to the outside eye of the offensive guard, 4 to 5 yards deep.

The linebacker keys the backfield set and is aware of the blocking scheme and the quarterback. He keys the near back to the far back to the ball. Against a full backfield flow to his outside, he flows down the line of scrimmage, inside-out on the ball, ready to take on blockers. He keeps his outside arm free and his shoulders parallel. Once the ballcarrier turns up, the linebacker attacks up at him, playing inside-out. When all backs go away, he steps to the center and flows down the line of scrimmage, staying inside-out on the ball. He flows only if all backs go wide. If a back comes inside, he plugs into the center's head, reading a possible trap or cutback by the inside ballcarrier. He must not let the blocker drive him past the cutback by the second back. When backs cross or one back comes straight at him, the linebacker doesn't plug or scrape. He hangs there and is prepared to jam straight ahead, protecting his B gap if the near back gets the ball or pursuing if the ball goes wider. If both backs come straight ahead (isolation), the linebacker attacks the first blocker with his inside forehand and outside arm free.

The linebacker's responsibility is the B gap. He stays inside-out on the ball.

To execute his responsibility, the linebacker takes a short step in the direction of flow with the foot away from the flow to keep from being overextended or from flowing too quickly. If a guard attacks, the linebacker attacks him using a forehand hit. As the guard attempts to gain position on the linebacker, the linebacker moves laterally as he moves up into the guard so he is always hitting into the guard head on. The linebacker is in a crouched position to keep the blocker away from his legs. If the linebacker is being isolated, he runs at it as hard and fast as he can. He hits right in the gap responsibility, with his outside arm free. Against flow away, the linebacker's second step is at a 45-degree angle to the center's head to protect against the cutback. The backside linebacker is the slow flow linebacker. He keeps his backside arm free for tackling the cutback.

4 Technique

For the 4 technique, the linebacker uses a two-point stance with feet parallel and weight on the balls of his feet (see figure 5.14). He's in a relaxed semicrouch with arms hanging in front so his hands hang below his knees. He aligns nose on to the nose of the offensive tackle, 4 to 5 yards deep.

The linebacker keys the backfield set and is aware of the blocking scheme and the quarterback. He keys the near back to the far back to the ball. Against a full backfield flow to his outside, he flows down the line of scrimmage, inside-out on the ball, ready to take on blockers. He keeps his outside arm free and his shoulders parallel. Once the ballcarrier turns up, the linebacker attacks up at him, playing inside-out. When all backs go away from him, he steps to the center and flows down the line of scrimmage, staying inside-out on the ball. He flows only if all backs go wide. If a back comes inside, he plugs into the center's head, reading a possible trap or cutback by the second back. The linebacker must not let the blocker drive him past the cutback. When the backs cross or one back comes straight at him, he doesn't plug or scrape. He hangs there and is prepared to jam straight ahead, protecting his B gap if the near back gets the ball or pursuing if the ball goes wider. If both backs come straight ahead (isolation), the linebacker attacks the first blocker with his outside forehand and inside arm free.

The linebacker's responsibility is the B gap to his side and then the ball.

To execute his responsibility, the linebacker takes a short step in the direction of flow with the foot away from the flow to keep from being overextended or from flowing too quickly. If the flow is to him and past the B gap, he continues to flow laterally, keeping an inside-out position on the ball. He keeps the ball in front of him. He must not overrun the ball and must be ready for the cutback. If the flow is away from him, he checks his B and A gaps for counters and cutbacks and then flows slowly to the ball, checking for cutbacks.

5 Technique

For the 5 technique, the linebacker uses a two-point stance with feet parallel and weight on the balls of his feet (see figure 5.14). He's in a relaxed semicrouch with arms hanging in front so his hands hang below his knees. He aligns nose on to the outside eye of the offensive tackle, 4 to 5 yards deep.

The linebacker keys the backfield set and is aware of the blocking scheme and the quarterback. He keys the near back to the far back to the ball.

Plug: Against a full backfield flow at him, the linebacker moves up hard, ready to jam the tackle if he blocks the linebacker, step into the tight end's down block if the tight end comes at him, or take on the fullback if the fullback leads on the linebacker at the line of scrimmage. The linebacker holds his ground and must not be driven inside or off the line of scrimmage. He fights to keep his outside arm free to force the ball back inside or to bounce deep into pursuit.

Scrape or flow: Against a full backfield flow to his outside, the linebacker flows down the line of scrimmage, inside-out on the ball, ready to take on blockers. He keeps his outside arm free and his shoulders parallel to the line of scrimmage. Once the ballcarrier turns up, the linebacker attacks up at him, inside-out.

The linebacker plugs or flows when all backs go away from him. He flows very slowly down the line of scrimmage, checking for counters and cutbacks. If a back comes inside, he steps behind the end, reading for a possible trap or cutback by the inside ballcarrier. He must not let the offensive tackle drive him past the countering back or the cutback by the second back.

The linebacker plugs or flows when all backs go away from him. The strong-side linebacker steps up into the A gap, checking for counters and cutbacks. The weak-side linebacker steps up into his B gap and then flows slowly down the line of scrimmage, checking for cutbacks and counters. He must keep deep enough to avoid tangling in the linemen's feet and be ready to take on blockers as he flows.

Hang: When backs cross or one back comes straight at him, the linebacker doesn't plug or scrape. He hangs there and is prepared to jam straight ahead, protecting his C or B gap if the near back gets the ball, or pursue if the ball goes wider. If both backs come straight at his gap, he attacks the first blocker with his inside forehand and outside arm free.

The linebacker's responsibility is the C gap to his side and then the ball.

To execute his responsibility, the linebacker takes a short step in the direction of flow with the foot away from the flow to keep from being overextended or from flowing too quickly. If the offensive tackle attacks, the linebacker uses a forehand hit. As the tackle attempts to gain position on the linebacker, the linebacker moves laterally as he moves up into the tackle so he's always hitting into the tackle head on. The linebacker stays crouched, protecting his legs and keeping his power. If he's being isolated, he runs at it as hard and fast as he can. He hits right in the middle of it. He makes the heap as deep in the backfield as possible. He controls his gap responsibility with his outside arm free.

Against flow away, the linebacker's second step is short and slow, maintaining his relation to the ball to protect against the cutback. The backside linebacker is the slow flow linebacker. He keeps his backside arm free for tackling the cutback.

Outside Linebacker Techniques

Now let's look at the outside linebacker techniques, including stance, alignment, depth, keys, responsibilities, and execution. The following techniques are usually assigned to outside linebackers.

5 Technique

For the 5 technique, the linebacker uses a two-point stance with feet parallel and weight on the balls of his feet (see figure 5.14, p. 76). He's in a relaxed semicrouch with arms hanging in front so his hands hang below his knees. He aligns nose on to the outside eye of the offensive tackle, 4 to 5 yards deep.

The linebacker keys the backfield set and is aware of the blocking scheme and the quarterback. He keys the near back to the far back to the ball. Against a full backfield flow at him, he moves up hard, ready to jam the tackle if he blocks him, step into the tight end's down block if the tight end comes at him, or take on the fullback if he leads on him at the line of scrimmage. The linebacker must hold his ground and not be driven inside or off the line of scrimmage. He fights to keep his outside arm free to force the ball back inside or to bounce deep into pursuit. Against a full backfield flow to his outside, he flows down the line of scrimmage, inside-out on the ball, ready to take on blockers. He keeps his outside arm free and his shoulders parallel to the line of scrimmage. Once the ballcarrier turns up, he attacks up at the ballcarrier, inside-out. When all backs go away from him, he plugs or flows. He steps up into the A and B gaps and then flows slowly down the line of scrimmage, checking for cutbacks and counters. He stays deep enough to avoid tangling in the linemen's feet and is ready to take on blockers as he flows. When backs cross or one back comes straight at him, the linebacker doesn't plug or scrape. He hangs there and is prepared to jam straight ahead, protecting his C gap if the near back gets the ball or pursuing if the ball goes wider. If both backs come straight at his gap, he attacks the first blocker with his inside forehand and outside arm free.

The linebacker has C gap responsibility.

To execute his responsibility, the linebacker takes a short step in the direction of flow with the foot away from the flow to keep from being overextended or from flowing too quickly. If the tackle attacks, he attacks him using a forehand hit. As the tackle attempts to gain position on him, he moves laterally as he moves up into the tackle so that he's always hitting into the tackle head on. He stays crouched, protecting his legs and keeping his power. If he's being isolated, the linebacker runs at it as hard and fast as he can, hitting right in the middle of it. He makes the heap as deep in the backfield as possible. He controls his gap responsibility with his outside arm free. Against flow away, his second step is short and slow, maintaining his relation to the ball to protect against the cutback. The backside linebacker is the slow flow linebacker. He keeps his backside arm free for tackling the cutback.

Inside 6 Technique

The linebacker uses a two-point stance with his inside foot slightly back and his weight off his heels (figure 5.15). His feet are no wider than

Figure 5.15 Linebacker's initial position in the inside 6 technique.

shoulder-width apart. He holds his hands in to his body near his waist and inside his hips. He is ready to deliver a blow with his forehands on the first movement.

The linebacker's alignment depends on the position of the offensive player opposite him. Against a tight end or tight slot, he aligns with his outside eye on the tight end's or tight slot's inside eye. He sets up at the line of scrimmage.

The linebacker feels the tight end and keys the offensive tackle to the backfield. On a run toward him, he has the quarterback (the end has the pitch) and must make a "me" call against the option. On a run toward him against power or sweep, he attacks through interference with an inside-out relationship to the blockers leading to the ballcarrier. On a run away from him, he drops straight back into the shallow hook area (8 yards) and then takes his normal pursuit course.

The C gap is the linebacker's first responsibility. He keeps his inside arm free. He must slow the tight end's release and never be blocked out. Against the option, the linebacker has the quarterback. Against a pass, he plays the pass coverage called.

To execute his responsibilities, the linebacker jams the tight end hard, staying on the line of scrimmage and reading the offensive tackle to the backfield. He reads the offensive tackle's block for clues to the play. He must be ready for a guard or the near back to come to kick him out. If this occurs, he stays low and holds his ground. As the blocker approaches, the linebacker steps into the guard with a side step or into the back at an angle to intercept his course. The linebacker creates a stalemate in the hole. He forces the ballcarrier to cut back into pursuit or bounce deep to the defensive end. Against a pass, he drops to his coverage. He must know the tight end's pattern by feel. He locates the wide receiver as he drops, keeping his head on a swivel to read the quarterback and any backfield patterns in front of himself.

6 Technique

The linebacker uses a two-point stance with feet parallel and no wider than shoulder-width apart and his weight off his heels (figure 5.16). His hands are in to his body near his waist and inside his hips. He is ready to deliver a blow with his forehands on the first movement. He aligns his nose to the tight end's nose. He sets up at the line of scrimmage.

The linebacker keys through the tight end to the ball. First, he reads the tight end's movement. If the tight end blocks him, he fights the tight end. He must keep the tight end from getting position on him. If the tight end tries to block him, he works to stay head up on the tight end, driving him off the line of scrimmage.

Figure 5.16 Linebacker's initial position in the 6 technique.

If the tight end tries to move inside, the linebacker rides him in, keeping him off the inside linebacker and keeping leverage on the play. The linebacker looks for a back or guard to come to kick him out. If the tight end releases outside, the linebacker jams him as he takes a mirror step with his head turned back inside to check for run or pass, taking the option or run responsibility or the pass drop. If the tight end pass blocks, the linebacker takes his pass drop, watching for a screen or delayed release.

The linebacker has D gap responsibility. Against the running game, his responsibility is to contain the outside play and help squeeze the off-tackle play. Against the option, he has the quarterback or pitch man based on his "you-me" call. Against the pass, he takes the responsibility defined by the coverage call, usually squat or trail.

To execute his responsibility, the linebacker reads the tight end's head and takes a quick jab step in the direction it moves. At the same time, he hits the tight end's front numbers with his forehands. If the tight end goes in, the linebacker rides him down the line of scrimmage, keeping him off the inside linebackers or from double-teaming the tackle. He looks for the kickout guard or back or backside pull. The linebacker must not let the tight end block him out. He keeps the tight end from getting into position and helps to squeeze the off-tackle play. He does not let the tight end hook him. He works upfield through his outside shoulder, turning wide plays back into pursuit. Against the pass, he holds the tight end on the line of scrimmage as long as possible. He checks for the wide screen as he takes his pass drop. Against flow away, he checks for the counter or reverse and then gets into his proper pursuit course, looking for a cutback.

7 Technique

The linebacker uses a two-point stance with feet parallel and no wider than shoulder-width apart and his weight off his heels. His hands are into his body just above his waist and inside his hips. His palms are out and his fingers up, ready to deliver a blow with his forehands on first movement. He aligns with his inside eye on the tight end's outside ear, 18 inches off the line of scrimmage.

The linebacker keys through the tight end to the ball. He reads the tight end's movement first. If the tight end blocks him, he fights the tight end to keep the tight end from getting position on him. If the tight end tries to hook, the linebacker works to stay head up on the tight end while driving him off the line of scrimmage. If the tight end tries to move inside, the linebacker rides him in, keeping him off the inside linebacker and keeping leverage on the play. The linebacker looks for a back or guard to come to kick him out. If the tight end releases outside, the linebacker jams him and mirrors his step and then steps back inside, keeping his shoulders square as he checks for option or pass. If the tight end pass blocks, the linebacker checks for a screen or draw and then rushes with outside contain.

The linebacker's responsibility is the D gap. His running game responsibility is to contain the outside play and help squeeze the off-tackle play. Against the option, he has the pitch. Against the pass, he has the contain rush.

To execute his responsibilities, the linebacker reads the tight end's head while getting into the tight end by jamming his hands and helmet into the tight end's numbers. If the tight end goes in, the linebacker rides him in, keeping him off the linebackers. The linebacker looks for a trapping guard or back. He does not let the tight end block him out. He must keep the tight end from getting into position. He helps squeeze the off-tackle play. He does not let the tight end hook him. He works upfield through his outside shoulder, turning wide plays back into pursuit. Against the pass, he holds the tight end on the line of scrimmage as long as possible. He checks for the wide screen and then rushes the quarterback, keeping him contained. Against flow away, he checks for the counter, squeezes through the C gap, and pursues through the backfield, staying as deep as the ball and watching for the reverse.

8 Technique

For the 8 technique, the linebacker uses a two-point stance with feet closer than shoulder-width apart, his inside foot slightly back, and his weight off his heels. His shoulders are parallel to the line of scrimmage. His head is turned so he can read the widest tight offensive lineman. His base alignment is 2 to 4 yards outside the widest tight offensive lineman at a depth of 2 to 5 yards off the line of scrimmage.

The base 8 technique can be played from three other alignment and depth combinations. In walk alignment (figure 5.17), the outside linebacker should split the distance between the last tight offensive lineman (offensive tackle or tight end) or tight slot and the widest wide receiver. The wider this distance is, the deeper the outside linebacker may align, up to a depth of 5 yards. If there is no wide receiver, the outside linebacker comes back in and plays his base alignment.

For up alignment (figure 5.18), the outside linebacker moves up directly on the line of scrimmage 2 yards outside the widest tight offensive lineman.

For face alignment (figure 5.19), the outside linebacker aligns in the face of the first receiver (split end, flanker, or slot) outside the last tight offensive lineman. The outside linebacker should be 4 to 5 yards off the line of scrim-

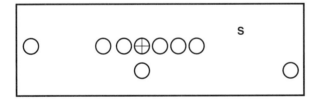

Figure 5.17 Outside linebacker's walk alignment for 8 technique.

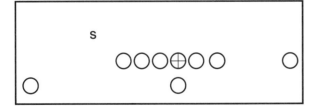

Figure 5.18 Outside linebacker's up alignment for 8 technique.

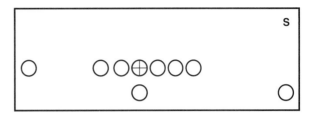

Figure 5.19 Outside linebacker's face alignment for 8 technique.

mage. If there is no wide receiver, the outside linebacker goes back to his base alignment.

The outside linebacker's alignment is dictated by the coverage and front. The alignment option desired will be stated after the coverage.

The linebacker keys through the widest tight offensive lineman to the ball. He reads the tight end's or offensive tackle's block on the defensive end. If the tight end or offensive tackle blocks straight ahead on the defensive end, the linebacker holds his ground and finds the ball, expecting an inside play. He makes sure the ballcarrier does not bounce outside and is ready to get into his pursuit course. If the tight end goes inside, the linebacker holds his ground and finds the ball. If the ball is on the line of scrimmage, he moves up, ready to play his option responsibility. If the ball is off the line of scrimmage, he checks for a run coming to him. If the run is off-tackle, he waits for the ball to break outside until the ball has crossed the line of scrimmage. If the ball is run outside, he moves up to the line of scrimmage, taking on the lead blocker, stringing out the run, and turning it back inside. If the ball is passed, he drops to his responsibility. For a pass going away, he gets into his pursuit course, deeper than the inside linebackers and underneath the secondary, watching for cutbacks. If the offensive tackle goes inside, the linebacker checks for a run in the B or A gap and then gets into his pursuit course for a run away. If the widest lineman tries to hook the defensive end, the linebacker immediately comes up to the line of scrimmage, getting as close to the block as possible without being hooked by the lead blocker, ready to stop the sweep. If the tight end takes an outside release, the linebacker collides with him while finding the ball. If the ball is on the line of scrimmage, he controls the tight end and works to his option responsibility. If the ball is off the line of scrimmage, he drops to his pass responsibility.

The linebacker has D gap responsibility. Against the running game, he must contain the outside play, stringing it out and turning it back inside. Against the option, he has the quarterback or pitch man, based on the coverage and the secondary alignment. If a secondary man has flat coverage outside of the linebacker, the linebacker has the quarterback. If the linebacker is responsible for flat coverage, he has the pitch man. On each down, the linebacker must know his option responsibility and communicate with the defensive end on who will take the quarterback. This is done by a "you–me" call, which is made by the linebacker. "You" tells the defensive end that he has the quarterback on the option. "Me" tells the defensive end that he should take the dive against the option because the linebacker has the quarterback. Usually there is a "you" call unless in the coverage a back who can take the pitch rolls up or aligns outside the linebacker.

To execute his responsibilities, on movement the linebacker steps forward with his inside foot, bringing it even with his outside foot. If the read indicates a run inside, he hangs back to make sure it cannot break outside and then goes to the ball. If the read indicates a run outside, he continues up to the line of scrimmage to take his option responsibility or to take on the lead blocker on the sweep, slowly stringing out the play by facing the lead blocker and trying to drive him back upfield, turning the play in. If the read indicates a run away, he gets into his pursuit course across the field, deeper than the inside linebackers and underneath the secondary, checking for the cutback. If the read indicates pass, he drops to his coverage assignment based on the call, offensive alignment, and any motion.

Pass Coverages

Defensive backs have a large role to play in good pass coverage, but linebackers also are called on to protect against the pass. This section describes key techniques for various pass coverages.

Outside Third Zone

The defensive back keys the first receiver and the ball. The defensive back aligns 8 to 10 yards deep and 2 yards outside the widest offensive man but never outside the numbers. His first step is always back toward his zone as he reads the receiver and the ball. He must shuffle back and to the outside, working toward the middle of his zone. He keeps a cushion between himself and the deepest receiver in his zone. This cushion reduces as the receiver nears the point at which he likely will break to receive the ball (12 to 15 yards). The defensive back looks for anyone entering his zone and listens for his teammates' warnings of an approaching opponent. He communicates with his teammates, alerting them to any receivers entering their zones by calling "inside" and "ball" when the ball is in the air. The defensive back has secondary run support on a run to his side. On a run away from him, he pursues through the middle third zone.

Middle Third Zone

The defensive back keys the ball and the receivers looking inside and out. He aligns 8 to 10 yards deep and over the ball to the outside shoulder of the wide guard when the ball is on a hash. His first step is always back toward his zone as he reads the ball. He must read the quarterback and scan the receivers to find the threat to the deep middle. He keeps a cushion between himself and the deepest receiver in his zone. He looks for anyone entering his zone and listens for his teammates' warning of an approaching opponent. He communicates with his teammates, alerting them to any receivers entering their zones by calling "outside" and "ball" when the ball is in the air. He has secondary inside-out run support on runs to either side.

Half Zone

The defensive back keys through the first receiver to the ball. He aligns 10 to 12 yards deep. If the ball is on his hash, he aligns 7 yards outside the hash. If the ball is on the opposite hash, he aligns on his hash. He moves laterally 1 yard for every 2 yards that the ball is in from the hash. He shuffles backward, maintaining his relation to the hash mark and keeping everything in front of him. The deep half zone defenders communicate with each other, warning of receivers threatening their zones. The defensive back knows how the underneath help is playing:

- Cover 2 funnels receivers inside and plays zone.
- Cover 5 plays man on the receivers.
- Cover 7 trails receivers and plays man.

If the run shows to his side, the defensive back has secondary contain. If the run shows away, he has fill pursuit. In cover 5 and cover 7, he has immediate pitch responsibility on an option to his side. He must communicate run to his teammates covering underneath him.

Curl to Flat Zone

The linebacker keys the last tight lineman or tight slot to the ball. His alignment is dictated by the defensive front, coverage, and the offense. He knows where the potential receivers are and where he is on the field before the snap. He brings his back foot even as he reads his key. If he reads pass, he drops to the curl zone, keeping his head on a swivel to find the receivers who threaten. He knows what the quarterback is doing. If the tight end or slot releases inside, he alerts the inside linebackers and finds the wide receiver. If the tight end attacks the curl zone, the linebacker gets underneath the tight end and makes the quarterback throw over him. If the tight end goes upfield, the linebacker widens his route and gets under the tight end while checking for a back coming underneath into the flat. He plays the deeper receiver in his zone and breaks on the ball. If the tight end or slot releases into the curl zone, the linebacker keeps a cushion, ready to break on the ball. If the tight end or slot releases outside, the linebacker deepens and finds the wide receiver. If the tight end attacks the curl zone, the linebacker gets under the tight end and intercepts his pattern. He finds the ball and breaks to the flat receiver. If the tight end continues inside, the linebacker alerts the inside linebackers and widens to the receiver in the flat. If the wide receiver breaks out, the linebacker widens to get under his pattern and runs parallel with his pattern, ready to break on the ball. If the wide receiver goes deep, the linebacker widens to cover the flat, breaking to the tight end's upfield shoulder if the tight end runs a quick out or getting underneath the tight end if he runs a deeper out.

If there's no tight end or slot, the linebacker finds the wide receiver as he drops. If the wide receiver threatens the curl zone, the linebacker gets under him, finds the quarterback, and watches for a back into the flat. The linebacker stays with the curl until the wide receiver goes further inside or until the inside linebacker releases him. If this does not happen, the linebacker plays the curl and breaks on the ball if it's thrown to the flat. If the linebacker is released, he widens, ready to break on the receiver in the flat if the ball is thrown.

If the run is to the linebacker, he has immediate contain. If the run is away, he takes a pursuit course between the inside linebacker's and the secondary's levels, watching for the cutback.

Hook to Curl Zone

The linebacker keys the backfield to the ball. His alignment is dictated by the defensive front. He knows where the potential receivers are and where he is on the field before the snap. He reads his key and steps with the foot away from flow. As he reads pass, he turns and drops to his zone, finding the receiving threats (tight end, tight slot, or near back) and watching the quarterback.

If the tight end or slot comes inside, the linebacker alerts the other inside linebacker by calling "drag" and checks for the wide receiver to attack the curl. If the wide receiver attacks the curl, the linebacker gets underneath the wide receiver and finds the ball. If the wide receiver doesn't attack, the linebacker continues dropping and breaks on the ball.

If the tight end or slot attacks the hook, the linebacker plays loosely behind him, keeping his head on a swivel to check for the wide receiver coming into the curl. The linebacker covers over the hook until the ball is in the air or the wide receiver leaves his zone.

If the tight end or slot releases out, or there is no tight end or slot, the linebacker checks for the near back to hook as the linebacker drops and then deepens for the curl and finds the wide receiver. As he gets there, the linebacker releases the outside linebacker to cover the flat. The linebacker plays under the curl and breaks on the ball.

If no one threatens the hook or curl, the linebacker continues to deepen, watching for delays into his area and reading the quarterback, ready to break on the ball.

Hook to Hole Zone

The linebacker keys the backfield to the ball. His alignment is dictated by the defensive front. He knows where the potential receivers are and where he is on the field before the ball is snapped. He reads the flow and steps with the foot away from the flow. If he reads pass, the linebacker drops to the hook zone and finds the immediate threats (tight end or tight slot and near back).

If the tight end or tight slot releases inside and continues across, the linebacker alerts the inside linebacker by calling "drag" and looks for the back to hook and the wide receiver to post to the hole. The linebacker gets deep in his zone and plays the deepest receiver.

If the tight end or tight slot hooks, the linebacker covers him loosely from behind, alert for an outside threat to the hole. He plays underneath such a threat, ready to break up to the hook if the quarterback throws there.

If the tight end or tight slot comes inside and continues through the hook to the hole, the linebacker turns into the tight end or tight slot and goes with him, forcing the quarterback to loft the ball over him to throw to the tight end or tight slot.

If the tight end or tight slot releases outside, or there is no tight end or tight slot, the linebacker deepens in his zone. He checks the back's threat to the hook zone and watches and listens for the backside tight end to threaten the hole. He plays off the hook, reading the quarterback, ready to protect the hole first.

If no one immediately threatens the hook or hole, he continues to drop to the hole, looking for threats from the wide receivers, ready to break on the ball.

Press

The defensive back keys the ball and through the number-one receiver to the near back. He aligns 4 to 5 yards deep on the outside eye of the number-one receiver. On the snap, he squares up on the number-one receiver and drives him back or funnels him to the inside. He harasses him physically or by his position. If the number-one receiver moves outside, the defensive back flattens him into the sideline and prevents him from turning upfield, while looking over his inside shoulder to see if the flat zone is threatened underneath. If the number-one receiver gets inside, the defensive back sinks on him (deepens and widens) while checking to see if the flat zone is threatened. He does not let the number-one receiver release inside and move immediately outside behind him and up the sideline. He must not let the number-one receiver get outside of him. If he does, he runs with him, playing man and abandoning his flat. The defensive back must stay with the receiver to help his teammate who has half coverage. This is why he must force the number-one receiver inside on the press.

If the flat zone is threatened, the defensive back hangs in the flat. Otherwise, he continues to deepen with the number-one receiver, getting under him as he gets to the cruise zone.

If run shows to his side, the defensive back has primary contain. If run shows away, he rotates through his pursuit course.

Squat

The defensive back keys the ball and through the number-two receiver to the near back. He aligns in base alignment on the number-two receiver if he is tight. If the number-two receiver is flexed or a wide slot, the defensive back aligns 4 to 5 yards deep on his inside shoulder.

On the snap, the defensive back squares up on the number-two receiver, dropping with and funneling him to the outside. He continues to drop in the curl area and watches for an outside receiver coming inside. If the number-two receiver does get inside of the defensive back and threatens to split the deep zone, the defensive back alerts the inside linebacker and the safety of the threat.

If run shows to his side, the defensive back has primary contain. If run shows away, he has cutback pursuit.

Trail

The defensive back keys his receiver and the ball. When on a wide receiver, he aligns 4 yards off the ball on the receiver's inside eye. When on a tight receiver, he plays base technique with his inside leg on the receiver's outside leg.

On the snap, the defensive back straddles the inside leg of his receiver. He lets the receiver come to him and turns the receiver to the outside as he gets there. He jams the receiver back hard. He must not let the receiver get inside of him. He releases the receiver to the outside, letting him feel he beat him, and then gets on the receiver's inside hip, keeping off him 3 to

4 yards with the inside of the receiver's hip on the outside of his hip.

The defensive back reads the receiver's waist. As the receiver lowers his hips, the defensive back is prepared for the receiver to make a cut. If the receiver turns inside, the defensive back turns underneath the receiver the same way and looks for the ball. The defensive back's inside position allows him to stay even with the receiver as the receiver makes the first break. The defensive back plays for the interception or the knock down. He must not stop running. If the receiver turns outside, the defensive back breaks underneath him, running parallel to his pattern and looking for the ball. The angle between the receiver and the quarterback allows the defensive back to be in the quarterback's vision continuously, even though the receiver breaks first, as long as the defensive back is playing 4 yards off the receiver and breaks immediately parallel to the receiver's pattern. The defensive back plays for the interception or the knock down. He must not stop running.

If run shows and crosses the line of scrimmage, the defensive back gets into a pursuit course.

Man

The defensive back keys his receiver and the ball. He plays his receiver man to man on the receiver's outside shoulder. The defensive back plays his pattern aggressively, keeping outside leverage and maintaining a cushion. If the receiver breaks a short pattern, the defensive back moves up on him but maintains position and body control so the receiver cannot break past him without a collision. The defensive back attacks the receiver's upfield shoulder. If the receiver runs a deep pattern, the defensive back decreases his cushion as he runs his cutting area (12 to 15 yards) but never allows the receiver to beat him on a go. As the receiver gets within 3 to 4 yards of the defensive back, the defensive back begins to turn his hips. If the receiver breaks inside and the defensive back closes on him and the receiver then breaks back out, the defensive back turns into the receiver and gets his head around quickly. If the receiver is breaking a corner, the defensive back will be right on the receiver. If the receiver is breaking an out, the defensive back will at least have him contained, preventing him from getting upfield.

As the receiver nears, the defensive back collides with him using his hands. The defensive back stays square to the receiver, knocking him back and out of his pattern. The defensive back must not lunge at the receiver with his upper body, but he jolts him by explosively thrusting his arms. The defensive back knows where his help is coming from (deep half or free).

If run shows to his side, the defensive back has slow secondary contain. If run shows away, he rotates through his pursuit course.

Free

The defensive back keys the ball and the entire offensive picture. On the snap of the ball, he takes his read steps backward. He watches the quarterback for down-the-line or off-the-line actions. If the ball comes off the line (a dropback or sprint out), he gets depth and plays center field. He reads the quarterback's eyes and front arm for the throw. He breaks from depth to intercept the course of the ball and the receiver. If the ball comes down the line, as in option, he's ready to play the pitch to either side. If run shows, he communicates to the rest of the defense and works for primary contain.

Ice in Goal Line Quarter Zone

The defensive back keys his receiver and the ball. He plays his receiver man to man within his quarter outside zone. He lines up on the receiver's outside shoulder but steps to the inside of his receiver without turning his shoulders, keeping 2 to 3 yards deep. He anticipates the quick slant.

The defensive back stays shallow in the end zone and lets the receiver come to him. He plays his pattern aggressively, keeping inside

leverage. He collides with the receiver, disrupting his pattern, ready to play off his block at the line of scrimmage. The defense has only 13 yards to defend. The defensive back's collision must jar the receiver as the defensive back maintains a low, balanced football position. He knocks the receiver back, out of his pattern. He doesn't lunge at the receiver with his upper body but jolts him by explosively thrusting his arms. The defensive back is a barrier as the receiver tries to run a pattern upfield or inside.

As soon as his hands are on the receiver, the defensive back takes a quick glance into the backfield while listening for his teammates' calls of run or pass. He looks for the quarterback's throwing motion and checks whether the number-two receiver is trying to break a quick out underneath him. If the receiver tries to go upfield, the defensive back stays in front of him, constantly jamming him, checking the quarterback action, and listening for "ball" calls. If the receiver breaks a short pattern, the defensive back collides with him but maintains position and body control so the receiver cannot break past him. His only help is from the inside linebackers (after they have checked run) and the pressure of the rush.

If the receiver runs a fade, the defensive back immediately turns toward the receiver and runs with him, keeping his eyes on the receiver. As the receiver's arms go up for the ball, the defensive back puts up his outside arm to disrupt the receiver's vision and sweeps through the receiver's outside arm to prevent his holding onto the ball.

If the ball is run to his side, the defensive back drives the receiver or blocker back toward the line of scrimmage and does not leave the receiver or blocker until he's sure he has a clean shot at the ballcarrier and the receiver cannot screen the defensive back. The defensive back must be most aggressive because the defense has 3 yards or less to defend. If the run is away, the defensive back stays with his man and watches for the runner being forced to reverse his field.

A defense must work very hard at disguising coverages. The goal is to keep the offense guessing what the coverage is in its presnap read. Line up three deep, and then, at the last second, squirm to two deep or vice versa. The underneath defenders should also move around to avoid tipping off the coverage. They should all be free to move up to the point where they can get back to effectively employ the coverage called.

Intercepting the Ball

Whether playing man or zone, defenders must play the man until the ball is in the air, and then play the ball. Until the ball is thrown, the receiver can hurt the defender. Once the ball is released, the receiver can no longer hurt the defender; only the ball can do that.

The mechanics of catching the ball are the same regardless of which side the catcher is on, whether he's on offense or defense. The receiver catches the ball with his fingertips, where there are more nerve endings, not with the flesh of his hands. One difference in catching on offense and intercepting on defense, which should be reflected in interception drills, is that often the defender is moving toward the line of scrimmage. The defender must attack the ball and catch it at the highest point possible. Interception drills should stress playing through the receiver to the ball, catching the ball at a high point, increasing the distance that the defender can cover while the ball is in the air, and being physical, ensuring that if the defender can't catch the ball, the receiver can't either.

JUMP BALL

Stand side by side against a receiver. A coach throws the ball up as a basketball referee would for a tipoff. Practice jumping as high as possible, timing the jump so you contact the ball at the maximum height of your jump. Control the ball and come down with it.

HAIL MARY

Working against receivers, sprint 40 yards into the end zone and time your jump to come down with the ball to win the game. Practice reacting to a tipped ball, which is usually what happens with a Hail Mary in a game.

INTERCEPTION CHALLENGE DRILL

Two players stand 15 yards in front of a coach and 7 yards apart. The coach throws the ball between them, and both players go after it. Players must play the ball, and the best man comes down with it. Players try to intercept the ball at its highest point.

COVERING THE HOOKS

Two receivers stand 12 yards deep and 7 yards apart. The linebacker is in his normal starting position. He quickly drops between the two receivers as the quarterback begins his drop. Without faking, the passer throws to one of the receivers. The linebacker makes the interception and returns it at full speed. If you have enough quarterbacks, use the scout team quarterback for this drill.

COME TO DRILL

The defensive backs line up 20 yards in front of the coach. At the signal, the first back starts forward at full speed. The coach passes the ball to him. The defender catches the ball and sprints to the coach. The coach throws the ball high most of the time so the defender must judge the height of the ball. Sometimes the coach throws the ball slightly to the right or left of the defensive back.

GOAL POST DRILL

This drill increases the interception distance of the defensive backs. Two defenders stand under the goal post. A receiver stands in each corner of the end zone. The quarterback takes a five-step drop, stops, and throws to one corner. The defensive backs sprint for the corner as soon as the quarterback moves. They must get to the corner in time to intercept the ball. If you have enough quarterbacks, use the scout team quarterback for this drill.

LONG-BALL DRILL

As the quarterback retreats to throw, the defensive back moves laterally to cover the out route. The quarterback sets up and either throws to the defensive back in the flat or makes the motion, pats the ball, and brings it back to throw the long one. When the quarterback pats the ball, the defensive back turns upfield and races for the interception. If you have enough quarterbacks, use the scout team quarterback for this drill.

PLAY THE BALL DRILL

Place two cones 15 yards apart where the defensive back lines up, and two more cones at a point 20 yards downfield. Receivers station just inside the two cones at the line of scrimmage. The defensive back stations midway between the other two cones. When the quarterback starts the play, the receivers sprint downfield just inside the cones, and the defensive back backpedals. When the quarterback throws to one of the two downfield cones, the defensive back reacts and intercepts the ball. Start with the cones 15 yards apart; as the defensive back gains confidence, widen the distance to 20 yards. If you have enough quarterbacks, use the scout team quarterback for this drill.

6

Team Offense

In this chapter we look at a method for organizing a comprehensive offensive play package. We begin with a running play and its coaching points and blocking rules. Next we examine a reverse off that same running play action. Then we move to a companion play that features a play-action pass, in other words faking the running play and throwing a pass off that action. We then look at a bootleg pass after faking that run, and also a screen pass off the same running play action. As you'll see, a single simple running play can open many possibilities.

After the run and play action, we move to three-step and five-step drop-back passes, with the option of a seven-step pass when using a deeper route, complete with coaching points and blocking rules. We then look at some drop-back screens, and finally at a draw play in which the quarterback begins the dropback and then hands the ball to the running back to keep the defense honest rather than allow them to lay back and rush the quarterback.

Formations and Backfield Alignments

Numbers are used to designate the desired basic formation. For instance, 1 is Pro Right, 9 is Pro Left, 2 and 8 are Twins (right or left), 3 and 7 are Power I three-back formations (right or left), and 4 and 6 are the same spacing as 1 and 9 but with the tight end (Y) off the line of scrimmage to facilitate his shift or motion and Z (a wide receiver) on the line of scrimmage (figure 6.1). The wide receiver, who in most formations is on the line of scrimmage, is designated as X, whereas the wide receiver off the line of scrimmage is designated as Z.

The placement for the tailback may be designated by a letter immediately following the number, such as 1I, 1A, or 1B, in which case the fullback (R) will be behind the quarterback and the tailback (T) will be in the area designated by the letter. If no letter is given after the number of a two-back formation, the backs are

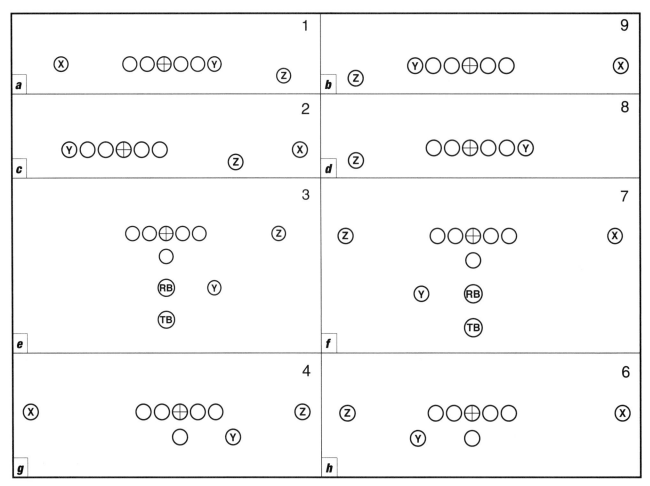

Figure 6.1 Base formations: *(a)* Pro Right; *(b)* Pro Left; *(c)* Twins Right; *(d)* Twins Left; *(e)* Power I Right; *(f)* Power I Left; *(g)* Pro Right with Y off the ball; *(h)* Pro Left with Y off the ball.

split (figure 6.2). If two letters are given, such as 9CI, the fullback will be in the area of the first letter and the tailback in the area of the second letter. In one-back formations, the fullback is directly behind the quarterback unless I is part of the call, in which case the tailback is directly behind the quarterback. If E and F are called, additional wide receivers are added and placed in the E or F positions, thereby limiting running backs to routes run from backfield or tight slot positions and permitting wide receivers to run all patterns from detached positions.

To get X (wide receiver) to reduce his split to 3 to 5 yards, we use the term *close*. To bring X all the way in, we use the term *tight*. If a tight receiver is to split out to 3 to 5 yards, he will be told to *flex*, and if he is to go all the way

out and become the widest receiver, he will be told to *split*. To move wide receivers to the opposite sides (right receiver to the left and left receiver to the right), presumably to take advantage of a physical mismatch, we use the term *flip*. For a formation with Twins with the inside receiver on the line of scrimmage and the outside receiver off, we call *change*.

All motion is initiated when the quarterback lifts his near heel, thereby giving the quarterback complete control of the 25-second (or 40-second) clock. The quarterback checks everyone. One second after every player is motionless, he starts the motion. During any motion, if the quarterback, or any other player, notices that someone moved or that the motion started while someone was moving, he hollers

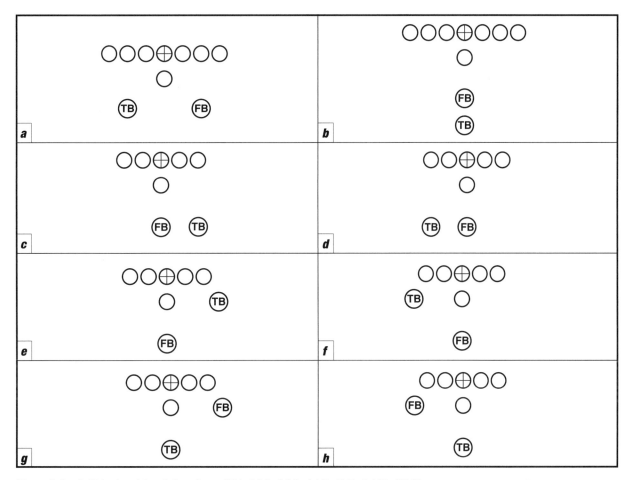

Figure 6.2 Split backs: *(a)* no letter given; *(b)* I; *(c)* A; *(d)* B; *(e)* C; *(f)* D; *(g)* CI; *(h)* DI.

freeze. At that point all 11 players freeze and stay motionless for one full second before the motion continues. In this way an illegal motion penalty is avoided.

In all types of motion, if only the word indicating motion is called, the motion refers to either Z or to the tight end, whichever is the slot or flanker in the given formation. If the fullback, tailback, or X is to go in motion, their position name will be called with the motion.

The play call might include the word *motion* followed by the formation and play. This tells Z (unless another position is specified) to line up anywhere that creates a formation normally used and then go in motion to the prescribed formation (figure 6.3).

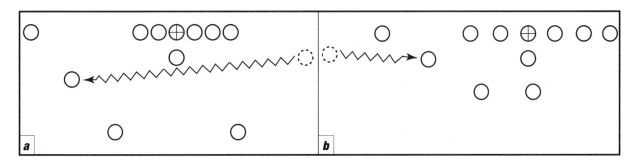

Figure 6.3 Z in motion: *(a)* Motion 8 911—Z motions from 1 to 8; *(b)* Motion 8B 122—Z motions from 8B Change to 8B.

Motion is close to full speed, so the quarterback must anticipate that speed and snap the ball before the man in motion arrives at the designated spot.

If the word *stack* follows the formation call, Z (unless another player is designated in the call) goes in motion until he is directly behind the widest receiver on the line of scrimmage. The ball is snapped when the motion player is stacked behind that receiver. Depending on the formation, the man in motion might move in or move out. If the man in motion moves out, as in 2I (figure 6.4a), the man in motion (Z) becomes the number-one receiver and X, the receiver on the line of scrimmage, becomes number two. If the man in motion moves in, as in 1 Flex I (figure 6.4b), the man in motion (Z) becomes the number-two receiver and the tight end, the receiver on the line of scrimmage, becomes number one.

Shifts

Often the backs or tight end shift prior to the snap. If the word *pound* is used at the end of the play call, the backs know to line up in any alignment used, and then when the quarterback, in his cadence, says *down*, the backs shift to the called formation. It might be as simple as moving from 1I to 1 or as complex as shifting from 2 Flex FI to 9FI (doubles to trips); see figure 6.5.

If the word *Main* is used at the end of the play call, the tight end knows to line up on the opposite side of the formation called. On the signal *down*, the tight end shifts to the position called. The wide receivers must also be aware that the tight end is shifting and accommodate him by their alignment relative to the line of scrimmage, making sure that, both before the shift and after, they keep the tight end eligible.

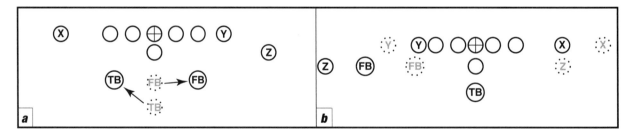

Figure 6.4 Stack: *(a)* 2I Stack; *(b)* 1 Flex I Stack.

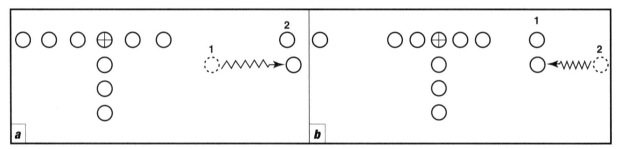

Figure 6.5 Shifts: *(a)* shift from 1I to 1; *(b)* shift from 2 Flex FI to 9FI.

The shift might be as simple as moving from 9I to 1I or 9EI to 1EI (doubles to trips) or as complex as moving from 2FI to 1 Flex CI (again doubles to trips); see figure 6.6.

Formations by Personnel Packages

As personnel enter and leave the playing field, each player entering the game must know what position he is representing and who he is replacing. It is his responsibility to holler the personnel package being employed, the letter of the position he is representing, and the name of the player being replaced. The quarterbacks standing beside the coach who is calling the play holler the personnel package and show the hand signal that represents each personnel package as soon as it is called so that players on the field can anticipate when they are being replaced.

There are many reasons to use several personnel packages (table 6.1) and to move often from one to the other. One reason is that it allows players to specialize, rather than trying to be all things in all situations. Running backs can spend the majority of their time practicing running plays and their ball carrying, faking, and blocking responsibilities. Receivers can spend most of their time practicing patterns, blocks from receiver alignments, and releases. One group of players, not two, can practice pat-terns from wide receiver alignments. Running backs practice only routes run from A, B, C, D, I, and Split Back alignments.

Numbering System

The offensive numbering system is not simple, but it gives specific information that is consistent and thorough. It's not based on rote memory; there is a rationale behind it. Once the philosophy of the system is learned, the player can reason out the information needed. All plays are three-digit numbers, with each number relating to the type of play it is.

The first digit indicates whether the play is a run or a pass and also signals which direction (right or left) the play is designed to go. The first digit of a run play is 1 (run to the right) or 9 (run to the left). The first digit of a drop-back pass is 2 (primary read to the right) or 8 (primary read to the left). The first digit of a play-action pass is 3 (to the right) or 7 (to the left). The first digit of a screen pass is 4 (receiver to the right) or 6 (receiver to the left).

The second digit indicates what series the play belongs to. For example, if the play is a run and the second digit is a 1, the play belongs to the teen, or zone, series. The 20s is the misdirection series, the 30s is the power series, the 40s is the trap series, the 50s is the shotgun cross series, and the 60s is the belly series.

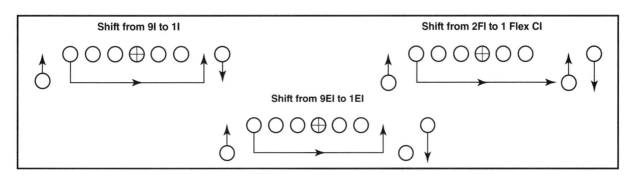

Figure 6.6 Tight end shifts.

TABLE 6.1 Personnel Packages

Personnel package	Required positions	Formations				
Regular	Two WRs (X and Z), one TE, two backs (FB and TB)	1/9 1I/9I 1A/9B 1B/9A 1C/9D	1CI/9DI 1D/9C 1DI/9CI 2/8 2I/8I	2A/8B 2B/8A 2C/8D 2CI/8DI 2D/8C	2DI/8CI 4/6 4I/6I 4A/6B 4B/6A	4C/6D 4CI/6DI 4D/6C 4DI/6CI 2D Strong/8C Strong
Fox	Three WRs (X, Z, and TE), two backs (FB and TB)	1 Flex/9 Flex 1 Flex I/9 Flex I 1 Flex A/9 Flex B 1 Flex B/9 Flex A 1 Flex C/9 Flex D 1 Flex CI/9 Flex DI		1 Flex D/9 Flex C 1 Flex DI/9 Flex CI 2 Flex/8Flex 2 Flex I/8 Flex I 2 Flex A/8 Flex B 2 Flex B/8 Flex A		2 Flex C/8 Flex D 2 Flex CI/8 Flex DI 2 Flex D/8 Flex C 2 Flex DI/8 Flex CI 1 Bunch/9 Bunch 1 Bunch I/9 Bunch I
Wolf	Two WRs (X and Z), two TEs, one back (FB)	1-9/9-1 1 Over Strong 9/9 Over Strong 1 1 Tight E Over Strong/9 Tight F Over Strong 1 Tight E Over Strong Left/9 Tight F Over Strong Right			1 Bunch Right/9 Bunch Left 1 Bunch Left/9 Bunch Right 1 Tight E/9 Tight F Run-the-clock-out formation.	
Hawk	Four WRs (X, Z, Y, and FB), one back (TB)	1 Flex CI/9 Flex DI 1 Flex EI/9 Flex FI 2 Flex CI/8 Flex FI 2 Flex EI/8 Flex FI 1 Bunch I/ 9 Bunch I			1 Flex DI/9 Flex CI 1 Flex FI/9 Flex EI 2 Flex DI/8 Flex EI 2 Flex FI/8 Flex EI	
Tiger	Three WRs (X, Z, and FB), one TE, one back (TB)	1 EI/9 FI 2 EI/8 FI 2 FI Stack/8 EI Stack 2 EI Strong/8 FI Strong 2 EI Over/8 FI Over			1 FI/9-EI 2 FI/8 EI 2 EI R Stack/8 FI R Stack 2 DI Over/8 CI Over	
Crow 2	Two WRs (X and Z), three backs (TE, FB, and TB)	3/7 4/6 4I/6I			4A/6B 4B/6A 4D/6C	
Crow 1	One WR (X), one TE, three backs (FB, TB, Z)*	1 PIR/9 PIL 1 Wing/9 Wing 1 Wing A/9 Wing B 1 PIL/9 PIR			1 Wing I/9 Wing I 1 Wing B/9 Wing A 1 Wing D Strong Left/9 Wing C Strong Right 1 Wing D Over/9 Wing C Over	
Crow 0	Two TEs, three backs (FB, TB, and Z)*	1 Tight PIR/9 Tight PIL 1 Tight WR/9 Tight WL 1 Tight WR A/9 Tight WL B			1 Tight PIL/9 Tight PIR 1 Tight WR I/9 Tight WL I 1 Tight WR B/9 Tight WL A	
Empty	Five WRs (X, Z, TE, FB, and TB)	1 Flex EF/9 Flex FE 1 Flex FD/9 Flex EC 1 Flex EC/9 Flex FD			1 Flex ED/9 Flex FC 1 Flex EF Stack/9 Flex FE Stack 2 Flex FC/8 Flex ED	

*Could have extra TE at wing.

If the play is a drop-back pass, the second digit tells the blocking protection to be used. When calling a play-action or screen pass, the series that is being faked is indicated by the second digit.

The third digit provides even more information. If the play is a run, the third digit indicates the area to be attacked or faked—1 is outside, 2 is off tackle, 3 is dive hole, 4 is center-guard gap, and 5 is over the center. If the play is a five- or seven-step drop-back pass, the third digit is simply rote memory. If the play is a play-action pass or a screen, the third digit notes the hole to which the ball is being faked. If the pass is a three-step drop (50 pass protection), the third digit refers to a pass tree—1 is a quick out, 2 is a diagonal, 3 is a hitch, and 4 is a fade. For some plays, a special number indicates bootleg (6), counteroption (7), or reverse (8).

Audibles

The head coach—or quarterbacks coach, if you have one—spends a tremendous amount of time with the quarterback leading up to game day. As soon as the coaching staff develops the offensive game plan, they meet with the quarterback and describe the game plan in detail to him. Each day of game week, review the plan with him. Bring him to the point where he can explain the game plan and rationale to you. Have him look at each of the opponent's defenses and coverages and tell you which plays he will audible out of and the possible plays that he can choose from when he automatics, the plays that he will railroad (same play as called but run to the opposite direction), or the receiver who should be open because of the coverage being employed. Use diagrammed cards, video, and PowerPoint presentations. If the quarterback railroads the play, the snap count stays the same as called in the huddle. If he audibles to a new play, the snap count is the first sound.

Running Game

The running game is put in a series—zone, counter, power, trap, and belly. Each play has its own blocking rules and techniques, coaching points, and tips for blocking each defense faced during the season. The plays are shown with various personnel packages and formations.

111 (911) Zone

Call-side wide receiver: deep third (stalk and circle)

Backside wide receiver: middle third (stalk and circle)

Call-side slot: area, slip technique with offensive tackle or lead block

Backside slot: inside release crossfield

Call-side tackle: area, combo slip with slot or offensive guard

Call-side guard: area, combo slip with offensive tackle or center, possible horn to inside linebacker

Center: slip with call-side or backside offensive guard, possible man

Backside guard: possible man

Backside tackle: seal, slip technique

The fullback (or the tailback, if in A) aims for the outside hip of the slot or offensive tackle to the split-end side. He makes sure his block is sealed and then goes on to block force.

The tailback (or the fullback, if in A) takes a 45-degree directional step at the offensive tackle's outside leg. He receives the ball from the quarterback as deep as possible. He pockets the ball, reads the tackle's block, and then runs to daylight. The play can break at the two hole or outside, or bend all the way back.

The quarterback moves away from the line of scrimmage at a 45-degree angle and pushes the ball back into the pouch of the ballcarrier. After the exchange, he immediately jerks his head and shoulders around to set up the bootleg fake or comes straight off to set up a regular play-action fake.

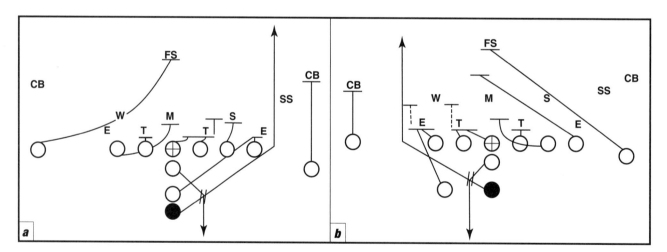

Figure 6.7 111 (911) Zone: *(a)* Regular 1I 111; *(b)* Regular 1B 911.

Personnel Packages and Formations for 111

Regular: two wide receivers (X and Z), one tight end, two backs (FB and TB)

1I/9I	1D/9C	2C/8D	4A	4DI/6CI
1A	1DI/9CI	2CI/8DI	6A/4B	2C Strong
9A/1B	2I/8I	2D/8C	4C/6D	2D Strong
1C/9D	2A	2DI/8CI	4CI/6DI	
1CI/9DI	8A/2B	4I/6I	4D/6C	

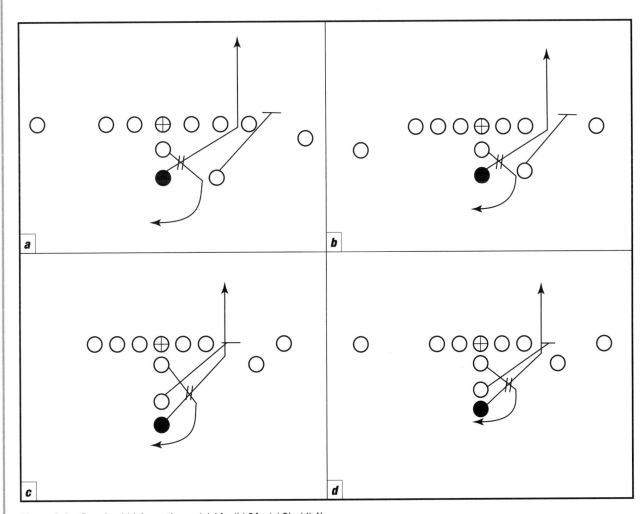

Figure 6.8 Regular 111 formations: *(a)* 1A; *(b)* 9A; *(c)* 2I; *(d)* 4I.

(continued)

Personnel Packages and Formations for 111 *(continued)*

Fox: three wide receivers (X, Z, and Y), two backs (FB and TB)

1 Flex I/9 Flex I	1 Flex D/9 Flex C	2 Flex C/8 Flex D	1 Bunch/9 Bunch
1 Flex A	1 Flex DI/9 Flex CI	2 Flex CI/8 Flex DI	1 Bunch I/9 Bunch I
1 Flex C/9 Flex D	2 Flex I/8 Flex I	2 Flex D/8 Flex C	
1 Flex CI/9 Flex DI	2 Flex A	2 Flex DI/8 Flex CI	

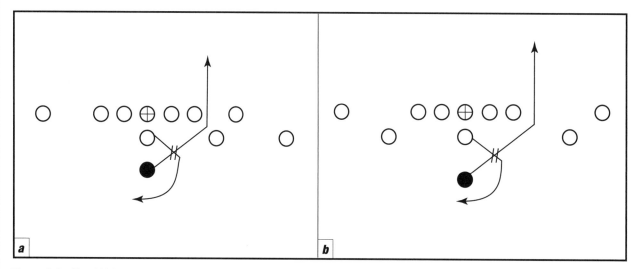

Figure 6.9   Fox 111 formations: *(a)* 1 Flex C; *(b)* 2 Flex DI.

Wolf: two wide receivers (X and Z), two tight ends, one back (FB)

1-9/9-1	1 Bunch Right/9 Bunch Left
1 Tight E/9 Tight F	1 Bunch Left/9 Bunch Right
1 Over Strong 9/9 Over Strong 1	
1 Tight E Over Strong/9 Tight F Over Strong	
1 Tight E Over Strong Left/9 Tight F Over Strong Right	

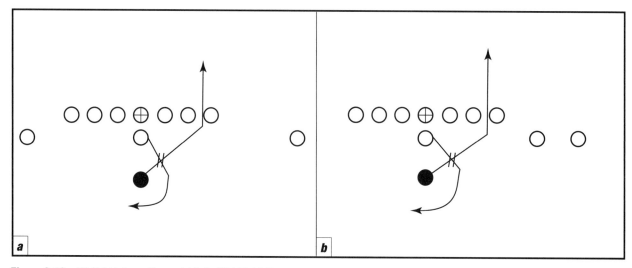

Figure 6.10   Wolf 111 formations: *(a)* 1-9; *(b)* 1 Tight E.

Hawk: four wide receivers (X, Z, Y, and FB), one back (TB)

1 Flex CI/9 Flex DI	1 Flex FI/9 Flex EI	2 Flex EI/8 Flex FI	1 Bunch I/9 Bunch I
9 Flex DI/1 Flex CI	9 Flex EI/1 Flex FI	8 Flex FI/2 Flex EI	8 Flex DI/2 Flex CI
1 Flex EI/9 Flex FI	2 Flex CI/8 Flex DI	2 Flex FI/8 Flex EI	8 Flex EI/2 Flex FI
9 Flex FI/1 Flex EI			

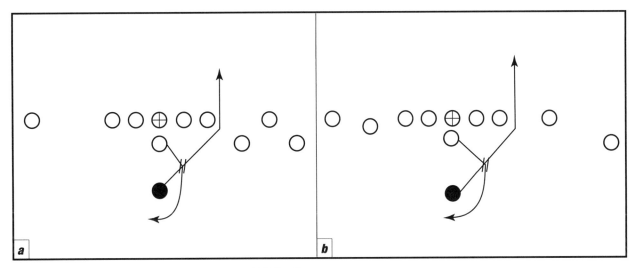

Figure 6.11 Hawk 111 formations: *(a)* 1 Flex EI; *(b)* 8 Flex EI.

Tiger: three wide receivers (X, Z, and FB), one tight end, one back (TB)

1-8I/9-2I	2-9I/8-1I	2 DI Over/8 CI Over
9-2I/1-8I	8-1I/2-9I	2 EI Strong/8 FI Strong
1 EI/9 FI	2-9I Stack/8-1I Stack	8 FI Strong/2 EI Strong
9 FI/1EI	2 EI R Stack/8 FI R Stack	
2 EI/8 FI	2 EI Over/8 FI Over	

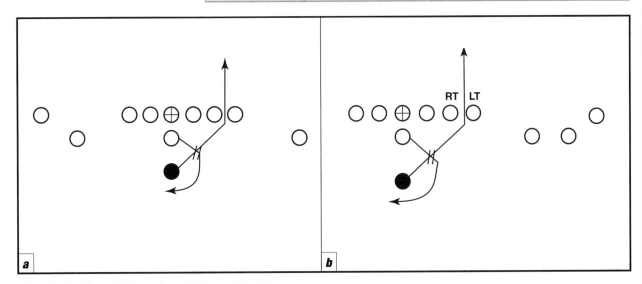

Figure 6.12 Tiger 111 formations: *(a)* 1FI; *(b)* 2 EI Strong.

(continued)

Crow 2: two wide receivers (X and Z), three backs (FB, TB, and Y)

3/7	6I/4I	4D/6C
7/3	4A	6C/4D
4I/6I	6A	

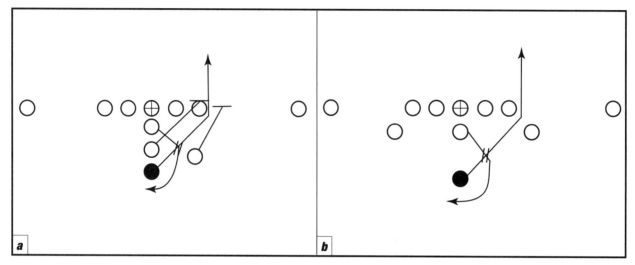

Figure 6.13   Crow 2 111 formations: *(a)* 3; *(b)* 4D.

Crow 1: one wide receiver (X), one tight end, three backs (FB, TB, and Z); could have an extra tight end at wing

1 PIR/9 PIL	1 Wing A
1 PIL/9 PIR	9 Wing A
1 Wing I/9 Wing I	

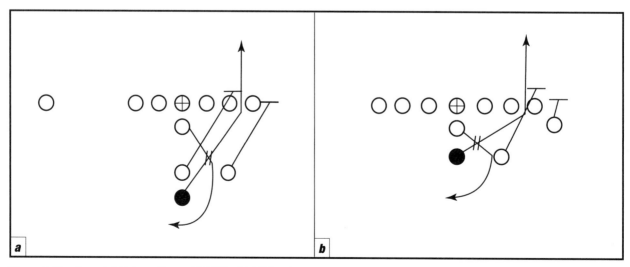

Figure 6.14   Crow 1 111 formations: *(a)* 1 PIR; *(b)* 1 Wing A.

Crow 0: two tight ends (X and Y), three backs (FB, TB, and Z); could have extra tight end at wing

1 Tight PIR/9 Tight PIL	**1 Tight WR A**
1 Tight PIL/9 Tight PIR	**9 Tight WL A**
1 Tight WR I/9 Tight WL I	

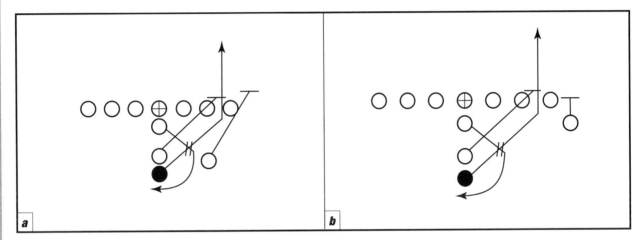

Figure 6.15 Crow 0 111 formations: *(a)* 1 Tight PIR; *(b)* 1 Tight WR I.

918 (118) Zone Reverse

When defenses begin to fly to the ball versus this zone play, they are ripe for the reverse off the zone action, as shown in figure 6.16.

Call-side wide receiver: deep 1/3 (stalk and circle).

Backside wide receiver: go in motion then aim a little deeper than the zone fake; hide the ball and read the guard's block.

Call-side slot: area, slip technique with offensive tackle or lead block.

Backside slot: inside release crossfield.

Call-side tackle: area; slip with slot or offensive guard.

Call-side guard: area; slip with offensive tackle or center.

Center: area, block lead half; backside area for pulling guard.

Backside guard: pull and lead reverse.

Backside tackle: area, block lead half; horn.

Fullback (tailback if in A): aim for the outside hip of slot or offensive tackle (to split-end side); make sure block is sealed and go on to block force.

Tailback (fullback if in A): take 45-degree directional step at outside leg of offensive tackle; make a big pocket and clamp hard; sell the fake; make someone tackle you.

Quarterback: move away from the line of scrimmage at a 45-degree angle and carry out a great 111 fake; put the ball on your hip and push it into the reverse man's belly; you are responsible for the exchange; drop and sell a play-action pass.

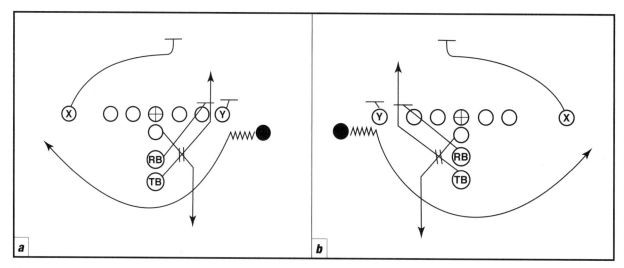

Figure 6.16   918 (118) Zone reverse: *(a)* Regular 1I March; *(b)* Regular 9I Winter.

Passing Game

The passing game consists of the three-step drop, five-step drop, seven-step drop, moving pocket, play action, bootleg, drop-back screen, moving pocket screen, play-action screen, and draw. The flexibility of this system allows teams to be successful with a small number of actual plays, although it appears to the defense that the offense has hundreds of plays.

Make sure all backs and receivers learn the philosophy of the play, including memorizing all five patterns of each play. They learn the play not by what patterns they run, because their positions relative to each other will change depending on the formation called, but by what patterns are run by 1 callside, 2 callside, 3, 1 backside, and 2 backside, numbering from outside in. Each receiver must also know and understand the hot-read system. The receivers and the quarterback must know who the hot-read defensive player is on each play and from each formation as well as which offensive receiver runs the hot route.

Run the basic play from a number of personnel packages: Regular, Fox, Wolf, Hawk, Tiger, Crow, and Empty. Run the basic play from many different formations, with and without motion and with and without shifting. For example:

- Motion 1B 285—Z lines up anywhere he chooses and motions to a 1 formation.
- 2CI Stack 285—Z lines up in 2 formation and motions out to a stack position behind X and becomes number one; X becomes number two.
- 1 Flex I Stack 285—Z lines up in 1 Flex and motions in to a Stack position behind Y and becomes number two; Y becomes number one.
- 2CI R Stack 285—the fullback lines up in 2CI and motions out to a Stack position behind X and becomes number one; X becomes number two and Z becomes number three.

- 9I Main 285—Y lines up as a tight end on the right side and shifts to tight end on the left side; wide receivers on both sides line up in 1 formation before the shift and 9 formation after the shift.
- 1C Pound 285—the fullback and tailback line up in any formation normally used and shift to a 1C formation.

Use tag words that change patterns between receivers. For example, *21 285 X and Z Change* means that X (1 callside) runs Z's (2 callside) pattern, and Z runs X's pattern. All other receivers run their basic patterns.

Use tag words in which one of the receivers is told what pattern to run in place of his basic pattern. For example, in 1I 282 X, Seam X (wide receiver) runs a seam pattern instead of the prescribed pattern in the basic 282 play. All other receivers run their basic patterns.

At the snap, when four receivers are from head-up on the ball to one side of the formation, do not count Z if he is given a tag-word pattern. Do this only from formations in which the backside receiver is tight. In this case, that backside tight receiver becomes number two to the backside. For example, in Regular 2A 282 Z Corner X is 1 callside. Z is given the tag word so he is not counted. The tailback is number two, fullback is number three, and because Y is tight on the back side, he is 2 backside. Another call might be Tiger 2EI 282 Z Corner. Again, X is 1 callside, Z is given the tag word and not counted, the fullback is 2 callside, and the tailback is 3, with the tight end being 2 backside.

For a drop-back pass, teach the entire philosophy of the play the first day, including the hot-read system, multiple personnel packages and formations, and the misdirection that must accompany every individual pattern. You might not incorporate motion, shifts, adjustments to coverages, and tag words the first day, but do this by the second or third day. It is vital for players to thoroughly understand the philosophy of the play, reaction to coverages, and blocking responsibilities. They should not have to rely on rote memory.

Three-Step Drop

251/851: 1 callside and 1 backside work a quick out. They take a minimum split with their inside feet back. After five steps, they work back toward the sideline. The pass is at the far hip. The receiver must not overrun an out pattern.

252/852: 1 callside or 1 backside works a diagonal. The receiver takes a minimum split with his inside foot back. After four steps, he drives hard off his outside foot, breaking in at a 45-degree angle. The pass is at the upfield receiver's chest. The receiver catches the ball with his fingers up and thumbs in.

253/853: 1 callside or 1 backside works a hitch. The split varies based on the coverage and the horizontal field position. The receiver's inside foot is back. After four steps, the receiver pumps his arms, plants his outside foot, turns to the quarterback, sits down, and works back toward the ball. Against man coverage or press coverage, the receiver works toward the defender's inside shoulder and forces him back and to the outside. The receiver must get separation. The pass will be at the middle of the receiver's chest. The receiver gets his fingers up and thumbs together.

254/854: 1 callside or 1 backside works a fade. There is a minimum split if to the open field, or an average split otherwise. The receiver's inside foot is back. The receiver works upfield and then gets some width.

If the ball is on or near his hash, the receiver aims for a spot 18 to 20 yards deep and 4 yards from the sideline. He must give the quarterback that 4-yard alley. Until the ball is in the air, the receiver must not close that gap or look back.

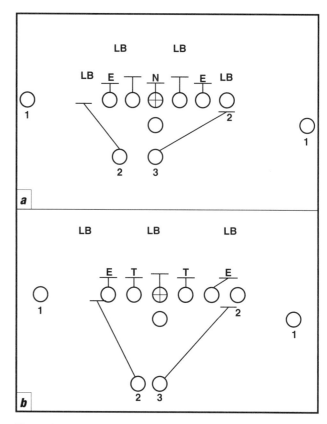

Figure 6.17 Three-step drop: *(a)* odd; *(b)* even.

If multiple receivers are to one side and one receiver is the designated route runner (in 1 Flex EI 254Y, the tight end [Y] runs the fade), the other receivers must know who runs the companion route and what that companion route is. Often the call is simply the formation and 250, which is to line up in the called formation and run a three-step drop route to be decided. The quarterback evaluates the coverage and calls the desired route or else signals that route to the receiver. If there are two wide receivers to the side being signaled, the signal refers to the receiver off the line of scrimmage (for example, in 2A 250 if the quarterback signals or calls 253, Z runs the hitch). If there are three wide receivers to one side and two of them are off the line of scrimmage, the call refers to the widest receiver off the line (for example, in 1 Flex EI 250, if the quarterback signals or calls 254, Z runs the fade).

The blocking protection begins with the interior line. They use aggressive area protection in which they line up on the ball and flash and cut. The number-two receiver in the backfield of a one-back formation blocks away from number three if tight or to the callside if not. He blocks the first man to show outside the offensive tackle's block to his side. He steps up and attacks the defender at the line of scrimmage, getting his hands down.

The number 2 call-side receiver (251/851, 252/852, and 253/853) runs a 5-yard middle hook as he takes an inside release. He gets head up on the ball as he slides to get open. If three receivers are to the callside and number three is not tight, he runs a fade. If he is tight, multiple receivers are on the backside, and none of them is tight, he blocks the first man to show outside the offensive tackle's block to his side. He steps up and attacks the defender at the line of scrimmage, getting the defender's hands down.

On 254/854, if in a two-back formation or if the inside receiver on the backside is tight, the number 2 call-side receiver runs a middle fade. He releases outside and then works back to the middle and gets deep. If wider than 5 yards, or if three receivers are to callside and number three is not tight, he runs a diagonal. If three receivers are to callside and number three is tight, or if the number 2 call-side receiver is in C or D, he runs a middle hook.

The number 2 backside receiver runs a middle hook if there is only one receiver to the callside. If two receivers are to callside and the number 2 backside receiver is tight, he blocks the first man to show outside the offensive tackle's block to his side. He steps up and attacks the defender at the line of scrimmage, getting his hands down. If two receivers are to callside and the number 2 backside receiver is not tight, or if three receivers are to backside, the number 2 backside receiver runs a fade.

If in the backfield of a one-back formation, number three blocks the first man to show outside the offensive tackle's block away from the slot's block, or to callside if no slot. He steps up and attacks the defender at the line of scrimmage, getting his hands down.

The number 3 call-side receiver runs a middle hook. If he is tight and number two away from the call is not tight, the number 3 call-side receiver blocks the first man to show outside the offensive tackle's block to his side. He steps up and attacks the defender at the line of scrimmage.

Five-Step Drop

The five-step drop centers on an important philosophy. Players should learn the philosophy of having a minimum number of plays and then tag-wording those plays to create versatility and to attack every zone on the field.

Stretch zone coverage horizontally, vertically, or both. Put three receivers in an area that can be covered by only two defenders. Isolate a receiver.

No matter how few or how many rushers, block them all and decrease the number of receivers or hot-read the blitzer. Depending on the defensive alignment, employ 80 or 40 blocking on five-step drop-pass plays to ensure that all potential rushers are accounted for and blocked (these blocking schemes are described in the next section). If you hot-read the blitzer, replace the blitzer with a receiver, get the ball to him, and don't block the blitzer.

If they continually bring maximum rush, go to Twins to ensure you have two receivers to the same side running companion patterns. Also place a greater emphasis on the three-step game.

Referring to the 280s when discussing five-step drop-pass plays means to employ 80 blocking rules.

When you tag-word an alternate pattern, you are not telling the quarterback that this is the receiver he must throw to but that you are tag-wording the pattern based on something seen. You feel there's a good chance that pattern will be successful. Thus the quarterback should view this tag-word pattern with some degree of credibility before going to other options. For any tag-word pattern that breaks inside (seam, post, square, across, inside go, bend in, hook and go, zig in, choice, option, bake), there is an automatic fake draw to hold the linebackers. The draw fake is always to the fullback unless the tailback is the only back directly in the backfield. When executing the draw fake, the quarterback hollers "draw!" while his back is to the defense.

80 Protection

Call-side tackle: number 2 line of scrimmage (possible gone call).

Call-side guard: number 1 line of scrimmage (possible gone call).

Center: area; bump or pat call, backside inside linebacker.

Backside guard: area.

Backside tackle: area (possible fan call).

Number 2 backside: area (first man outside backside tackle's block, controlled

release); bib call versus closedown, Bob call versus regular.

Number 3: call-side inside linebacker.

Use 88 or 88 read protection (figures 6.19 and 6.20) versus even eight-man fronts against odd fronts with strength to callside, or when faced with the threat of a four-man rush to callside or 4-1/2 men to callside (when a defensive player is playing head up on the offensive center, he's considered half to the strong side and half to the weak side). Use 48 or 48 read protection (figures 6.22 and 6.23)when facing an eight-man front with strength to the backside or 4-1/2 men to the backside. Number 2 callside blocks the widest rusher outside of the offensive tackle's block whether 88 is called or not. If 88 read is called and the defender rushes, number 2 callside flattens out as soon as the defender passes and looks for the ball. If 88 or 88 read is called and the defender drops, number 2 callside runs his pattern. All other blocks remain the same as in 80 protection.

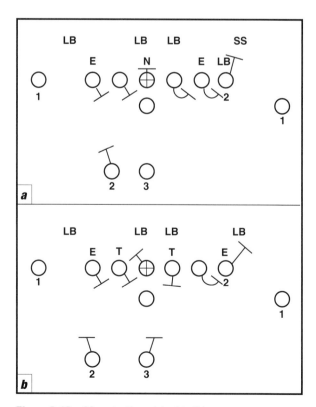

Figure 6.18 80 protection: *(a)* odd; *(b)* even.

Figure 6.19 88 protection: *(a)* odd; *(b)* even.

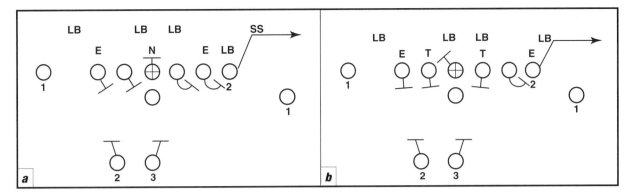

Figure 6.20 88 read protection: *(a)* odd; *(b)* even.

40 Protection

The first uncovered man from the backside guard to the call-side guard slides to the back-side area (figure 6.21).

Call-side tackle: area (possible fan call).

Call-side guard: area, uncovered, slide to center's area.

Center: if covered, attack weak-side half of man on and peek to backside inside linebacker, then bump to inside linebacker when call-side guard blocks nose; if uncovered, slide to backside area.

Backside guard: slide to backside area.

Backside tackle: slide to backside area.

Number 2 callside: check inside linebacker and, if he rushes, check outside linebacker and block him if he rushes; if either drops, run route.

Number 2 backside: pattern.

Number 3: Molly inside linebacker to outside linebacker.

Use 48 or 48-read protection (figures 6.22 and 6.23) against odd or even eight-man fronts with 4-1/2 men to the backside. Number 2 callside blocks the widest rusher outside of the offensive tackle's block whether or not 48 is called. If 48 read is called and the defender rushes, number 2 callside flattens out as soon as the defender passes and looks for the ball. If 48 or 48 read is called and the defender drops, number 2 callside runs his pattern. Number 2 backside blocks the widest rusher. All other blocks remain the same as in 80 protection.

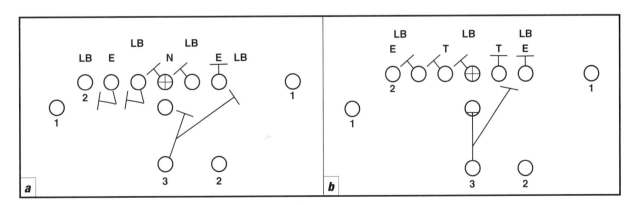

Figure 6.21 40 protection: *(a)* odd; *(b)* even.

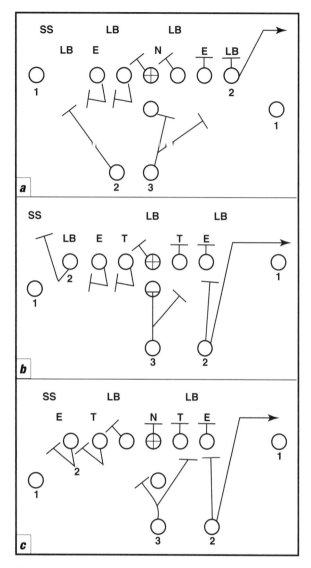

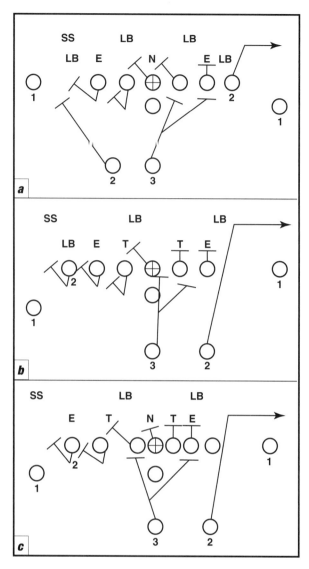

Figure 6.22 48 protection: *(a)* call-side guard uncovered; *(b)* center uncovered; *(c)* backside guard uncovered.

Figure 6.23 48-read protection: *(a)* call-side guard uncovered; *(b)* center uncovered; *(c)* backside guard uncovered.

Seven-Step Drop

Take a seven-step drop when playing 285/885 and passing to the underneath delay route or when using deep-breaking tag-word patterns for 281/881, 282/882, and 285/885, such as shake (post-corner) and bake (corner-post). The bake pattern will necessitate the draw fake because it breaks to the middle. Use the same blocking rules for a seven-step drop (80, 48) as employed for a five-step drop but with slightly different coaching points because of the increased depth of the quarterback's drop.

282 (882) Curl

Against seven-man fronts, use 80 blocking. Use 88 blocking versus a balanced eight-man front or an unbalanced eight-man front with strength to the tight end. Use 48 blocking versus an unbalanced eight-man front with strength to the split-end side.

Number 1: run a 12-yard read curl pattern.

Number 2 callside: if from the line of scrimmage, run a 5-yard speed turn out; if from the backfield, run a 3-yard speed turn out.

Number 2 backside: check flare if from backfield; check alley if from line of scrimmage; check seam if split.

Number 3: run a 6-yard hook, level off, and slide away from coverage; block if linebacker rushes.

The quarterback reads the defender responsible for the curl area. If the defender gets more depth than width, number 1 will run a tight bracket and come right back to the ball. If the defender gets more width than depth, number 1 will run inside around the defender, looking for the open window in which to settle. Against man or trail, number 1 takes two steps toward a corner before running inside. Against zone, if the defender responsible for the flat drops curl to the flat, the quarterback hits number 2 early or waits for number 1 to come open late. If the defense has only number 2 to cover underneath to the callside, the inside defender must choose between number 1 (curl) and number 3 (hook).

Against man-to-man pass coverage, make it impossible for the defense to stay with one receiver. If the defense plays bump and run, number 1 gets his 12 yards and then runs over the top to the inside. If they play man from head up, number 1 gets his depth and then pivots inside into the defender and comes back to the ball. Use tag words to take advantage of man coverage. Sending number 1 backside on a seam or square in can make coverage difficult. Sending number 1 callside on a shake is also difficult to defend. 1A 282 T and Y Change almost assures the tailback of being open, especially if Y runs his pattern to make it difficult for the linebacker covering the tailback to get past him to the outside.

Against zone coverage, stretch their coverage, which this play does horizontally. Create a triangle in which two defenders are stretched to try to cover three receivers. If they play five under, make side covered by two underneath the callside. If they play six under, they will be two deep. Tag-word the backside receiver to a seam and split the two deep.

Run the read curl. The receivers take a presnap read, attempting to determine who has responsibility for the curl area. The misdirection should appear to be a Go pattern to make the cornerback back off the receiver and

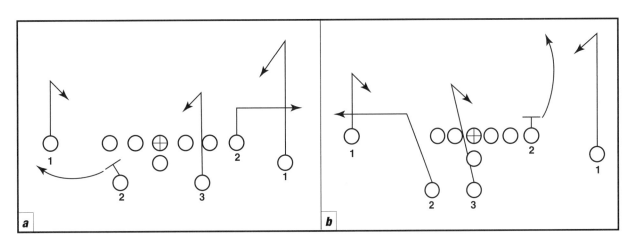

Figure 6.24 282 (882) Curl: *(a)* Regular 1 282; *(b)* Regular 1B 882.

give some cushion. As the receiver releases from the line of scrimmage, he uses his peripheral vision to determine who has curl responsibility and to view his drop. At 10 yards, the receiver starts to settle, pumping his arms as he sits down, aiming slightly toward the sidelines. As he gets to 12 yards deep, the receiver uses the defender's path to tell him what to do. If the defender coming to the curl area gets more depth than width, the receiver keeps a tight bracket and comes right back to the ball. If the defender flies out horizontally, gaining more width than depth, the receiver circles around him and looks for the open window. Regardless of which path the defender takes, the receiver must get 12 yards deep before finishing the route. The quarterback makes the same read, so he anticipates the receiver's route and throws the ball as the receiver makes the break.

For the speed turn-out pattern, the receiver cuts over his outside foot instead of planting his inside foot and turns. If number 1 callside runs the out (2I 282 X and Z Change), the pattern becomes a 10-yard out. If tag words such as "shake" or "bake" are given to one of the receivers, the play becomes a seven-step drop for the quarterback to accommodate the lengthier pattern.

Play-Action Pass

A well-balanced offense has at least one play-action pass off every running play. Success in the running play helps sell the companion play-action pass. Success in the play-action pass significantly aids the running game.

To create diversity, make sure every receiver learns the philosophy of the play and memorizes each route. Then run the play from a variety of formations with and without motion and tag words.

311 (711) Zone Pass

Use 330 pass protection.

Number 1 callside: corner.

Number 2 callside: out.

Number 1 backside: diagonal.

Fullback: if in I, block first man to show outside call-side tackle's block; if behind quarterback in any other formation, fake 111; clamp down dramatically, leaving room for the quarterback to keep the ball; carry out run fake and make defense attempt to tackle you; if unblocked rusher shows, become a blocker.

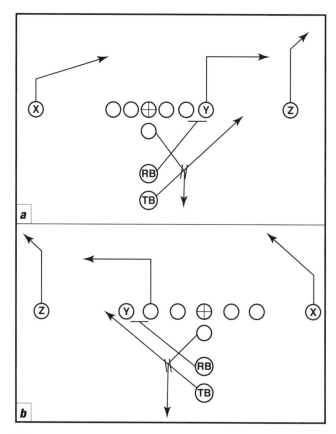

Figure 6.25   311 (711) Zone Pass: *(a)* Regular 1I 311; *(b)* Regular 9I 711.

Tailback: if in A set, block first man to show outside call-side tackle's block; if no rusher and you are number 2 callside, run an out; if in B set, come over the top and block first man to show outside call-side tackle's block; if in I, fake 111; clamp down dramatically, leaving room for the quarterback to keep the ball; carry out run fake and make defense attempt to tackle you; if unblocked rusher shows, become a blocker.

Quarterback: super fake of 111 with open hand (ball fake on 711); hide the ball and drop straight back off the fake; read short to deep.

311 (711) Zone Drag Pass

Use 330 pass protection.

Number 1 callside: run a hitch.

Number 2 callside: block aggressively for two counts or drop down on all fours as if staying and blocking, then drag across field under the sneak route but gaining depth; become primary receiver.

Number 1 backside: run sneak route; must be deeper than the drag and take coverage off the drag.

Fullback: if in I, block first man to show outside call-side tackle's block; if behind quarterback in any other formation, fake 111; clamp down dramatically, leaving room for quarterback to keep the ball; carry out run fake and make defense attempt to tackle you; if unblocked rusher shows, become a blocker.

Tailback: If in A set, block first man to show outside call-side tackle's block; if in B set, come over the top and block first man to show outside call-side tackle's block; if in I, fake 111; clamp down dramatically, leaving room for the quarterback to keep the ball; carry out run fake and make defense attempt to tackle you; if unblocked rusher shows, be a blocker.

The quarterback fakes 111 with his open hand (ball fake on 711). He hides the ball and drops straight back off the fake. He looks off to the receivers on the right until the last minute, then drops another two steps, turns to the left, and hits the drag pattern.

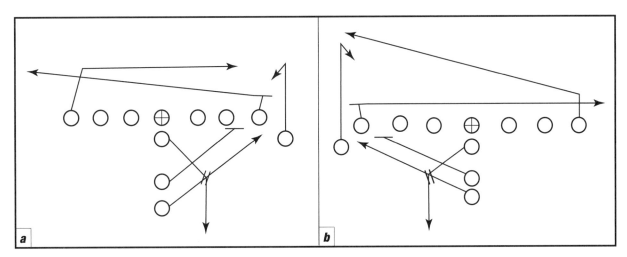

Figure 6.26 Zone drag pass: *(a)* Crow 0 1 Tight WR I (311 Drag); *(b)* Crow 0 9 Tight WL I (711 Drag).

316 (716) Zone Bootleg

Use 330 pass protection.

Center or call-side guard, or backside guard if both center and call-side guard are covered: Molly; take inside linebacker if he rushes, otherwise pull and block call-side outside linebacker.

Number 1 callside: zig out; make first move look as though you are going crossfield for a block on the outside zone play; if a slot, block for three counts and then slide to flat.

Number 2 callside: fake 911; become a blocker; if a slot, block for three counts and then slide to flat.

Number 1 backside: run a good stalk block and then break a short post.

Number 2 backside: block and then slide off and sneak across the middle, looking for the open slot between the far-side inside linebacker, outside linebacker, and cornerback; get depth from tackle to tackle according to linebacker drop and then level off and get width, working from hook to curl to flat.

Number 3: block the first man to show outside the tackle's block; if lined up behind the quarterback, fake 911.

Quarterback: fake 911; put the ball on your hip, look the faker into the line, then whip head around and sprint to the right; look for 1 callside then 2 backside to be open, deep to short.

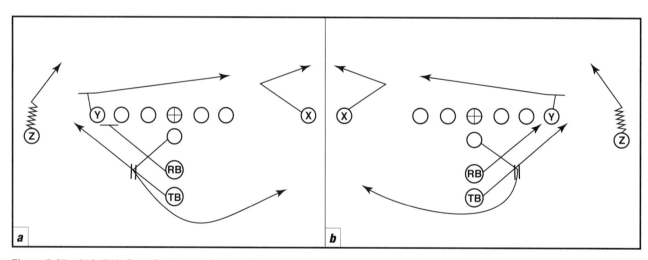

Figure 6.27 316 (716) Zone Bootleg: *(a)* Regular 9l 316 Bootleg; *(b)* Regular 1l 716 Bootleg.

Play-Action Screen

Effective screens have a definite impact on the defense's rush and aggressiveness. You should not only have a play-action pass for each run but also a play-action screen. The examples that follow describe a play-action screen with a reverse fake and a play-action screen with bootleg action. With a variety of formations and personnel packages, you can get the ball in your playmaker's hands.

411 (611) Zone Fake Reverse Screen

Use screen right pass protection.

Number 1 callside: block deep third.

Number 2 callside: sprint inside hollering "reverse"; super fake with quarterback; clamp and dip inside shoulder; carry out the fake; take people with you.

Number 1 backside: stalk and block deep third.

Fullback: block first man to show outside tackle's block; slide outside, turn and find ball; wave hands to help quarterback find you; if behind quarterback in a one-back formation, first fake 111.

Tailback: if in I or A, block widest rusher; if in one back I, first fake 111 and then slide outside, turn, and find ball; wave hands to help quarterback find you.

Quarterback: quick fake of 111, then show reverse and holler "reverse"; follow fake to behind the backside guard and then turn toward the line as you prepare to throw the screen so that you can see if anyone has read the screen.

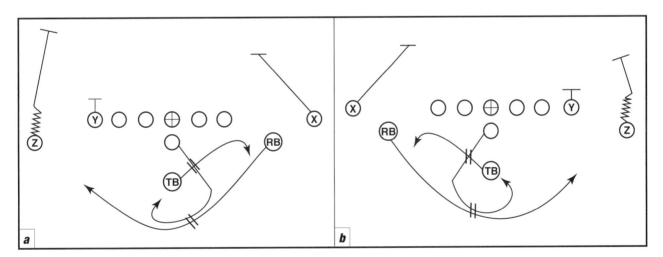

Figure 6.28   411 (611) Zone Fake Reverse Screen: *(a)* Tiger 9 2I 411T; *(b)* Tiger 1 8I 611T.

416 (616) Zone Bootleg Screen

Use screen right pass protection.

Number 1 callside: zig out and block deep third.

Number 2 callside: area, then block middle third.

Number 1 backside: block deep third.

Fullback: block first man to show outside tackle's block; slide outside, turn, and find ball; wave hands to help quarterback find you; if behind the quarterback in a one-back formation, first fake 111.

Tailback: if in I or A, block widest rusher; if in one back I, first fake 111 then slide outside, turn, and find ball; wave your hands to help quarterback find you.

Quarterback: quick fake of 111 and then show bootleg quickly; sell the bootleg and holler "boot"; boot to behind the backside guard and then turn toward the line as you prepare to throw the screen so that you can see if anyone has read the screen.

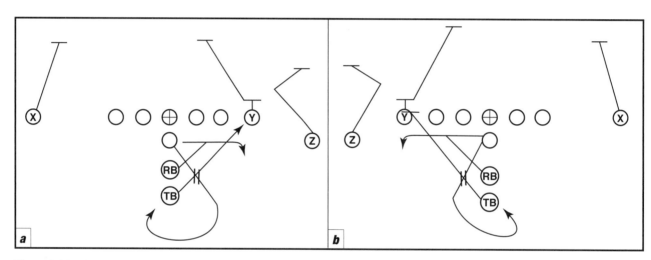

Figure 6.29 416 (616) Zone Bootleg Screen: *(a)* Regular 1I 416R; *(b)* Regular 9I 616R.

Drop-Back Screen

Drop-back screens are important to the drop-back passing game. An effective screen has a great impact on the pass rush and helps you determine whether or not to stunt linebackers regularly. There are many types of drop-back screens—quick, delayed, middle screens, outside screens, double screens, and fake double screens.

401 (601) Quick Screen

Line: screen the pass rush away from the call-side guard–tackle gap, center, call-side guard, or backside guard; if both center and call-side guard are covered, aggressively attack call-side linebacker.

Number 1 callside: block deep third.

Number 1 backside: block deep third.

Number 2 backside: aggressively attack backside linebacker.

Tight end: aggressively attack middle linebacker.

Tailback: move to call-side guard–tackle gap, turn, and face quarterback with arms waving to help him find you.

The quarterback quickly moves from a five-step drop to a seven-step drop as he looks off to the backside. He finds the receiver and steps into the pass.

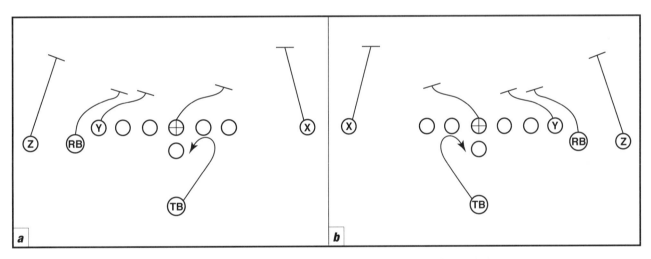

Figure 6.30   401 (601) quick screen: *(a)* Tiger 9DI 401 T Screen Right; *(b)* Tiger 1CI 601 T Screen Left.

403 (603) Double Screen

Use drop-back screen-pass protection. The backside tackle blocks for two counts and then sprints to the fullback.

Number 1 backside: block middle third.

Number 2 backside: block call-side deep third.

Number 3 backside: block call-side linebacker.

Tight end: block and then slide to the outside hip of the call-side offensive tackle; look for the ball.

Fullback: align to the right of the quarterback; sprint to the line of scrimmage 1 yard outside of backside offensive tackle, turn, wave, and look for the ball; then block deep third.

From the shotgun, the quarterback drops, looking to the fullback until the last minute. Then he turns and finds the tight end.

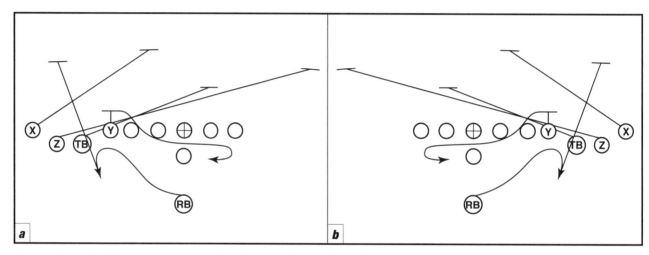

Figure 6.31 403 (603) double screen: *(a)* Tiger 8F Over 403 Y; *(b)* Tiger 2E Over 603 Y.

Draw

The draw (figure 6.32) goes hand in hand with the screen in controlling the defensive pass rush. It demands just as much coaching and practice time as the most dominant running play in your offense.

Call-side wide receiver: blocks outside third.

Backside wide receiver: blocks middle third.

Call-side slot: releases outside, looks and hollers for ball; if outside linebacker is playing tight and threatens inside charge, releases inside and delays his charge; if one-back formation, calls *down* and blocks area.

Backside slot: releases inside to the second level; blocks ahead of play.

Line: uses 80 pass protection rules and techniques and exhibits total aggression.

Call-side tackle: number 2 line of scrimmage (fan); on *down* call, blocks area.

Call-side guard: number 1 line of scrimmage (fan); on *down* call, blocks area.

Center: blocks area, backside inside linebacker.

Backside guard: sets area; offers outside rush lane and soft shoulder.

Backside tackle: sets area; offers outside rush lane and soft shoulder.

Fullback (tailback if in I): sets up as in pocket pass protection and is patient; does not look for ball, makes pocket at last second; clamps on ball and picks way off center's block.

Tailback (fullback if in I): sets up as in pocket pass protection, then blocks first linebacker past center to callside; works inside out and keeps body between linebacker and ball.

The quarterback starts his regular five-step drop. He continues back and places the ball on the fullback's belly. The quarterback is responsible for the exchange.

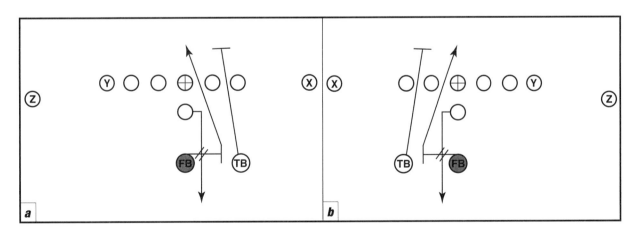

Figure 6.32 195 (995) draw: *(a)* Regular 9A 195; *(b)* Regular 1B 995.

7

Team Defense

The first thing to do when designing a front or an adjustment to a front is to subject that design to several tests. First, look at balance. A balanced formation has 5-1/2 men (when a player is playing head-up on the offensive center, he's considered half to the strong side and half to the weak side), or at least 6 and 5, on each side of the ball. Once in a great while you might consider an alignment that is 6-1/2 and 4-1/2, but only if there's a tremendous tendency for the offense to go to the strong side. This count is not just from how you line up prior to the snap but also after execution of a called stunt. If the offense is not balanced, adjust to their formation. It is essential to match the offensive alignment.

Consider the option responsibility. Review dive, keep, and pitch responsibilities, ensuring players are totally sound in the distribution of their responsibilities. You do not want to be caught in a front in which you're attacking the dive only from the inside out. That isn't sound if offensive and defensive personnel match up evenly. Neither do you want to be predictable in quarterback and pitch responsibility, so that

the quarterback can easily read his key. Attack the quarterback with different people coming from different locations, but avoid having a defensive back as the primary player taking any phase of the option unless the underneath coverage is some form of man.

Look at zone coverage. Pure man pass coverage might not be comfortable. The offense can create a mismatch, and if the defense doesn't get to the quarterback quickly, the quarterback can find the mismatch and get the ball to the open man. Mix up your coverages and do your best to disguise the coverage, but you may want to avoid pure man coverage.

Alternate between a seven- and eight-man front. Stop the run first. If you can't stop the run, your opponent won't need to throw the ball. So you must have the flexibility to align in either a seven- or an eight-man front, depending on what your opponent wants to do to attempt to move the ball.

Both the gaps and alignments are labeled in relation to offensive line personnel. The gaps between the offensive guards and center are called the A gaps. Moving from inside out, the

B gaps are between the guards and tackles, the C gaps between the tackles and tight ends, and the D gaps between the tight ends and wings (figure 7.1).

Whereas gaps are denoted by letters, alignments and techniques are denoted by numbers. (See figure 5.2, page 65, for illustrations of defensive alignments.) Head up on the offensive center is called a 0 alignment. A 1 alignment is shading the shoulder of the center. Shading the inside shoulder of the guard is an inside 2. Head up on the offensive guard is a 2

alignment. A 3 alignment is shading the shoulder of the guard. Shading the inside shoulder of the tackle is an inside 4. Head up on the offensive tackle is a 4 alignment. A 5 alignment is shading the shoulder of the tackle. Shading the inside shoulder of the tight end is an inside 6. Head up on the tight end is a 6 alignment. A 7 alignment is shading the shoulder of the tight end. Shading the inside shoulder of the wing is an inside 8. Head up on the wing is an 8 alignment. Finally, a 9 alignment is shading the shoulder of the wing.

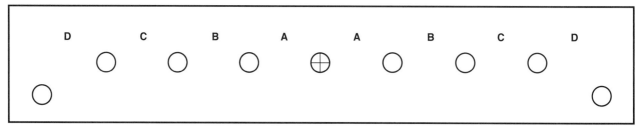

Figure 7.1 Gaps.

3-4 Defense

Secondary: two or three deep; corners are right and left.

Strong safety: 8 technique to tight side.

Tight tackle: 4 technique.

Split tackle: 0 technique.

Tight end: 6 technique to a tight end; 5 technique to a split end.

Split end: 5 technique or 5-off technique to a split end; 4 technique to a tight end.

Sam linebacker: 3 technique to tight side.

Mike linebacker: 3 technique to split side.

Will linebacker: 8 technique to split side versus a split end; 6 technique on line of scrimmage versus a tight end. Still has pass coverage.

In the 3-4 defense pursuit course (figure 7.4), the pursuit of the inside linebackers is rather deep to avoid the pileup at the line; they correctly estimate the speed of the ballcarrier

and are moving toward the line of scrimmage with positive momentum when the tackle is made. The inside linebacker away from flow steps up to check the A gaps before flowing slowly along the line of scrimmage, checking for the cutback or counter. The end away from flow trails through the backfield at ball depth, looking for counters and reverses until the ball crosses the line of scrimmage. The defensive backs make sure to keep receivers in front of them until the ball crosses the line of scrimmage. A defensive back must not move to another zone until the defensive back behind him has entered his zone and is in position to cover any receiver in his zone.

The path that each defender takes to pursue to the ballcarrier is fundamental. A fundamentally sound team will practice this over and over. In a stunt call, the linebacker involved is called as is the gap he is to stunt through. The defensive linemen in that area stunt to the adjoining gaps.

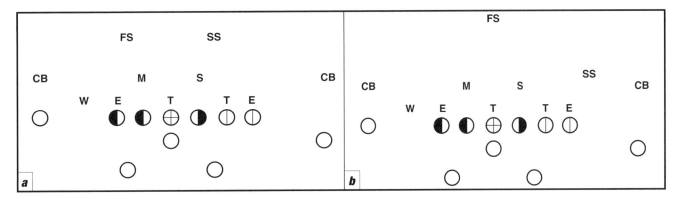

Figure 7.2 3-4 defense: *(a)* cover 2; *(b)* cover 3.

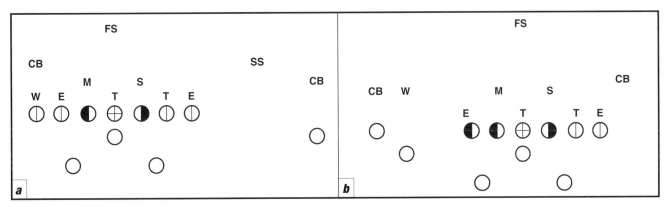

Figure 7.3 3-4 defense cover 3: *(a)* versus double tight end; *(b)* versus twins.

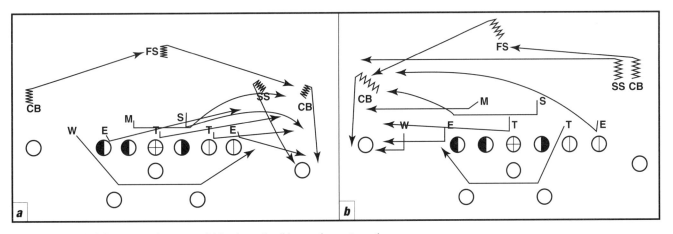

Figure 7.4 3-4 defense pursuit course: *(a)* to strength; *(b)* away from strength.

Twist-in stunts (figure 7.5). The inside line-man pulls his man into the outside gap. Once his shoulders are turned, he releases for the pass rush. He must remember he is the widest rusher and has contain duties. The outside lineman takes a lead step and then moves upfield off his teammate's butt.

Twist-out stunts (figure 7.6). The outside line-man pulls his man into the inside gap. Once his shoulders are turned, he releases for the pass rush. The inside lineman takes a lead step and then releases upfield off his teammate's butt. The outside lineman is the widest rusher and has contain duties.

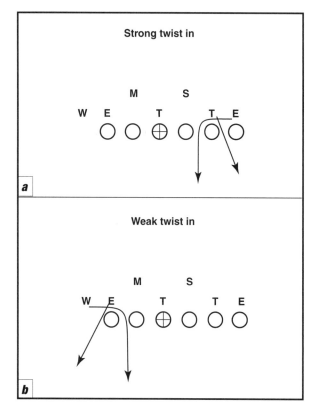

Figure 7.5 Twist-in stunts.

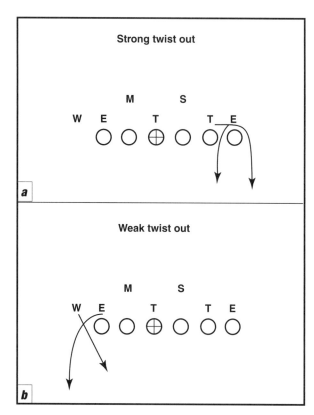

Figure 7.6 Twist-out stunts.

Fold-in stunts (figure 7.7). The outside line-man jams his man and then goes off the butt of his teammate to move upfield into the backfield. The inside lineman must beat the offensive lineman into the gap and then work a contain rush because the stunt makes him the widest rusher.

Fold-out stunts (figure 7.8). The inside lineman jams his man and then goes off the

butt of his teammate to move upfield into the backfield. He works a contain rush because the stunt makes him the widest rusher. The outside lineman must beat the offensive lineman into the gap.

Many other stunts could be called from this defensive alignment. Additional stunts might include the secondary.

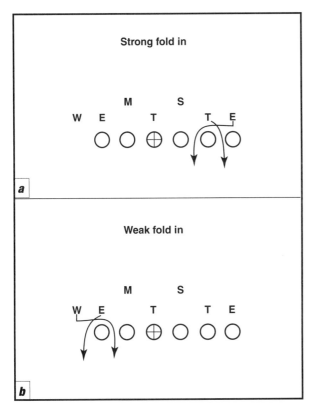

Figure 7.7 Fold-in stunts.

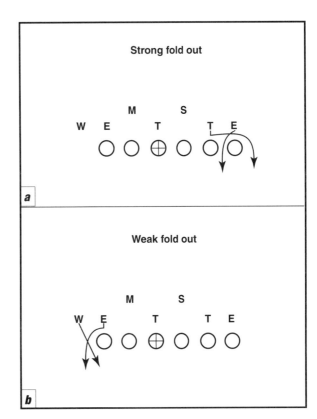

Figure 7.8 Fold-out stunts.

4-3 Defense

The 4-3 defense (figure 7.9) usually involves three alignments. The shades change depending on the offensive tendencies, especially on how tight-end oriented the offense is in its running game.

Secondary: two or three deep; corners are right and left.

Strong safety: tight side.

Tight tackle: 3 technique.

Split tackle: inside 2 technique.

Tight end: inside 6 technique to a tight end; 5 technique to a split end.

Split end: 5 technique or 5-off technique.

Sam linebacker: 5 technique to tight side.

Mike linebacker: 0 technique.

Will linebacker: 5 technique to split side; 7 technique versus tight end.

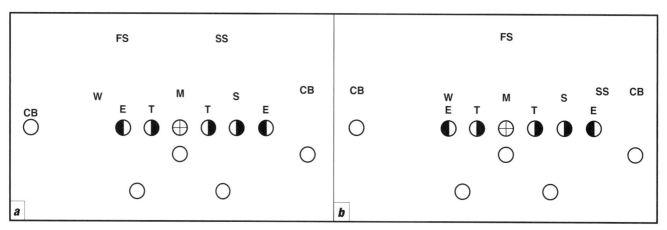

Figure 7.9 4-3 defense: *(a)* cover 2; *(b)* cover 3.

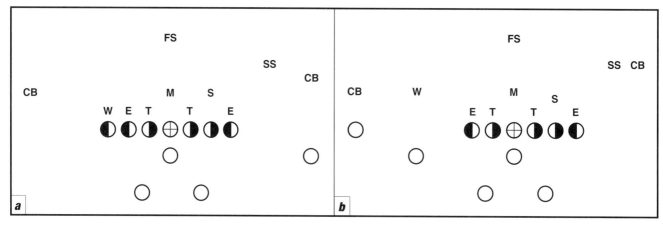

Figure 7.10 4-3 defense cover 3: *(a)* versus double tight end; *(b)* versus twins.

In the 4-3 defense pursuit course (figure 7.11), the pursuit of the inside linebackers is rather deep to avoid a pileup at the line; they correctly estimate the speed of the ballcarrier and are moving toward the line of scrimmage with positive momentum when the tackle is made. The linebacker away from flow steps up to check the A and B gaps before flowing slowly along the line of scrimmage, checking for the cutback or counter. The end away from flow trails through the backfield at ball depth, looking for counters and reverses until the ball crosses the line of scrimmage. The defensive backs make sure to keep receivers in front of them until the ball crosses the line of scrimmage. A defensive back must not move to another zone until the defensive back behind him has entered his zone and is in position to cover any receiver in his zone.

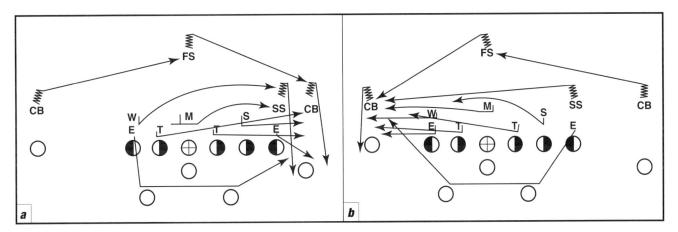

Figure 7.11   4-3 defense pursuit course: *(a)* to strength; *(b)* away from strength.

4-3 Shade Defense

Secondary: two or three deep; corners are right and left.

Strong safety: tight side, unless both corners are to one side, then go opposite.

Tight tackle: 3 technique.

Split tackle: 1 technique.

Tight end: inside 6 technique to a tight end; 5 technique to a split end.

Split end: 5 technique or 5-off technique.

Sam linebacker: 5 technique to tight side.

Mike linebacker: 0 technique.

Will linebacker: 5 technique to split side; 7 technique versus double tight end.

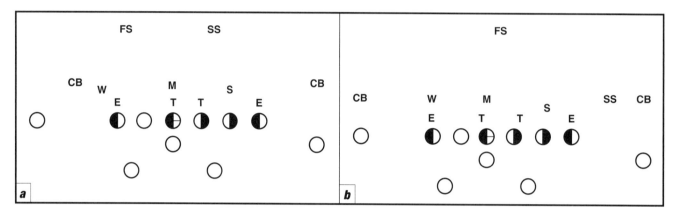

Figure 7.12 4-3 shade defense: *(a)* cover 2; *(b)* cover 3.

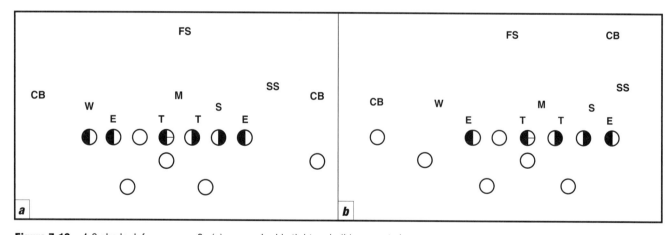

Figure 7.13 4-3 shade defense cover 3: *(a)* versus double tight end; *(b)* versus twins.

4-3 Odd Defense

Secondary: two or three deep; corners are right and left, unless no wide receiver, and twins or trips on other side; both corners go to twins or trips.

Strong safety: tight side.

Tight tackle: inside 4 technique.

Split tackle: 1 technique.

Tight end: inside technique to a tight end; 5 technique to a split end.

Split end: 5 technique or 5-off technique.

Sam linebacker: 5 technique to tight side.

Mike linebacker: 0 technique.

Will linebacker: 5 technique to split side; 7 technique versus tight end.

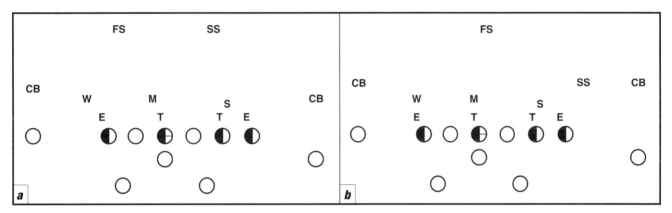

Figure 7.14 4-3 odd defense: *(a)* cover 2; *(b)* cover 3.

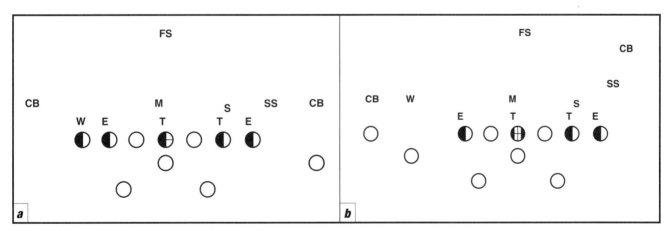

Figure 7.15 4-3 odd defense cover 3: *(a)* versus double tight end; *(b)* versus twins.

Nickel Defense

The nickel back refers to a fifth defensive back in a game (figure 7.16). That fifth back might enter the game in place of a linebacker or might replace a defensive lineman, limiting the defense to a three-man line. You might choose a nickel package in a long-yardage situation, to counter a fourth-down play, or versus a two-minute offense. You don't necessarily need to go to a new coverage with a nickel back in the game. Using a nickel package simply means you should have better pass coverage regardless of what pass defense you employ.

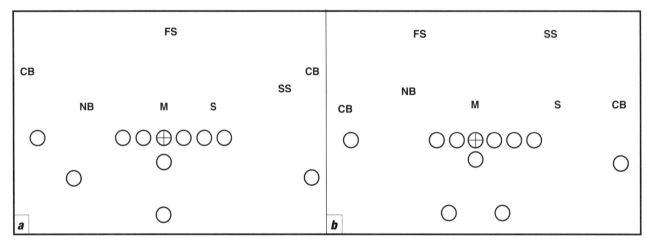

Figure 7.16 Nickel defense: *(a)* vs. one-back formation; *(b)* vs. two-back formation.

Dime Defense

Now that most teams use four or five receivers as a regular part of their passing game, defenses must counter with more defensive backs. Hence the dime defensive back, or sixth back. Now unless only one linebacker is used, teams using the dime defense will be in a three-man line.

Nickel and dime back: aligns on number one if a wide receiver or tight wing and plays press technique with flat responsibility; if no wide receiver, goes to other side and plays squat technique on number two with curl responsibility.

Corner: outside third coverage; keeps everything in front of him.

Free safety: deep middle third coverage; keeps everything in front of him.

Strong safety: plays squat on the widest number two with curl responsibility; if nickel and dime are on the same side, goes opposite and presses number one with flat responsibility.

Mike linebacker: hook or hook to hole pass responsibility.

Sam linebacker: hook or hook to hole pass responsibility.

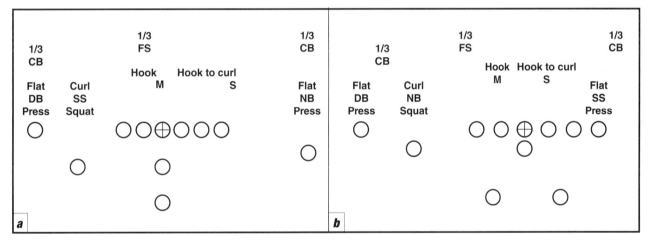

Figure 7.17 Dime defense: *(a)* vs. one-back formation; *(b)* vs. two-back formation.

Goal-Line Defense

Figure 7.18 shows the goal-line defense to use inside the 5-yard line, depending on the down and distance and when expecting a compacted offensive alignment. Including the stunting free safety, commit at least seven to the run or pass rush. You might also stunt either or both linebackers.

Corners: ice technique on wide receivers while covering outside fourth width of end zone; corners are right and left.

Free safety: either stunts or plays spy from 3 to 5 yards deep but is never deeper than 2 yards in the end zone.

Tight nose: 3 technique.

Split nose: 0 technique.

Tight tackle: 6 technique.

Split tackle: 3 technique.

Tight end: 8 technique.

Split end: 5 technique or 5-off technique to a split end; inside 6 technique to a tight end.

Mike linebacker: 5 technique; coverage is inside fourth zone of end zone.

Will linebacker: 5 technique; coverage is inside fourth zone of end zone.

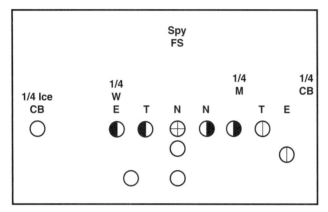

Figure 7.18 Goal-line defense.

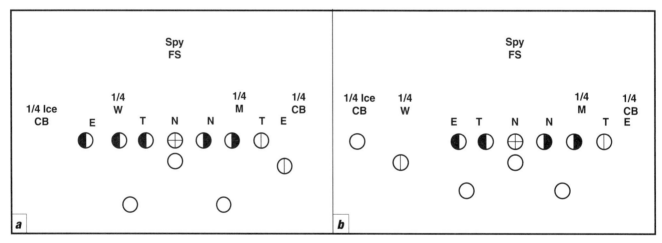

Figure 7.19 Goal-line defense: *(a)* versus double tight end; *(b)* versus twins.

8

Special-Teams Play

Some people are amazed by how many football games are won or lost on the execution, or lack thereof, of some phase of the kicking game. But should this really be a surprise? No, because in an average football game at least 25 to 30 percent of plays directly involve some phase of the kicking game. Break down a game in which the winner has 30 points or more and the loser 20 points or more, and you'll see how frequently a kicker, punter, or placekicker is on the playing field. Special teams really are special because of the tremendous impact they have on most games. This is seen in dramatic shifts in field position, momentum, and scoring.

Special-teams play involves many aspects. There is regular kickoff coverage as well as coverage for pooch and onside kicks. The receiving team must be ready to return regular kickoffs or pooch kicks or recover onside kicks. Extra-point offense for regular and faked extra points must be practiced. Extra-point defense focuses on blocks for regular extra points and readiness to cover faked extra points. Field-goal offense includes regular and faked field goals and planning for pooch punts out of a field-goal alignment. Field-goal defense must plan for blocks, fakes, or pooch punts. Punt coverage for regular punts, rugby punts, and fake punts are key. Punt defense must plan on fakes, wall returns, hold returns, and blocks. Then there are quick kicks from the shotgun and quick kick returns.

Unfortunately, few coaches spend enough practice time on the kicking game. For players to get sufficient kicking game practice, every coach on a staff must have kicking game responsibilities. At least one third of every practice should be devoted to the kicking game. Before a head coach writes in offensive and defensive plans on a practice schedule, he should block out one third of the practice time for the kicking game and itemize that part of the schedule.

Practice for every phase of the kicking game should begin with individual and group drills before progressing to team play. This should happen every day throughout the season.

Don't disregard individual and group drills once a segment has been introduced. Teams don't do that for offense and defense, and they shouldn't for the kicking game. Of course, players not involved in a particular area of the kicking game practice may practice offensive or defensive play while the rest of team focuses on special-teams play.

If a team is going to treat the kicking game with the same respect it shows offense and defense, the coach must select the best players on the field to execute the special-teams assignments. You don't start your second team on offense or defense, so why do it in the kicking game? Special teams is not the place to put second-teamers or to give game-time auditions to those you think might become key players. Special teams is for your best athletes, your established playmakers.

On game day, put a 4-yard square on the 50-yard line where the next special-teams unit will assemble one play prior to taking the field. In other words, if you are on defense in third down and three territory, the punt block or punt return unit assembles in that 50-yard line square with the special-teams coach. Assign one player on each special-teams unit the responsibility of being the captain of that special-teams group. The captain has certain duties to perform to keep that unit accountable (table 8.1).

TABLE 8.1   Responsibilities of Special-Teams Captains

Special-teams unit	Captain	Duties
Field goal and extra-point offense	Holder	• Count number of players in time so an extra player can get on or off without calling time-out. • Call the side of the overload rush. • Call off the fake if the defense is aligned to stop it.
Field goal and extra-point defense	Free safety	• Count number of players in time so an extra player can get on or off without calling time-out. • Alert team if there is a substitute jersey number at any of the key positions (kicker, holder, wing, tight end). • Alert team when the offense comes out in nonkicking formation. Yell for a new defense and get people in proper alignment.
Kickoff coverage	Safety	• Count number of players in time so an extra player can get on or off without calling time-out. • Alert team to the location of the key returner. • Alert team if the return team is in an unusual alignment or if a key new person is on the field, such as someone in position to take a reverse handoff. • Keep team in the huddle until the official puts the ball in play. • Be aware of the 25-second clock.
Kickoff return	Fullback	• Count number of players in time so an extra player can get on or off without calling time-out. • Alert team of clues that the kicking team might try an unusual kick (onside, line drive, squib, pooch, sideline). • Watch the ball. • Remind the front line to stay until the ball goes over their heads.

Special-teams unit	Captain	Duties
Punt coverage	Up back	• Count number of players in time so an extra player can get on or off without calling time-out. • Call the side of the overload rush. • Call off the fake if the defense is aligned to stop it. • Call the direction of the punt.
Punt defense	Free safety	• Count number of players in time so an extra player can get on or off without calling time-out. • Alert team if there is a substitute jersey number at any of the key positions (punter, up back, wide receiver, spear, tight end). • Alert team when the punting team comes out in nonpunting formation. Yell for a new defense and get people in proper alignment. • If ball is not to you, yell "poison" to teammates to alert them to face the ball and get away from it.

Kickoff Return

For the kickoff return, use an open huddle, facing the kicking team, with the fullback in front of the team calling the play. Players wait with their hands on their knees until the fullback is ready and in the huddle. During this time, the fullback counts to be sure that all 11 players are present. The fullback steps up to the huddle and calls, "Ready." The huddle snaps up with their hands together behind their backs. The fullback runs through his cadence, for example, "kickoff return middle, kickoff return middle, you got it? Ready, hit." All players shout "hit" as they clap their hands and break the huddle.

Middle Return

All blocks must be above the waist. The left guard watches the kick clear him, then drops back to the 30 and moves up to block 3. The left tackle watches the kick clear him, then drops back to the 30 and moves up to block 4. The center watches the kick clear him, then drops back to the 30 and moves up to block 5. The right tackle watches the kick clear him, then drops back to the 30 and moves up to block 6. The right guard watches the kick clear him, then drops back to the 30 and moves up to block 7. The ends watch for a short kick. Then the left end drops slightly and sprints across the field, trap blocking 2. The right end drops slightly and sprints across the field, trap blocking 8. The fullback blocks the first man downfield and stays with him. The left halfback and right halfback are 5 yards shallower than the safety. The left halfback helps the left guard or left tackle. He must be prepared to catch and return the kick. The left halfback is responsible for any ball on the left side that the safety cannot get to. The right halfback helps the right guard or right tackle. He also must be prepared to catch and return the kick as he is responsible for any ball on the right side that the safety cannot get to.

The safety is the returner. Every kick is his unless he cannot get to it, in which case he calls to the back who's in position to catch the ball to go ahead and do so. If the safety concedes the return to another back, he then assumes that back's blocking responsibility. The return man takes the ball straight upfield and uses his blockers, running full speed and looking for a seam to open.

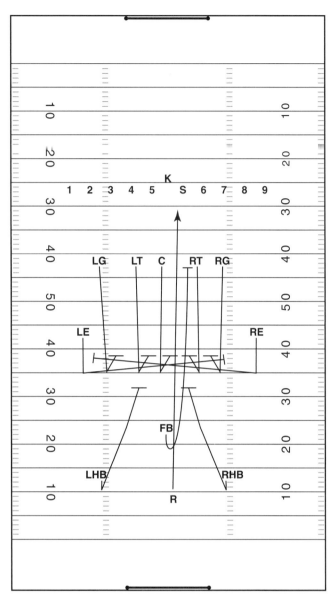

Figure 8.1   Kickoff middle return.

Right Return

The left guard, left tackle, center, right tackle, and right guard watch for the kick to clear them. Once the kick clears, the left guard drops back and then moves upfield and to his right to block the safety. The left tackle drops back and across the field and then moves upfield to block 4 to the side of the return. The center and right tackle drop back and across the field and then move upfield to block 3 to the side of the return. The right guard drops back and blocks 2, taking him inside. The left end makes sure the kick goes deep, drops back and across the field, and then moves upfield to block 5 to the side of the return. The right end makes sure the kick goes deep and then moves up on 2, blocking him inside with the right guard. The right halfback moves upfield and blocks 1, taking him to the sidelines. The left halfback and fullback lead the way for the return, blocking anyone in their way. They lead between 1 and 2. Initially, the safety runs straight upfield to get the coverage to commit. He gets to the sideline and follows the blocks.

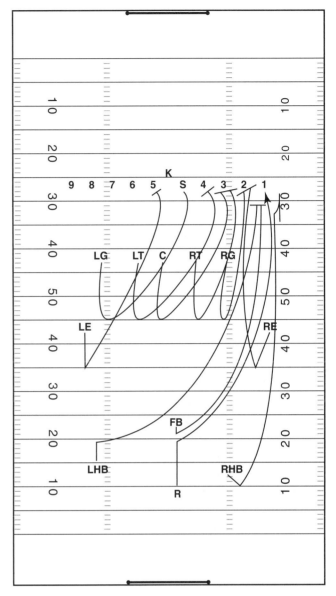

Figure 8.2   Kickoff right return.

Reverse Left Return

When opponent coverage starts to overcommit to what appears to be a return to one side, you might feel it's time to begin that return and then employ a reverse back to the opposite side. The left guard, left tackle, center, right tackle, and right guard watch the kick clear them. The left guard drops back and blocks 3 so that he gets the advantage to the side to which he thinks the return is going. The left guard must wall off 3 and prevent him from getting back on the reverse. The left tackle drops back and blocks 4 to get the advantage to the side he thinks the return is going. The left tackle walls off 4 and prevents him from getting back on the reverse. The center drops back and blocks 5, getting the advantage to the side he thinks the return is going. The center walls off 5 and prevents him from getting back on the reverse. The right tackle drops back and blocks 6 to get the advantage to the side to which he thinks the return is going. The right tackle walls off 6 and prevents him from getting back on the reverse. The right guard drops back and then sprints across the field, blocking out on the widest rusher. The right guard lets the return go inside him. The left end makes sure the kick goes deep and then gets across the field and blocks. He must not let anyone cross his face while working back toward the reverse. The right end makes sure the kick goes deep and then starts upfield, peels around, and receives the ball outside the safety. The right end pours it on and gets upfield and outside. The left halfback and fullback move upfield and to the right, blocking the first rushers they see. They make it look like a right return. The right halfback starts upfield and then swings to the left and leads the reverse. He mows down the first rusher he sees. The safety secures the ball and starts on a right return. He hands off the ball to the right end on an outside exchange, pressing the ball into the right end's chest. The safety continues upfield, faking a right return.

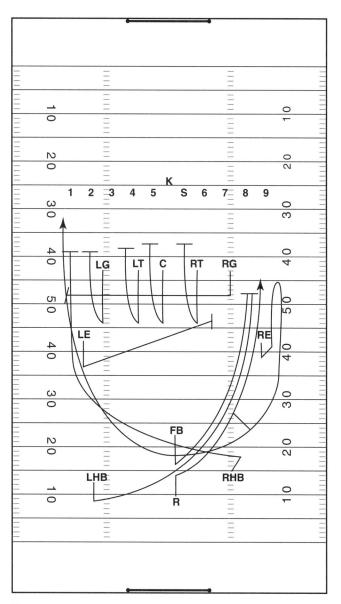

Figure 8.3 Kickoff reverse left return.

Kickoff Coverage

The skill of the kicker and the speed and disciplined coverage of the attacking players are vital to the success of a special-teams squad. Obviously, you want to force the opponent's offense to face a very long field.

Use an open huddle, facing the receiving team with the safety in front of the team calling the play. The kicker is in the middle of the front row so that an onside kick, or a muddle huddle with a deep kick, can be employed directly from the huddle. Players wait with their hands on their knees until the kicker is ready and in the huddle. During this time, the safety counts to be sure that all 11 players are present. When the kicker enters the huddle, he puts his hands on his knees. The safety steps up to the huddle and calls, "Ready." The players in the huddle snap up with hands together behind their backs.

The safety calls the coverage, including five points:

1. The formation the coverage team will assume—either right or left, which indicates the side of the field on which 1 will align.

2. The positioning of the ball—either right hash, middle of the field, or left hash.

3. The desired direction of the kick—either right, middle, or left.

4. The final call "avoid right" or "avoid left," telling the team which direction to take to avoid the blocks of the front line.

5. As a changeup, the numbers of the players that may exchange coverage routes.

For example, the safety might call "right, left, right, avoid right," meaning a right formation (1 to the right side of the field), a kick from the left hash across the field to the right hash, and avoidance of the front line of blockers by moving to the right. He then says "You got it? Ready, hit!" The players in the huddle shout

"hit!" and clap their hands to break the huddle. They sprint to their alignment. Because the hit man's coverage is directly to the ball, he can line up anywhere he feels will give him quickest access to the receiver. Remember there must always be at least four players on each side of the kicker at the time of the kick.

Each player kneels on his right knee with his right hand on the yard stripe 5 yards behind the ball. In an upright stance, the safety takes his spot beside the ball and faces the kicker. When the kicker signals to the safety that he's ready and the referee blows the ball live, the safety raises his hands to shoulder height, shouts "Ready!" and brings his hands to his sides. On "ready," the coverage goes to a three-point stance, looking in toward the ball. The safety moves to the position he'll take for coverage. As soon as he's in position, the kicker approaches the ball and kicks it. The coverage players take off as soon as the kicker enters their line of vision, sprinting downfield in their lanes. The 25-second clock is in effect on this play and begins with the referee's whistle.

Alignments

1: 5 yards from the sideline

2: 6 yards inside 1

3: 3 yards outside hash

4: 1 yard inside hash, unless kick is from his hash, then 1 yard outside hash

5: center of goal post

6: 1 yard inside hash, unless kick is from his hash, then 1 yard outside hash

7: 5 yards outside hash

8: 6 yards outside 7

Players adjust their spacing slightly to accommodate where the hit man chooses to align.

Coverage for 1 through 8 is the designated base alignment point. 7 and 8 contain on their side of the field should the opponent return the kick there. They turn such a return back into pursuit. They cover hard in their lanes, gradually closing in on the ballcarrier as they get deeper upfield and keeping a steady relationship to the coverage men inside them. They avoid the front-line blocker to the side designated in the huddle. They get back in their lanes, ready to take on the blocker in the back of the return. They come under control without slowing down as they approach the ball, always moving so they have the ballcarrier as he comes upfield, without allowing him to break outside them.

Sometimes try trading coverage paths and responsibilities of the outside two players. For example, 1 and 2 trade so 2 becomes contain or 8 trades with 7. You even can trade 6 with 7 or 8, so 6 becomes contain, or 3 with 1 or 2, though only to the side away from the direction of the kick.

The hit man goes hard and fast directly to the ball. He must be reckless and make the play. He moves laterally back and forth before the kick so the receiving team doesn't know where he's coming from. He must not be more than one lane from his spot when the ball is kicked.

The kicker stays head-up on the ball. He must never cross the opponent's 40-yard line.

The safety stays head-up on the ball and must never cross the 50-yard line. The safety is the last line of support if the ball gets that far. He must make the tackle. He shouldn't try for a pretty tackle, just a sure tackle. He gets on the return man's back and rides him, if necessary, but he must make the tackle.

The kickoff coverage unit is not for the fainthearted or timid. It's for only the most disciplined players. They must be accountable and consistent in their coverage lanes.

Punt Defense

Sell your punt defense unit on the philosophy that the punt return is the first play of the offensive series and the last play of the defensive series. For all punt-defense situations, make two calls in the huddle: one anticipating a punt and one in case they run or pass from an offensive formation. If the safety is not a regular defensive back, he'll spend practice time versus the run and the pass as a defensive safety so the opponent can't exploit him.

No member of the return team may initiate contact with the offensive center for 1 second after the snap. Players must align no deeper than the 10-yard line and must not back up. If the ball goes over the head of the deep-return man, he gives the fair catch signal and simulates receiving the punt. He must be a great actor. That said, the objective is to catch every punt and to seldom employ the fair catch. If the ball is totally uncatchable, the safety calls "poison" and keeps his eyes on the ball as he backs away completely. He must never turn his back to the ball.

10 Punt Hold

The left and right corners hold up the widest players as long as possible and make them release outside. The corners turn and run with the widest players, continuing to force them away from the play. They stay with their targets throughout the play.

The Sam and Will linebackers hold up the second players from the outside (on or off the line of scrimmage) and make them release to the outside. Then they go to force the punt. The linebackers turn back outside and work upfield, looking for the most dangerous threats to the return.

The ends hold up the third players from the outside as long as possible and make them release inside. They then turn and run with their targets, forcing them inside and away from the return. The ends stay with their men for the duration of the return.

The tackles hold up the first players outside the center (on or off the line of scrimmage) and make them release inside. They then turn and run with their targets, continuing to force them inside and away from the return. The tackles stay with their men for the duration of the return.

The Mike linebacker holds up the center, staying with him all the way downfield. Mike must not let the center get by him. He can't make contact with the center until 1 second after the snap.

The strong safety stacks behind the Mike linebacker and sprints back to block the first man downfield to the side of the punt.

The punt is the free safety's to catch. The free safety looks for the seam to open between the end and the linebacker.

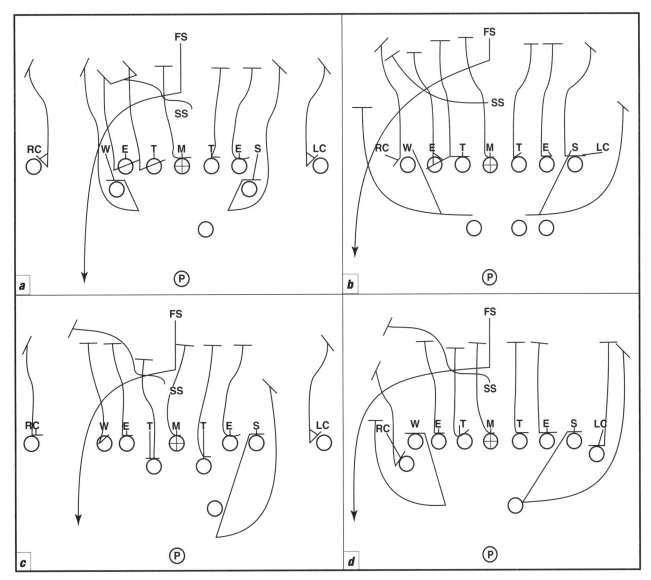

Figure 8.4 10 punt hold: *(a)* vs. Spread punt formation; *(b)* vs. Semispread punt formation; *(c)* vs. Spear punt formation; *(d)* vs. Tight punt formation.

9 Punt Hold

The left and right corners hold up the widest players as long as possible and make them release outside. The corners turn and run with their targets and continue to force them away from the play. The corners stay with their men throughout the play.

The Sam and Will linebackers hold up the second players from the outside (on or off the line of scrimmage) and make them release to the outside. They then go and force the punt. They turn back outside and work upfield, looking for the most dangerous threats to the return.

The ends hold up the third players from the outside as long as possible and make them release inside. Then they turn and run with their targets, continuing to force them inside and away from the return. The ends stay with their men for the duration of the return.

The tackles hold up the first player outside the center (on or off the line of scrimmage) and make him release inside. Then they turn and run with their men, continuing to force them inside and away from the return. The tackles stay with their men for the duration of the return.

The Mike linebacker holds up the center and stays with him all the way downfield.

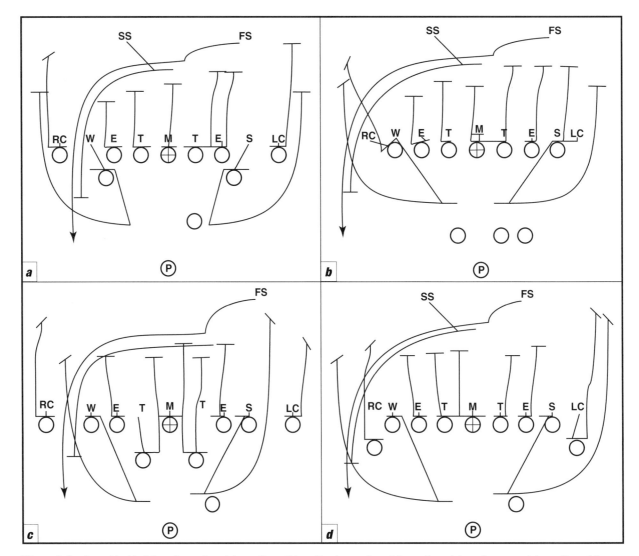

Figure 8.5 9 punt hold: *(a)* vs. Spread punt formation; *(b)* vs. Semispread punt formation; *(c)* vs. Spear punt formation; *(d)* vs. Tight punt formation.

Mike must not let the center get by. He can't make contact with the center until 1 second after the snap.

The strong safety gets in front of the free safety and leads him upfield, blocking the first immediate threat. He heads for the gap between the end and linebacker. The strong safety must be ready to catch the punt if the free safety calls for him to take it.

The punt is the free safety's to catch. The free safety follows the strong safety upfield, looking for the seam to open between the end and linebacker. If it's impossible for him

to get to the ball, the free safety calls for the strong safety to field the ball. In this case, the free safety leads the way for the return by the strong safety.

10 Wall

If the call is to his side, the right or left corner hits and forces his man to release to the outside. He sprints downfield and sets the wall. Everyone else sets the wall in relation to the corner. The corner aligns 5 to 7 yards upfield and 8 yards outside the returner but never

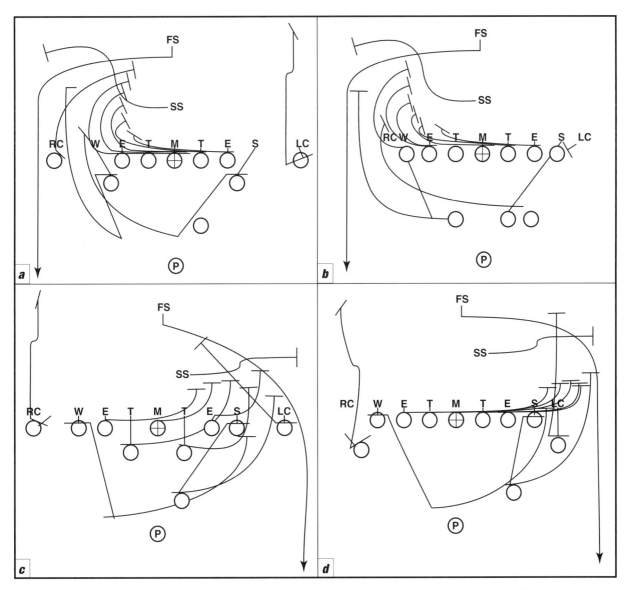

Figure 8.6 10 wall: *(a)* right vs. Spread punt formation; *(b)* right vs. Semispread punt formation; *(c)* left vs. Spear punt formation; *(d)* left vs. Tight punt formation.

inside the hash. If the call is away, the corner holds up the widest player as long as possible and makes him release outside. The corner turns and runs with his man, continuing to force him away from the play. The corner stays with him throughout the play.

If the call is to his side, the Sam or Will linebacker hits, penetrates, and makes the punter punt on schedule. He peels all the way downfield behind the wall, picking up anyone who is there. If the call is away, the linebacker hits into the second player from the outside (on or off the line of scrimmage) and makes him release to the outside. He penetrates and makes the punter punt on schedule. He peels back and becomes the last person on the wall.

The left and right ends, left and right tackles, and the Mike linebacker have the same responsibilities. Each one jams the man over him and then lets him escape. He flattens out and gets to the wall, setting himself 5 yards from his teammate. He blocks in front and above the waist. He lets the defender come to him. If his man is aligned off the line of scrimmage, the player hits and stays with him all the way, keeping himself between his man and the wall.

The strong safety sprints to where the wall will be set and blocks the first opponent who could prevent the returner from reaching the wall.

The punt is the free safety's to catch. He secures the catch, comes upfield slightly, and then sprints to the wall. He must be willing to give ground slightly to get behind the wall. If the ball is punted too far from the wall, the free safety takes it straight upfield.

9 Wall

If the call is to his side, the left or right corner hits and forces his man to release to the outside. He sprints downfield and sets the wall. Everyone else sets the wall in relation to the corner. The corner aligns 5 to 7 yards upfield and 8 yards outside the returner but never inside the hash. If the call is away, the corner holds up the widest player as long as possible and makes him release outside. He turns and runs with his man and continues to force him away from the play. He stays with his man throughout the play.

If the call is to his side, the Sam or Will linebacker hits, penetrates, and makes the punter punt on schedule. He peels all the way downfield behind the wall, picking up anyone who is there. If the call is away, the linebacker hits into the second player from the outside (on or off the line of scrimmage) and makes him release to the outside. He penetrates and makes the punter punt on schedule. He peels back and becomes the last person on the wall.

The left and right ends, left and right tackles, and the Mike linebacker have the same responsibilities. Each one jams the man over him and then lets him escape. He flattens out and gets to the wall, setting himself 5 yards from his teammate. He blocks in front and above the waist. He lets the defender come to him. If his man is aligned off the line of scrimmage, the player hits and stays with him all the way, keeping himself between his man and the wall.

The strong safety makes sure the catch is secured and leads the returner into the wall. He is ready to catch the punt if the free safety calls for him to take it.

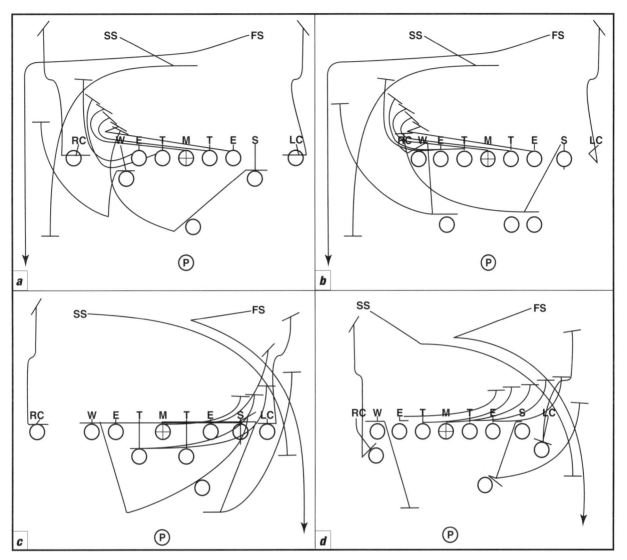

Figure 8.7 9 wall: *(a)* right vs. Spread punt formation; *(b)* right vs. Semispread punt formation; *(c)* left vs. Spear punt formation; *(d)* left vs. Tight punt formation.

The punt is the free safety's to catch. He secures the catch, comes upfield slightly, and then sprints to the wall, following the strong safety. He must be willing to give ground slightly to get behind the wall. If the ball is punted too far from the wall, the free safety takes it straight upfield. If it's impossible for him to catch the ball, the free safety calls for the strong safety to field the ball. In this case, the free safety leads the way for the strong safety's return.

10-Man Punt Blocks to Attack the B Gap

The illustrations in figure 8.8 show a way to attack the weak area of the punt formation, in this case the punting team's B gap.

If there are split receivers, the left and right corners go out on them and cover them man to man. If not, the corners align 1 yard outside the widest men and sprint to the ball.

If there's a wide receiver, the Sam and Will linebackers align 1 yard outside the widest tight men and sprint to the ball. If there's no wide receiver, they align on the widest tight men. The linebacker attacks the inside shoulder and pulls his man inside.

The ends align in an inside 4 technique and drive inside out into the second man past the ball.

If the call is to his side, the split tackle aligns in a 0 technique on the center. He draws the center's block as he attacks the callside A gap. If the call is away, the tight tackle aligns in a 2 technique on the first man past the ball away from the call. He drives across the first man's face to the outside, drawing his block.

The Mike linebacker stacks behind the defensive tackle in a 0 technique. He crashes through the A gap away from the call and goes to the ball.

The strong safety aligns off the line of scrimmage in the C gap. He slides inside as he times the snap. He attacks the B gap and goes to the ball.

The punt is the free safety's to catch. He secures the catch and comes straight upfield, getting as much as he can.

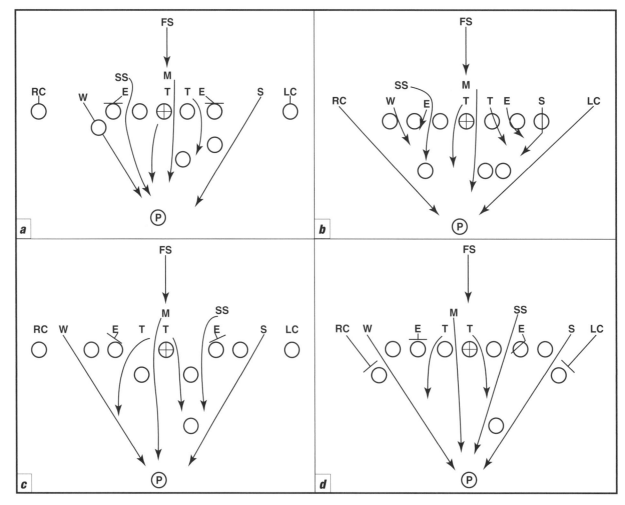

Figure 8.8 10-man punt blocks to attack the punting team's B gap: *(a)* right B; *(b)* right B; *(c)* left B; *(d)* left B.

If the block doesn't work and the ball is kicked, all players peel back and block. They must be sure to block in front and above the waist.

10-Man Punt Blocks to Attack the A Gap

The illustrations in figure 8.9 show a way to attack the weak area of the punt formation, in this case the punting team's A gap.

If there are split receivers, the left and right corners go out on them and cover them man to man. If not, the corners align 1 yard outside the widest men and sprint to the ball.

If there's a wide receiver, the Sam and Will linebackers align 1 yard outside the widest tight men and sprint to the ball. If there's no wide receiver, they align on the widest tight men. The linebacker attacks the inside shoulder and pulls his man inside.

The ends align in a 4 technique and drive hard into their men, occupying their blocks.

If the call is to his side, the tackle aligns in a 2 technique and drives hard to his outside, pulling his man outside. If the call is away, the tackle aligns in a 0 technique and drives hard away from the call, pulling his man to that side.

The Mike linebacker aligns slightly off the ball in the gap between the two defensive tackles. He gets in a three-point stance and drives straight through the gap, hard to the ball.

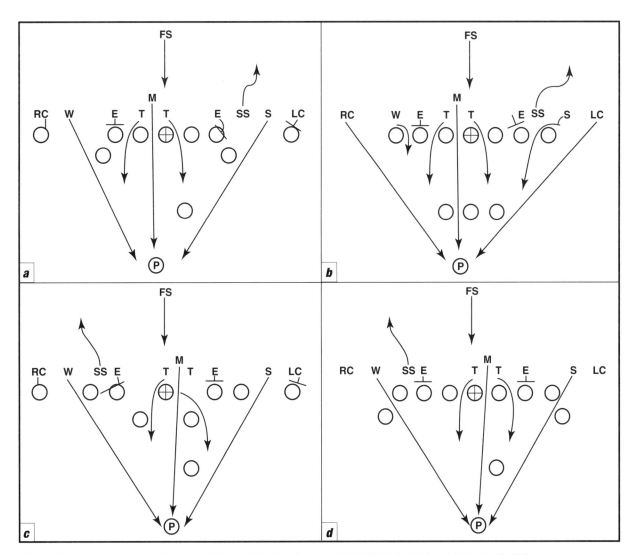

Figure 8.9 10-man punt blocks to attack the punting team's A gap: *(a)* right A; *(b)* right A; *(c)* left A; *(d)* left A.

The strong safety aligns on the line of scrimmage away from the call on the second man from the outside. On the snap, he drops outside into coverage, picking up the first tight receiver.

The punt is the free safety's to catch. He secures the catch and comes straight upfield, getting as much as he can.

If the block doesn't work and the ball is kicked, everyone peels back and blocks. Players must make block only in front and above the waist.

9-Man Punt Blocks

The left and right corners play the widest players man to man. If the corner's man is aligned tight and the call is to his side, the corner pulls him out. If the call is away, the corner keeps

his man on the line of scrimmage for as long as possible.

If the call is to his side, the Sam or Will linebacker stacks behind the widest tight player and rushes through the widest tight gap (C or D gap). If the call is away, the linebacker aligns on the second widest man to his side. He rushes outside, checking for the fake and keeping contain.

If the call is to his side, the end aligns on the second widest man and pulls him in (D call) or out (C call). If the call is away, the end aligns on the first man to the offside of the center. He pulls his man out and then plays for the fake.

If the call is to his side, the tackle aligns on the third widest man on the call side and pulls him in. If the call is away, the tackle aligns

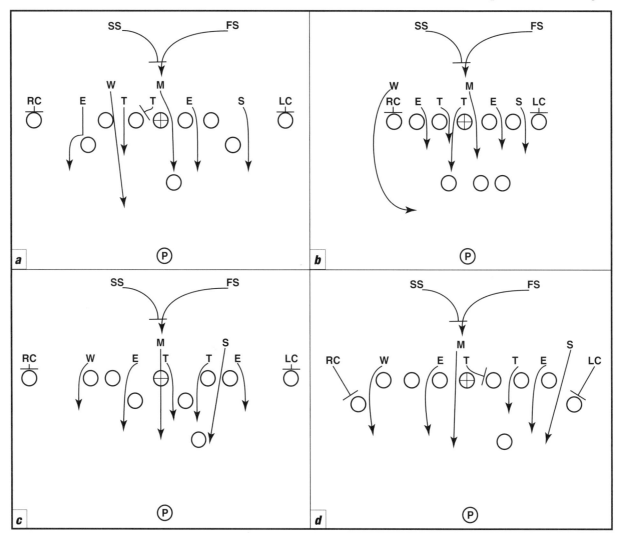

Figure 8.10 9-man punt blocks: *(a)* crash right C; *(b)* crash right D; *(c)* crash left C; *(d)* crash left D.

on the center and rushes callside, forcing the center to block him while he jams the first man from the center. If the punting team's formation is a three-man wedge off the line, the tackle goes through the center–guard gap and forces the middle man of the wedge to take him.

The Mike linebacker stacks behind the man covering the center and charges in the A gap away from the call.

The strong safety makes sure the catch is secured and leads the returner straight upfield. He must block and be ready to catch the punt if the free safety calls for him to take it.

The punt is the free safety's to catch. The free safety secures the catch and comes straight upfield, getting as much as he can. If it's impossible for him to get to the ball, he calls for the strong safety to take it. He then leads the way for the strong safety's return.

If the block doesn't work and the ball is kicked, everyone peels back and blocks. They must block in front and above the waist.

Punt Safe

The left and right corners line up head-on to the widest receivers on their sides and play them man to man. The Sam linebacker and strong safety line up on the second receivers from the outside and play them man to man.

The ends and tackles align as shown in figure 8.11. The strong end aligns head-up on the second lineman past the center. The strong tackle is head-up on the first lineman past the center.

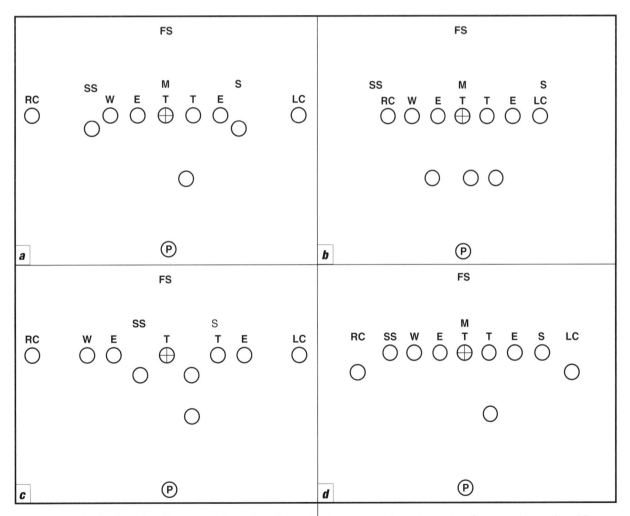

Figure 8.11 Punt safe: *(a)* vs. Spread punt formation; *(b)* vs. Semispread punt formation; *(c)* vs. Spear punt formation; *(d)* vs. Tight punt formation.

The weak-side tackle is head-up on the center, and the weak-side end is head-up on the first lineman past the center. They deliver into the men over them, hold them up, and find the ball.

The Mike linebacker stacks behind the 0 technique defensive tackle. He has the up-back man to man. The Will linebacker aligns on the line of scrimmage over the offensive left tackle. He has the punter man to man.

The punt is the free safety's to catch. He secures the catch and comes straight upfield, getting as much as he can. If the play is a fake, the free safety is free to play his instincts.

Go to punt safe when you are expecting a fake punt and are playing the fake all the way. When punt safe is called, the only substitution made from regular defensive personnel is the free safety, if he's not the regular punt returner.

Punt Coverage

You might want to use more than one punt formation. Also consider huddling before a punt instead of coming directly from the sideline to the line of scrimmage. From the huddle, sprint to the line and snap the ball quickly. This gives the defense very little time to recognize the play and employ an effective punt rush scheme.

Spread Punt

Use both man and zone blocking. Block man to man within a zone.

The gunners need speed and strength and must be good tacklers. They align outside the numbers. Their coverage key is the ball. They must not get held up. They have to get there and make the tackle.

Usually, defensive backs act as the wings. The wing splits the outside leg of the tackle. He stands in a staggered stance with his inside foot up, hands on thighs, and no weight on his back foot. On the snap, he kicks and slides— kicking with his back foot and sliding with his up foot—for two or three kick-slides. He keeps his thumbs to his nipples. He doesn't reach

for people. Instead he gets his back up and his hips down, keeping his butt vertical. He must not widen as he gets vertical. He always works inside out and lets the opponent come to him. He lets a twist stunt unfold before it gets to him. He has the 1 rusher from the outside. His coverage is halfway between the hash and the boundary.

The tackles are fast linebackers. The tackle splits 12 inches from the guard. He uses a staggered stance with the inside foot up, hands on thighs, no weight on his back foot. Like the wing, the tackle kicks and slides for two or three steps. Thumbs to nipples, he doesn't reach for people. Instead he gets his back up and hips down, keeping his butt vertical. He must not widen as he gets vertical. He always works inside out and lets the opponent come to him. He lets a twist stunt unfold before it gets to him. He has the number 2 rusher from the outside. His coverage is 2 yards outside the hash.

The guards are inside linebackers and tight ends, players who are bigger than the tackles and can run. The guard splits 6 inches from the center. He uses a staggered stance with his inside foot up, hands on thighs, and no weight on his back foot. Like the wing, the guard kicks and slides for two or three steps. Thumbs to

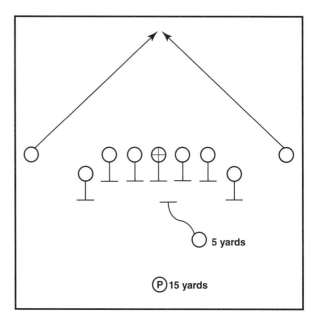

Figure 8.12 Spread punt.

nipples, he doesn't reach for people. Instead he gets his back up and hips down, keeping his butt vertical. He must not widen as he gets vertical. He always works inside out and lets the opponent come to him. He lets a twist stunt unfold before it gets to him. He has the 3 rusher from the outside. His coverage is 4 yards inside the hash.

The center must be an athlete who can protect and then run and cover. The center secures the snap and then kicks and slides for two or three kick-slides. Thumbs to nipples, he doesn't reach for people. He gets his back up and hips down, keeping his butt vertical. He must not widen as he gets vertical. He always works inside out and lets the opponent come to him. With his right hand, he holds up the 4 rusher from the right. When he reaches the vertical apex, he turns out on the 4 rusher to the left and blocks him to the outside. He lets a twist stunt unfold before it gets to him. His coverage is the ball.

The protector is the field general. He must be a good athlete and have the toughness to be a good blocker. Finding the right protector is a high priority. He aligns 5 yards behind the right guard. He must not back up. He has the 4 rusher from the right. His coverage is the middle of the goalpost.

The punter's coverage is head-up to the ball. He is the safety.

Spear Punt

The spear man must be an outstanding tackler and possess excellent speed. He must be a real head hunter. He needs to be a good blocker because he'll undoubtedly be covered and must, through his blocking, give the punter time to kick.

For the spear punt, there are 3 feet between the center and the guards, and 2-1/2 feet between the guards and tackles and between tackles and ends.

The blocking rules for the linemen are outside, on, inside, free. The order of counting off is from the outside in. For example, Y calls the number of the man on the outside he'll block. The right tackle then calls the number of the next man inside whom he can reach, followed by the right guard and the spear man.

Z and T are the spear men. They go right to the ball and make the ballcarrier commit. If two men are in Z's or T's area, they make a call ("Ringo" for Z and "Lucky" for T). This tells the end on that side that he is now the spear man. The end and tackle on the side of the call must decide between them which one will be the spear man based on the rush alignment in front of them. If the end has two men or a wide rusher and the tackle has no one on him, a "you-me" call determines the spear man. If after a Ringo or Lucky call, both the end and tackle have men to block, the end remains the spear man. A change can even be made on the run. If the tackle's man to block is over the end and, as the play begins, it's obvious he's not rushing but wants to hold up the end from coverage, the tackle can make a "me" call and become the spear man, going for the ball.

On the line, each blocker's inside foot is frozen in place. The lineman takes a short jab step back, then steps up and out into the rusher and jams him outside. A lineman who has a man on him and a man outside to block cannot jab. He must step directly out to get the outside man and give up his body to block the man over him.

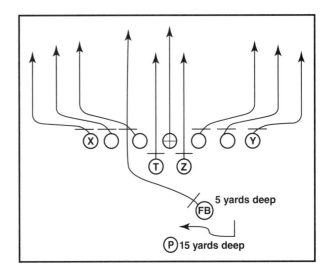

Figure 8.13 Spear punt.

Z and T begin in a two-point stance and jam a man in their areas. If there are two men in his area, Z or T makes the Ringo or Lucky call and then steps directly out to get the widest man while using his body and inside leg to block the inside man.

The fullback protects the kicker's foot. He blocks the first man who shows, checking from the inside out. He's alert for any overload before the ball is snapped. He stands his ground and cannot back up or be pushed back.

In coverage, X and Y go halfway between the hash and sideline and upfield for contain. If the ballcarrier runs away, X or Y cuts underneath the coverage, taking a pursuit course and watching for the cutback. The player who gets the Ringo or Lucky call to his side is the spear man and goes directly to the ball. If this player and the tackle decide the tackle should be the spear man, the player retains his original contain course halfway between the hash and the sideline.

The tackles take a course 2 yards outside the hash marks. If the ballcarrier runs away, the tackle closes off the field, checking for the reverse. He becomes contain and cannot let the ballcarrier outside him. If the tackle gets the Ringo or Lucky call to his side, the end on the same side becomes the spear man, and the tackle takes a course halfway between the hash and the sideline, serving as the contain man. If after a Ringo or Lucky call, the tackle and the end decide that the end must stay and block, the "you-me" call makes the tackle the spear man, and he goes directly to the ball. The guards cover 3 yards inside the hash marks.

Z and T are the spear men and go directly to the ball. If one has two men in his area and must make a Ringo or Lucky call, after blocking he takes a course 2 yards outside the hash marks. If the ballcarrier runs away, he closes off the field, checking for the reverse. He is now the contain man and must never let the ball outside him.

The center splits the goal posts. After the ball has been kicked, the fullback keeps lever-

age on the ball by staying head-up on the ball. The punter is the safety. He looks for the wall up a sideline, gets outside the wall, and keeps leverage on the ball.

Punt From Shotgun

A punt from the shotgun can be effectively employed, especially from midfield to the opponent's 30. The quarterback/punter pooch punts, rugby punts, or punts out of bounds.

The punter should practice situation punts instead of spending all his practice punting straight and deep. He should work on pooch punts that give the punt coverage more time to effectively cover or to force a fair catch. He should also practice directional punts that place the ball between the hash and boundary on either side away from the returner and negatively affect the timing of the return. Other situation punts call for punting out of bounds, getting added height if punting with the wind, and hitting line-drive punts into the wind. When punting out of bounds, the punter aims for the 8-yard line, not the 1-yard line. This gives him a margin for error in either direction. When done correctly, this ensures the punt goes out of bounds inside the 20.

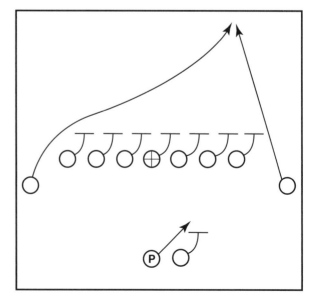

Figure 8.14 Wolf 1-9 shotgun punt.

Extra Point or Field Goal

For an extra point or field goal, linemen use no more than a 6-inch split. On the snap, the lineman takes a jab step with his inside foot and seals the inside gap. His jab step goes in front of and past the outside foot of his blocker to his inside. The lineman's coverage is straight downfield. He keeps his outside foot stationary.

The wings align 1 yard deep with their inside legs on the outside legs of the ends. The wing blocks the first man who shows outside the end's block. He keeps his outside foot stationary. On coverage, the wing has contain.

The holder aligns so the ball will be placed at 7 yards. He counts all players to ensure there are 11 and that they are properly aligned. He checks with the center to see that he's ready, and then checks with the kicker to see that he's ready. When the kicker is ready, the holder calls "ready!" His call tells all players to freeze. The holder presents his hands to the center, and the center snaps the ball when he's ready.

The kicker helps the holder find the right spot. The kicker aligns his steps and lets the holder know he's ready by nodding his head.

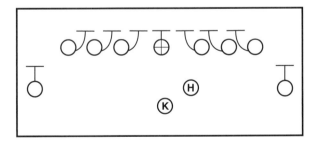

Figure 8.15 Alignment for extra point or field goal.

Field Goal Block

For each rush stunt, to employ the same rush to the other side, flip all personnel. This way, each position does the same thing whether rushing from the left or the right.

Left D

No defensive player may initiate contact with the center for 1 second after the snap. The strong safety aligns at an angle that gives him the best direct line to the block. The Sam linebacker rushes over the wing's outside shoulder, pulling the wing to the outside with him. The wing is his man on a pass. The Mike linebacker aligns on the tight end. He hits the tight end and pulls him inside down the line of scrimmage. The tight end is his man on a pass. The left corner aligns over the offensive tackle and then drops, playing free zone behind the block side. The right corner plays man to man on the wing away from the rush.

The tight-side end and split-side tackle are in 2 alignment. They block the offensive guards back into the backfield as hard and far as possible.

The tight-side tackle is in 0 alignment. He shoots the gap that he and the free safety designated ahead of time, helping the end or tackle drive the guard as far back into the backfield as possible.

The Will linebacker aligns over the tight end away from the rush. Will jams the tight end, checking for a fake run and playing man on the tight end on a pass. The split end aligns over the wing. The split end steps up to the wing and hits him and then checks for anyone swinging from the backfield.

The free safety jumps around to disguise his course. He plans a course from the ball to the middle of the goal post. He rushes behind the tight tackle's double team with the end

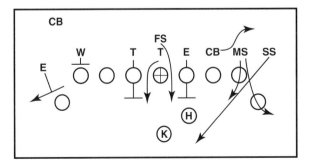

Figure 8.16 Left D field goal block.

or tackle. The free safety gets as deep into the backfield as he can. He extends his arms and jumps as high as possible.

Left C

The strong safety rushes and occupies the wing, taking the wing man to man. The Sam linebacker rushes flat through the outside hip of the tight end. The Mike linebacker aligns on the tight end. Mike hits the tight end and pulls him inside down the line of scrimmage. The tight end is his man on a pass. The Will linebacker aligns over the tight end away from the rush. Will jams the tight end, checking for a fake run and playing man to man on the tight end on a pass.

The left corner aligns over the offensive tackle and then drops, playing free zone behind the block side. The right corner plays man to man on the wing away from the rush.

The tight-side end and split-side tackle are in 2 alignment. They block the offensive guards back into the backfield as hard and far as possible.

The tight-side tackle is in 0 alignment. He shoots the gap that he and the free safety designated ahead of time, helping the end or tackle drive the guard as far back into the backfield as possible.

The split end aligns over the wing. He steps up and hits the wing and then checks for anyone swinging from the backfield.

The free safety jumps around to disguise his course. He plans a course from the ball to the middle of the goal post. He rushes behind the tight tackle's double team with the end or tackle. He gets as deep into the backfield as he can. He extends his arms and jumps as high as possible.

Left B

The strong safety rushes over the wing's outside shoulder, pulling the wing to the outside with him. The wing is his man on a pass. The Sam linebacker aligns on the tight end. Sam hits the tight end and keeps him on the line of scrimmage. The tight end is his man on a pass. The Mike linebacker aligns on the offensive tackle and pulls him outside. Mike must be ready to rush if the offensive tackle blocks down on the left corner. The Will linebacker aligns over the tight end away from the rush. Will jams the tight end, checking for a fake run and playing man to man on the tight end on a pass.

The left corner aligns in the offensive tackle–offensive guard gap and rushes that gap. The right corner plays man to man on the wing away from the rush.

The tight-side end is in 2 alignment over the offensive guard and pulls him hard inside. The tackles align over the center and left guard. The tackles double-team the left guard, driving him deep into the backfield.

The split end aligns over the wing. The split end steps up and hits the wing and then checks for anyone swinging from the backfield.

The free safety jumps around to disguise his course. He rushes the A gap behind the double team. The free safety gets as deep into the backfield as he can and then extends his arms and jumps as high as possible.

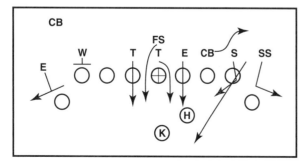

Figure 8.17 Left C field goal block.

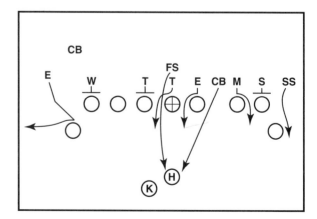

Figure 8.18 Left B field goal block.

Left A

The strong safety rushes over the wing's outside shoulder, pulling the wing to the outside with him. The wing is his man on a pass. The Sam linebacker aligns on the tight end. Sam hits the tight end and keeps him on the line of scrimmage. The tight end is his man on a pass. The Mike linebacker aligns on the tackle and pulls him outside. He must be ready to rush if the tackle blocks down on the left corner. The Will linebacker aligns over the tight end away from the rush. Will jams the tight end, checking for a fake run and playing man to man on the tight end on a pass.

The left corner aligns on the offensive guard in a 3 technique and pulls the guard outside. The corner must be ready to rush if the guard blocks down on the tight-side end. The right corner plays man to man on the wing away from the rush.

The tight-side end is in an inside 2 alignment over the offensive guard and rushes the A gap. The tackles align over the center and left guard. They double-team the left guard, driving him deep into the backfield.

The split end aligns over the wing. He steps up and hits the wing and then checks for anyone swinging from the backfield.

The free safety jumps around to disguise his course. He rushes the A gap behind the double team. He gets as deep into the backfield as he can and then extends his arms and jumps as high as possible.

Fake Field Goal Defense

This defense is called when the position of the ball and game circumstances make it unlikely that the kicking team will truly kick. The defense plays the fake all the way, without rushing.

The ends are in 4 alignment, playing 5 technique. When the ball is in the center of the field, the tackles are in 2 alignment, playing 2 gap responsibility. If the ball is within 6 yards of the hash, the tackle to the sideline slides to a 0 technique. The Sam linebacker and strong safety align over the tight ends. They jam the tight ends hard and play them man to man. The Mike and Will linebackers are in 3 alignment. If the ball is within 6 yards of the hash, they slide toward the wide side. They play man to man against the men in the backfield without the ball (the holder or kicker). The left and right corners align over the wings, playing them man to man. The free safety plays free, favoring the wide side of the field.

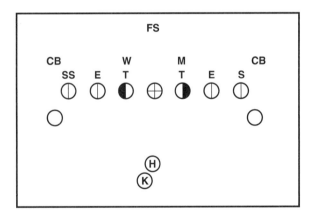

Figure 8.20 Fake field goal defense.

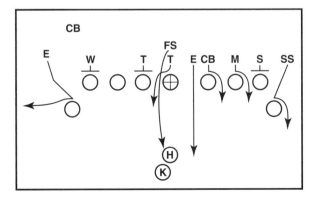

Figure 8.19 Left A field goal block.

9

Practices

Planning practices is a difficult and time-consuming task. Each practice must fulfill many objectives. As early as possible, players must attain a high level of cardiovascular fitness, so this is a focus throughout but particularly in the opening weeks of practice. Each practice should have a theme, something coherent that ties the workouts together. In each practice, coaches must challenge their players, reviewing what has already been taught as well as adding new material to work on. Ideally, practices will include nearly equal time for offense, defense, and special teams. Players in their practice sessions progress through individual, group, and team drills, all working toward the same goal. Boring routines must be avoided. In early practices, players should be ready for full-go contact, but drills that increase injury risk should be avoided until later in the practice season. Never waste practice time with filler. Practice time is precious. Make the most of every minute.

Practices are a race against time and must always be as efficient as possible. Avoid long lines of players waiting to perform a drill. If you are a coach, do not overlook teaching moments, but learn to coach on the run. Keep your comments brief, and provide feedback as the drills continue. Save longer comments for after practice.

All coaches should participate in the planning of every practice. Coaches know better than anyone what their players need to become game ready. The head coach should write down everything to ensure all coaches are on the same page and that practices progress in the most efficient and logical way.

In our program, prior to the start of practice, we have 30 minutes of individual specialty consisting of long snaps, punting, punt receiving, kickoff and kick receiving, extra point/field goal kicking with a snapper and holder, and passers working with receivers. Quarterbacks begin by executing all fundamental drills, from gripping the ball to passing from one knee; standing with feet parallel and then stepping in the direction of the pass with opposite foot forward; and taking drops and employing play-action footwork.

After individual specialty time, we begin practice with 15 minutes of jogging, stretching, and form running. We then proceed to individual position drills, followed by group work, and then team drills. In the final 5 minutes of every practice, we run our fourth quarter drill, which is at least a little different every day. During this 5-minute period, players give everything they have left. The result is a squad that is ready to give a total effort in the final minutes of games. In our fourth quarter drills, players are always executing football skills, not merely running for conditioning. Groups are typically 20 yards apart. Players shuffle and pivot, carioca, sprint backward, bear walk, sprint with a forward roll in the middle of the drill, and so on. Sometimes the drill is a competitive group relay. In any case, you want to really work them hard. You want to leave them totally exhausted.

Players finish practice excited as they compete among themselves with no thought of who is the star of the team, who is a starter, or who is a scout teamer. Players have had fun while improving their conditioning.

Position-Specific Work

Individual drills for each position are done at every practice, although players don't work on all these skills in every practice. Coaches determine which skills should be worked on based on the players' strengths and weaknesses, performances in the last game, and the upcoming opponent.

Wide Receiver

Wide receivers practice basics, such as the two-point stance (arms flexed and inside foot back) and start (accelerate full speed out of stance and into pattern). Repeatedly drill formation recognition. Call a formation and then have players get in proper alignment. Drills must become automatic, with each player immediately assuming his correct position. Work on this early in the season. Simply call a formation without calling and running a play.

Tight, flex, and close splits are drilled. When drilling on proper splits, stress under which conditions to use maximum and minimum splits, when a certain split will help fulfill the receiver's role for the called play, and how the receiver can influence the defender when the width of the split has no effect on the play. Put receivers in the best possible alignment to do the job required on the specific play. Teach receivers that if their splits have no effect on the outcome of the play called, they need to vary their splits to confuse defenders about what type of play has been called and where the attack might be going.

If motion is going to be in a play call, it becomes part of the call. Have a premotion call and a call for the formation at the snap of the ball. When in motion, receivers move under control but rapidly. This requires a good deal of practice because for the timing of the play to be correct all players must motion at the same speed. Make sure motion does not begin until all 11 players are motionless for one full second. When motion is called, the player going in motion is expected at a specific spot at the snap of the ball. This requires practice and coordination between the motion man and the quarterback.

Teach releases including head and shoulders, fake, rip, and swim (see chapter 4). The approach, move, misdirection, and burst—parts of running a pattern—are integral in the receiver's ability to get open and receive the pass. As each pattern is taught, emphasize each part of the pattern instead of simply telling the receiver, for instance, to "run an out at 10 yards."

When practicing catching and securing the ball, stress complete concentration on the ball. After catching the ball and securing it, the receiver starts moving upfield. It's never enough to only complete the pass. Stress attaining additional yardage either by breaking the tackle or making the tackler miss. The receiver catches the ball and immediately heads north and south to get the most additional yardage possible.

It's easy to get receivers to practice catching the ball. What takes more work is getting them excited about blocking. Remind them that they can be the difference between a 5-yard play and a touchdown. He can spring the ballcarrier with his block, opening the field for him. In both individual and team drills, emphasize to the receiver the importance of positioning himself between the ballcarrier and the opponent, breaking down, stalking him, and keeping his hands on the opponent's breast plate. The opponent will reveal where the ballcarrier is by trying to get to him. The receiver doesn't need eyes in the back of his head; he simply reacts to the opponent's movement and continually shifts his body to stay between the opponent and the ball. Receivers tend to get too many holding penalties, so have them work every day on keeping their hands in the framework of the body, thumbs pointing toward each other so the elbows are in, providing the greatest extension strength possible.

Running Back

Running backs drill both the two-point and three-point stances. Running backs are evaluated on their stances on every snap of every play because every offensive play starts with assuming the correct stance.

Effective faking is essential to a successful offensive attack. It's vital to make defenses believe that something other than the called play is going to take place. Run a drill in which only the quarterback knows what's going to happen when the ball is snapped. Include companion plays in your offense, such as a running play and a play-action pass that fakes the running play or two running plays that go together in which either running back could end up with the ball. The coach calls two plays that are companion plays, and the quarterback runs one of the two plays. The running backs do not know whether they will get the ball. This shifts the focus of a drill to making great fakes because the backs must be prepared to end up with the ball.

Running backs practice receiving handoffs and protecting the ball. Two lines of ballcarriers face each other. They run toward each other, and one player hands off to the player running toward him. The player with the ball places the ball into the belly of the player approaching him. The player receiving the ball has his near elbow up and thumb straight down and the far elbow 6 inches from his chest. This provides an adequate target or pocket for receiving the ball, and the position of the far arm prevents the ball from sliding through. As the player receiving the handoff feels the pressure of the ball against him, he clamps his arms over the ball to protect it. This puts the near arm over the top of the ball with that hand over the far point of the ball, and the far arm under the ball securing the near point of the ball. He should always keep both hands on the ball when going through traffic.

While running at full speed with the ball in hand, the ballcarrier practices getting too much weight forward to the point at which he loses his balance. He uses his hand to pop himself back up and attempts to regain his balance.

Running backs practice running with power, running with a forward lean, with shoulders out over their feet. These backs work hard year-round at developing leg strength and stamina. In practice, they might run with a parachute or pull a sled with a shoulder harness to build strength.

Running backs need to practice shedding tacklers. Stress to them to continue to chop their feet, never stopping their feet from moving. They should practice using a stiff arm and delivering a shoulder and forearm into the defensive man as he spins out.

Run blocking is part of individual drills for running backs. Players work on various run blocks, including isolation blocks, kickout blocks, or lead blocks on a linebacker.

Pass protection is rehearsed every day, either during individual drills (the back blocks a pass rusher), group drills (7 on 7 and 2-minute), or team drills. The running back must be an effective and consistent pass blocker. Essentially, he uses the same technique as a lineman, which is to establish the inside foot as the post foot and deny the rusher the inside lane to the passer.

Running backs practice patterns the same way wide receivers do, except the running back's patterns originate from the backfield, so no one is pressing him. Running backs also work on catching and securing the ball and gaining yards after the catch—same as for wide receivers.

Tight End

The tight end uses a three-point stance similar to an interior lineman's when tight, and a two-point stance with his inside foot back, similar to a wide receiver's, if he is flexed. Evaluate his stance on every play. On the snap, the tight end may step back to be in position for pass protection, may explode off the line of scrimmage to establish a key block, or may proceed into a pass route. All parts of the pass pattern—release, approach, move, misdirection, and burst—are the same as for wide receivers.

The terms "tight" and "flex" describe the split of the tight end. Teach tight ends to widen to the extent they can while still controlling the inside gap.

Tight ends practice receiving and protecting the ball. Many of a tight end's routes are underneath or down the middle, making him vulnerable to being hit hard at the same time he receives the ball. So he must concentrate fully on looking the ball in and securing it. Run distraction drills, in which the tight ends learn to focus entirely on the pass coming to him. To improve balance, stress footwork drills such as running the ropes, jump rope, and dot drills.

Like wide receivers, tight ends should practice gaining yards after the catch. The tight end must run with power, anticipate contact, and attack the tackler. Because many of his patterns are underneath cuts in which he's covered by a linebacker, he can help himself by faking. Misdirection is just as important for a tight end running a pattern as it is for a wide receiver. Tight ends must learn that though most of the time they should turn the closest direction and head upfield with the ball, it's

sometimes to their advantage to dip the inside shoulder and go the opposite way.

For run blocking, the tight end will sometimes block one on one and sometimes will slip block with the offensive tackle. He'll spend a great deal of practice time on blocking, getting this in all aspects of practice, including individual, group, and team drills.

In most passing situations, tight ends run patterns. However, maximum protection is sometimes needed, so tight ends stay in and block. In these cases, the tight end keeps his inside foot up, and this foot becomes his post foot.

Offensive Lineman

The center uses a balanced stance. Linemen on the right side use a right-handed stance, and those on the left use a left-handed stance. Evaluation of the stance should be ongoing. Offensive linemen use a variety of starts, from stepping back to pocket pass protection, to exploding straight ahead, to pulling, to getting in position to slip block.

In horizontal splits, teach linemen to take as wide a split as they can control. Linemen should experiment with splits when the play is going away from them and their split is immaterial to the success of the play.

If defenses are stunting, have linemen take maximum vertical splits so they have time to read the stunt and react to it. If the offense is going north and south with power plays, they should crowd the line of scrimmage to get contact quickly.

Drill daily on run-blocking technique for each play against the anticipated defensive looks. Practice each technique (drive block, trap, counter, sweep, crossfield blocking, slip) in a walk-through, ending with full-speed, full-hit one-on-one or two-on-two situations. Then put it all together against stand-up dummies or live in nine-on-seven or team drills.

Whether it is dropback, play action, screen, or cut blocking for a three-step drop, pass protection can be taught in a one-on-one drill versus the pass rush or in seven-on-seven and team drills. Include the draw as part of drop-back passing. Time each block and stress that linemen must give the quarterback 3 to 3-1/2 seconds to get the ball off.

Quarterback

The quarterback is the leader of the huddle and must practice his huddle procedure. He looks his teammates in the eyes and calls the play with complete confidence in his voice.

Evaluate the quarterback's stance on every play in every practice. He should bend his knees and hips and keep his back straight. Stress that his cadence must be loud and with authority. If the play calls for motion, the quarterback must time his cadence exactly with the motion. To initiate motion, he lifts his heel only after everyone is motionless for one full second.

The quarterback and center constantly practice their exchange. The quarterback places his hands well up under the center's butt and rides his hands and arms forward as the ball is snapped. The quarterback knows the center will explode straight ahead as he snaps the ball. The quarterback brings the ball into his belly and then begins the play. Every snap must be secure, which takes a lot of practice.

The quarterback emphasizes sprinting to his drop, whether it's a three-step, five-step, or seven-step drop. The quicker he gets to his drop, the more time he has to read the coverage, make the correct decision, and deliver the ball.

The quarterback should practice look-offs every day. Run drills in which he must see the receiver with his peripheral vision while his eyes are aimed at a different area.

The quarterback practices using the pocket. This can be done simply with a coach rushing and forcing the quarterback to step up into the pocket. However, the quarterback can get the true feel for this only by having the offensive line block a real rush, as occurs in team drills or nine-on-seven drills.

Passing fundamentals are practiced every day. The quarterback focuses on the mechanics of passing. In the stance preceding the release of the pass, he stresses keeping his toes pointed east and west, moving his feet, and stepping in the direction of the release. During the delivery, he stresses holding the ball high throughout, leading with his elbow, and bringing his hips forward in his follow-through.

Coverage reads can be taught in the classroom as well as on the practice field. This starts with the drawing of various coverages, progresses to video analysis of practices and games (your team's and your opponent's), and finally moves onto the practice field. Show your quarterback what could be the difference between a presnap read and a postsnap read. Explain each defender's responsibilities in pure zone, pure man, man-under two deep, man-free safety, press, trail, and squat.

Blitz reads also start in the classroom, proceed to video analysis, and then move to the practice field. Teach your quarterback who the hot read is, who the hot receiver is, and where he will be given the blitz. Make sure he understands the offensive blocking scheme and knows when the blitz will be blocked and when he'll come free.

The quarterback is responsible for the handoff. It's his job to press the ball into the running back's pouch. It's the running back's responsibility to form the correct pocket, but his eyes must be on the point of attack, not the ball. Emphasize that unless the quarterback is 100 percent sure of a secure exchange, he must keep the ball and follow the running back into the hole.

An effective quarterback is skilled at faking and takes great pride in this part of his game. He practices until his fake looks exactly like a true exchange.

In individual drills, a coach rushes to simulate a defender coming free and forcing the quarterback to abort the pocket and scramble. Let him know the receivers' responsibilities when a scramble occurs. Proceed to group and team drills in which the quarterback is forced to scramble and the receivers must read the scramble and react.

Defensive Back

The defensive back uses a two-point stance with a slight bend at the hips and knees. The defensive back must know not only his base alignment but also how that alignment will change when the offensive formation changes. As with alignment, the defensive back learns how his depth varies depending on the coverage called and the offensive formation he sees. Deep-coverage depth will vary from 8 to 12 yards. For underneath zone or underneath man coverage, depth is 4 to 5 yards.

Defensive backs are trained to think pass until the play proves to be a run. Thus, they step back and out on the snap of the ball. Defensive backs drill daily on backpedaling with their eyes on the quarterback. They learn to change direction instantly to get to the ball or plant and sprint back toward the line of scrimmage when they determine that the play is a run.

In man coverage, the defensive back aligns on his man's outside shoulder and plays his receiver and the ball. He plays his receiver aggressively, keeping outside leverage and maintaining a cushion. The defensive back makes contact with his receiver with his hands until the ball is in the air. When the ball is in the air, the defensive back plays the ball.

In zone coverage, the defensive back stays deeper than the deepest man in his zone. When a receiver enters his zone, the defensive back aggressively plays the receiver man to man as long as the receiver is in his zone. The defensive back communicates constantly with his teammate in the adjacent zone to let him know when the receiver is leaving his zone and entering the teammate's.

The defensive back plays the man until the ball is in the air, and then he plays the ball. Once the ball is released, only the ball, not the man, can hurt the defense. The defensive

back plays the ball all the way and aggressively attacks the ball. He doesn't wait for the ball to get to him.

To prevent the completion, the defensive back aggressively competes for the ball. If the receiver is closer to the ball, the defensive back plays through the receiver, jarring the ball loose.

For the interception, the defensive back is ready to go vertical and catch the ball at its highest point. He never goes underneath the receiver unless he's absolutely sure he can get to the ball. He's always ready to react to a tipped ball. The defensive back looks the ball in, catches it, and puts it away.

A defensive back must make the sure tackle. It need not be a pretty tackle—just a sure tackle. The defensive back knows he's the last line of defense.

The defensive back practices pursuit. When the ball goes away from him, he knows there's a definite pattern to get to the ball. He takes the path that puts him where the ballcarrier will be. Football is a team game, and the success of limiting the ballcarrier's run depends on each defender taking a prescribed course to get to the ball.

Success in forcing fumbles results from practicing several techniques to separate the ballcarrier from the ball. Depending on whether the tackler is coming toward the ballcarrier, attacking him from the side, or overtaking him from the rear, the technique could be driving the head into the ball, reaching in and pulling the ball out, raking the ball out with an overhand motion, or bringing the fist up into the ball and punching it out. Defensive backs drill for all of these.

Linebacker

Linebackers use a two-point stance with feet parallel. In some alignments, outside linebackers keep their inside foot slightly back. The weight is on the balls of the feet. The linebacker's alignment depends on the defense called.

An inside linebacker's depth is usually 4 to 5 yards. In some calls, outside linebackers are on the line of scrimmage, but in other alignments they are 2 to 5 yards deep.

Keys, responsibilities, and execution are taught by the particular technique that each linebacker finds himself in based on the called defense. In all techniques he must play run until the play is proven to be a pass. Thus his first step is forward toward the line of scrimmage. Playing linebacker requires great discipline—he must read his keys and react accordingly.

Each technique carries with it the keys and execution for that alignment. How to shed the block varies depending on the linebacker's alignment and area of responsibility. Everything comes down to teaching the linebacker to play the technique for the called defense.

For man coverage, the linebacker must get in the receiver's hip pocket and play him aggressively—he will be getting help from on top when the route goes deep. In zone coverage, there must be good communication with those covering zones on either side about when a receiver is entering one zone and leaving another.

Whether playing man under or zone, the linebacker plays the man until the ball is released. If his man goes deep, he turns and runs with him, even in zone coverage, as long as no one else is entering the vacated zone. Once the pass is thrown, the linebacker plays the ball all the way and gets a hand on it. If he can't get a hand on the ball, he times his hit to make contact at the exact time the ball arrives. Linebackers practice the tip drill repeatedly for proper reaction to tipped passes.

Just as blocking is the lifeblood of offense, tackling is the lifeblood of defense. Teach the correct form for both face-to-face tackles and side tackles. Tackling must be taught, retaught, and taught again; take nothing for granted. Tackling, in some form, must be practiced every day.

As he takes his pursuit course, the linebacker establishes and maintains leverage on the ball-carrier. The farther he is from the ballcarrier, the deeper his pursuit course will be.

Linebackers are the most aggressive players on defense. They enthusiastically receive instruction on how to strip the ball while making the tackle. They understand that if they can cause a fumble while making a tackle, that's great—but the most important thing is to consistently make the tackle.

Defensive Lineman

The defensive lineman uses a three-point stance with feet slightly staggered and no wider than shoulder-width apart. He uses his fingertips rather than his knuckles. His feet are extended back, putting much of his weight on his fingertips. His free hand is shoulder high, ready to jam the offensive lineman. The defensive lineman's alignment varies from head-up to shading the inside or outside of the offensive lineman. His depth varies from crowding the line of scrimmage to 18 inches deep, depending on the alignment called.

For every alignment, there are keys, responsibilities, and executions to learn. This is basic to playing any defensive line position.

To shed the block, the defensive lineman must get his pads under the blocker's pads. He must hit up with the outside forehand, bringing it clear up and locking the elbow. If he doesn't bring the forehand clear up, the blocker will get to his body.

For check draw, screen, counter, and reverse, defensive linemen, rather than flying to where they think the ball has gone, must be taught to read their keys and fulfill their responsibilities.

To knock down the pass when rushing the passer, the hands and arms are extended up to obstruct the quarterback's vision and ultimately knock down the thrown ball.

Most of the defensive lineman's tackles are not open-field tackles. They are usually in confined areas. The main emphasis is stopping the ballcarrier's momentum and driving the pile back away from the line of scrimmage.

The defensive lineman must close off each gap down the line of scrimmage as he moves along his pursuit course.

As one lineman applies the first hit, the next lineman rips the ball out of the ballcarrier's grip.

Group Work

Group work includes drills such as three-on-two, five-on-three, backfield running play drills, option read drills, option responsibility drills, and pass play drills such as one on one, two on two, and two on one. Move to more complex group drills including a seven-on-seven passing game versus linebackers and secondary and nine-on-seven running game drills including the defensive line and linebackers versus the offensive line and backs.

Team Drills

Team drills include pursuit course, running game, passing game, red-zone offense versus red-zone defense, goal-line offense versus goal-line defense, coming out (-1 yard line to -20) situation, two-minute work, and, finally, team scrimmaging.

Break up the kicking game in the same way, beginning with individual drills, moving to group work, and ending with team drills.

For all group and team drills, every play and defense is scripted. This guarantees you will see each play a set number of times from the formations you want to use in the upcoming game and against the defenses and coverages you expect to face. On defense, you ensure seeing each front, stunt, and coverage against the formations you will face, with and without motion. Use script forms for each of the following drills: nine on seven, seven on seven, goal line, team, and occasionally two-minute. Instead of lamenting that you forgot to practice a certain play or defense or that you didn't practice a play against a certain defensive alignment or a stunt against a par-

ticular formation, plan exactly what you want to practice.

Clock management is one of the biggest weaknesses I see in football at all levels. I shudder when I see a quarterback spike the ball and be asked to do in three downs what he has had trouble doing the entire game in four downs. If you have an automatic formation to use in this situation and a list of three or four plays that your team has practiced all week for the quarterback to choose from and call to the team, there should be no need to spike the ball. I also see losing coaches take unused time-outs into the locker room, and far too many blocking in-the-back penalties on punt returns. To make sure you don't fall prey to these problems, practice every conceivable clock-management situation daily and establish guidelines on when to use time-outs. You should spend one third of practice time on some phase of the kicking game.

Preparation During Game Week

When game week rolls around, it's important to have a game preparation checklist (figure 9.1) that includes every aspect of video breakdown on both your team and your opponent, the game plan, practice preparation, short lists, and wristbands.

On day five, counting down to game day (Monday if your team plays on Saturday; Sunday if your team plays on Friday), spend about 90 minutes critiquing the video of the previous game with your squad. Then, in helmets and sweats, have your players stretch and execute form running drills. Finally, present your offensive, defensive, and kicking game plans.

Players are in full pads for midweek practices (days 4 and 3). These are the only days with possible full contact. Rehearse your game plans for offense, defense, and the kicking game, including all adjustments made for the upcoming opponent. Offenses and defenses continue to change, sometimes dramatically.

Offensive Checklist

Day 6

___Video breakdown
___Offensive game plan
___Written evaluation of personnel
___Written evaluation of substitutions
___Evaluation of team video
___Postgame evaluation form

Tendency charts

___Down and distance
___Defensive alignment
___Motion adjustments
___Stunts and tendencies
___Coverage disguises

Day 5

___Video study with groups
___Pass coverage on scout cards
___Defensive stunts and alignments on cards

___Video shown to scout team
___Practice opponent's defense with scout team
___Hand out scouting report

Day 4

___Scout team in opponent's jersey numbers
___Players memorize names and numbers
___Wristbands

Day 3

___Breakdown of team's tendencies
___Vertical field position tendency chart

Day 2

___Video study with groups
___Drive lists
___Break down future opponent's video

Day 1

___Game plan short list

Figure 9.1a Sample game preparation checklist for offense.

Defensive Checklist

Day 6

___Video breakdown
___Defensive game plan
___Written evaluation of personnel
___Evaluation of team video
___Postgame evaluation form

Tendency charts

___Down and distance
___Formation
___Hash mark
___Gimmick plays

Day 5

___Video study with groups
___Pass pattern cards for secondary
___Blocking adjustment cards for linemen
___Plays and blocking on scout cards
___Video shown to scout team
___Practice of opponent's offense with scout team

___Scouting report

Day 4

___Scout team in opponent's jersey numbers
___Players memorize names and numbers
___Wristbands
___Short list of situations

Day 3

___Vertical field tendency chart
___Drive sheets
___Breakdown of our tendencies

Day 2

___Video study with groups
___Vertical field position
___Break down future opponent's video

Day 1

___Game plan short list

Figure 9.1b Sample game preparation checklist for defense.

Special-Teams Checklist

Day 6

_____Video breakdown
_____Punt rush
_____Punt return
_____Kickoff coverage
_____Kickoff return
_____Field goal
_____Extra-point block
_____Gimmick plays
_____Written evaluation of personnel
_____Evaluation of team video
_____Postgame evaluation form
_____Game plan

Game plan

_____Punt block it
_____Punt return
_____Punt coverage
_____Punt automatics
_____Kickoff coverage
_____Kickoff return
_____Onside kick

_____Field goal and extra point block it
_____Field goal and extra-point fakes

Day 5

_____Kicking game on scout cards
_____Video study with groups
_____Scout team reviews video
_____Scouting report
_____Practice kicking game with scout team

Day 4

_____Players memorize key names and numbers
_____Scout team in opponent's jersey numbers
_____Wristbands

Day 3

_____Breakdown of tendencies

Day 2

_____Video study with groups
_____Script

Day 1

_____Game plan short list

Figure 9.1c   Sample game preparation checklist for special teams.

Even so, the team that blocks and tackles best usually wins. So work on individual full-go blocking and tackling drills every contact practice.

Full-scale scrimmages are normally confined to summer camp. You could include game condition scrimmages (except that quarterbacks are not live) each Saturday during camp, but once into the regular season, rarely will you hold all-out scrimmages in practice. Do everything you can to reduce the risk of injury. Group and team drills are usually full speed with a quick whistle; full speed with no contact except at the line of scrimmage; or full speed but no tackle.

Day 2 features a practice with helmets and shoulder pads that emphasizes timing and execution of all three phases of the game plan.

The practice on the day before game day is brief, an hour or less, in helmets and T-shirts and shorts or sweats. Players break a good sweat and review all adjustments. Emphasize timing as you rehearse the game scripts.

Every minute of practice schedule must be accounted for on a written schedule. I recommend using forms similar to those shown in figures 9.2a, 9.3a, and 9.4a. These schedules are broken down by 5-minute periods. At the end of each period, a horn blows and the manager announces the number of the period the team is entering.

The sample offensive schedule shown in figure 9.2a breaks down as follows. Prepractice, which includes all specialty personnel practicing their particular specialty, lasts for 30 minutes.

Date **09/14**

(New run) new front   New pass / new stunt   New formation / new coverage   New personnel package

(Offense/Defense/kicking game)   Time **3:45–5:30**

| Film meeting ____ | Offense meeting ____ | Defense meeting ____ | Prepractice* **3:00** | Key words **Consistency** |
| Team meeting ____ | Offense lifting ____ | Defense lifting ____ | Running/stretching **3:30** | |

Period	Time	Line	WRs.	LBs	RBs and TBs	OLBs	QBs	DBs	Specialties
1	3:45	Special play—Regular 1B 948							
2	3:50	Duck walk and finish	Releases and blocking vs. DBs		Two-man sled		3-, 5-, and 7-step drops		
3	3:55	Seven-man sled	Jump ball and long ball vs. DBs		111/911 and 131/931 blocking		Pass off balance, step up in pocket, abort pocket		
4	4:00	Slip block	Comeback pattern		80, 88, and 48 blocking		Look offs, peripheral vision		
5	4:05	Horn block	Read curl		Receiving drills		254 target		
6	4:10	Polish run vs. 80, 90, and 00 defenses and stunts							
7	4:15		Polish pass						
8	4:20	1-on-1 pass pro vs. DL	Line pro drill, spread punt	Break the press drill	Center and protector vs. #4 in spread punt		411, 416, 431, and 436 mechanics		

(continued)

Figure 9.2a Sample offensive practice schedule.

Period	Time	Line	WRs./LBs	RBs and TBs/OLBs	QBs/DBs	Specialties
9	4:25		Deliver and cover drill, spread punt	Gunner coverage drill	Finding the screen receiver	
10	4:30	Group pass pro 80 and 48 vs. DL	Team spread and coverage vs. live rush and return		Reaction to covered screen receiver	Birthdays
11	4:35	Screen pass pro	411 and 416, 431 and 436 from all formations and packages with WRs, RBs, and TBs catching passes			
12	4:40	9 on 7, TEs split time between 9 on 7 and 7 on 7	7 on 7	9 on 7	9 on 7	
13	4:45		7 on 7	7 on 7	7 on 7	
14	4:50	Play-action pass pro vs. DL and LB 316/716, 326/726, 336/736, 333/733, 346/746, 352/752, 362/762	Two-minute drill: 1. -30, 1 time out, 75 seconds			
15	4:55		2. 50, 0 time outs, 38 seconds 3. -25, 2 time outs, 86 seconds			
16	5:00	Team offense				Announcements
17	5:05					
18	5:10	Reach block for shotgun punt	Break the press drill	Protect the punter		
19	5:15	Coverage for shotgun punt	Gunner coverage drill	Coverage drill	Scramble drill with some receivers	
20	5:20	Wolf 1-9 shotgun punt (rugby, boundary, and pooch)				
21	5:25	Fourth quarter				
22	5:30	Team dismissed				

* Prepractice begins 45 minutes before practice and lasts 30 minutes. Players involved include centers, long snappers, holders, kickers, punters, kick returners, punt returners, quarterbacks, and receivers (X, Y, Z, RB, and TB). Drills include center–quarterback exchange; shotgun snaps; quarterback passing to receivers on all basic individual routes; long snapper–holder–kicker kicking extra points and field goals; long snapper–punter–safety on punts and returns; and rushers vs. punts, extra points, and field goals. Then the whole team runs a lap around the perimeter of the field, stretches as a group, and performs form running drills, which takes 15 minutes.

Figure 9.2a *(continued).*

Offensive Script

Date _09/14_ 9 on 7

	Script #	Personnel package	Formation	Play	Blocking	Hash	Defense	Coverage
1	88	R	1I	162	Slip	Right	90	3
2	23	R	9I	911	Slip	Right	80 Up	2
3	57	R	Motion 1	131	BIB	Middle	00	5
4	53	T	8-1 I Stack	122	Guard only pull	Left	90 Mike B	3
5	41	C-0	1 Tight PIL	113	Team	Middle	90 Will Opp. A Mike B	3
6	97	H	9 Flex F	QB Sneak	Wedge	Right	80 Weak	2
7	76	W	Motion 9-1	944	Set	Middle	80	3
8	90	R	9I	162 Center Sweep	Zone, backside guard lead	Left	Sam D-80	2
9	42	W	1 Tight C Over Strong	113	Zone	Right	80	3
10	98	C-0	1 Tight PIR	QB Sneak	Wedge	Middle	30	3
11	96	T	2E	995	Down	Left	80 Weak	2
12	89	R	9I	962	Slip	Right	Sam A-80-Mike B	3
13	73	W	1 Tight E	144	Bump	Left	00	5
14	43	R	9	913	Team	Left	Sam C-00	3
15	4	R	8A	111	Slip	Middle	Sam A, Mike C 90	3

Figure 9.2b Sample offensive script.

Date <u>09/07</u>   New run / new front   New pass (new stunt)   New formation / new coverage   New personnel package

Offense/(defense)/kicking game   Time <u>3:45–5:30</u>

Film meeting _____   Offense meeting _____   Defense meeting _____   Prepractice* <u>3:00</u>   Key words <u>Emotion</u>

Team meeting _____   Offense lifting _____   Defense lifting _____   Running/stretching <u>3:30</u>

Period	Time	Line	WRs./LBs	RBs and TBs/OLBs	QBs/DBs	Specialties
1	3:45	Team pursuit				
2	3:50	Move, Remove, and Stem	Adjustments to all formations			
3	3:55	Giant Slant Weak BC 283 and Giant Slant Weak Sam B Mike C 283	Giant Slant Weak Sam B Mike C 283		Jump ball and long ball vs. rec.	
4	4:00	Form and perfect tackle	Leverage tackling drill	Skate drill	Interception drills	
5	4:05	Seven-man sled	Interception drills	Interception drills	Sideline tackling drill	
6	4:10	Pass rush drill vs. OL	Hook to hole vs. rec.	Option responsibility	Press and squat vs. rec.	
7	4:15	3 on 2 vs. OL	Hook to curl vs. rec.	Curl to flat vs. rec		
8	4:20	9 and 10 man crash left C vs. spread, semispread, and spear punt formation	Mike and Will–9 and 10 man crash left C	Sam–9 man crash left C		
9	4:25			Sam and RC–10 man crash left C		

Period	Time	Line	WRs./LBs	RBs and TBs/OLBs	QBs/DBs	Specialties
10	4:30	Team 9 and 10 man punt block, crash left C				
11	4:35	Polish team recognition vs. scout offense—formations and motion				Birthdays
12	4:40	9 on 7	9 on 7	9 on 7		
13	4:45		7 on 7	7 on 7	7 on 7	
14	4:50	Twist and fold 10, 20, 30, 50, and 90	Two-minute defense			
15	4:55					
16	5:00	Team defense				Announcements
17	5:05					
18	5:10	TE, tackles, and free left and right D field goal block	SS, Sam, and Mike left and right D field goal block	Corners, Will, and SE left and right D field goal block		
19	5:15	Team left and right D field goal block				
20	5:20	Team fake field goal defense from left, right, and middle				
21	5:25	Fourth quarter, last play of the game				
22	5:30	Team dismissed				

Figure 9.3a Sample defensive practice schedule.

Defensive Script

Date _09/15_ Team

	Script #	Personnel package	Alignment	Defense	Coverage	Stunt	Hash	Formation	Play
1	39	Regular	2	40	3	46 Sam C 243	Right	9I	931
2	44	Regular	2	40	3	243 Will opp. A Saber B	Left	Motion 1DI	122 R Pull
3	65	Leopard	2	70	3	273 Saber opp. A Will delay A	Middle	9I	346 R Flat
4	17	Regular	4	10	2	412 Slant	Left	1I	113 Option
5	23	Regular	3	20	3	Opp. B 323 Near A	Right	Motion 9I	933 Iso
6	70	Regular	2	70	3	Go Mike B 273	Middle	1I	333 815
7		Leopard	2	273	3		Right	8I	913 Z Rev
8	44	Bull	2	40	3	243 Will opp. A Saber B	Right	8I	133 Iso
9	12	Regular	9	10	3	Go 913 slant weak	Left	1DI	293
10	101	Puma	3	90	5	Fold tight 395	Left	2I	DB 096
11	103	Puma	4	90	2	Sam opp. B 492 Fold split	Middle	Motion 1	131
12	87	Regular	2	80	3	283 Corner C	Left	Tight 2I	Z Inside C
13	105	Regular	2	00	9	A 209	Right	9CI	891
14		Puma	2	287	7		Left	1I	DB 8+69
15	92	Regular	2	90	9	B Sam opp. A 299	Right	9I	913 Option
16	77	Regular	2	80	9	289 Will B	Right	1I	254
17	39	Bull	2	40	2	46 Sam C 242	Middle	1I	113
18	9	Puma	4	10	5	415 Pinch	Left	9I	336 80 Corner
19		Regular	2	292	2		Middle	9CI	922 R Pull
20	81	Regular	2	80	3	Free A 283	Left	2I	113 Option

Figure 9.3b Sample defensive script.

Date __08/18__   New run / new front   New pass / new stunt   New formation / new coverage   New personnel package

Offense/defense/(kicking game) Time __3:00–4:00__

Film meeting _____ Offense meeting __2:15__ Defense meeting __2:15__ Prepractice* __3:00__ Key words __Concentration__

Team meeting __9:00 p.m.__ Offense lifting __11:00__ Defense lifting __11:30__ Running/stretching __2:45__

Period	Time	Line	WRs./LBs	RBs and TBs/OLBs	QBs/DBs	Specialties
1	3:00	Red punt—Personnel from previous play stay in game. Practice every personnel package of every play from Green and Red. Also shift from Spread to I9 and pooch punt when safety comes up. Gunners get between ball and goal line.				
2	3:05					
3	3:10	Team red punt vs. scout defense				
4	3:15	Kickoff receive, front line drill		Deep six, cover the field drill, communicate		
5	3:20	Wedge, sink to 30, block dummies at 35		Wedge drill, live returner for timing		
6	3:25	Team middle return vs. scout team				
7	3:30	Field goal, interior five block all conceivable rushes	TEs and wings block perimeter rushes	Big 3 drill		
8	3:35					
9	3:40	Team field goal live vs. scout team from all angles and distances				
10	3:45	Field goal alert—Use every personnel package with only the kicker and long snapper entering the game. Have the clock running or temporarily stopped and then set in play				
11	3:50					Birthdays
12	3:55					
13	4:00	Team dismissed				

Note: Any time a player is not involved in a special team, he joins a station by his position (OL, DL, LB, secondary, RB and QB, and WR and QB). The stations today are jump rope, ladder, shuttle and box run, hill run, parachute, and position drills. Each station lasts 10 minutes.

Figure 9.4a   Sample kicking game practice schedule.

Kicking Game Script

Date *08/20*

	Script #	Offensive yard line	Unit	Formation	Play	Offensive hash	Coaching point
1	71	−49	Punt coverage	Spread	Punt, boundary left	Left	Punter reacts to getting bumped
2	119	−7	Punt block	10-man block	Crash left C	Right	
3	47	+3	Extra point	Extra point	Kick	Middle	Bad snap, fire right
4	57	+32	Field goal	Field goal	Pooch punt	Middle	
5	37	−35	Hands team	Kickoff receive	Onside kick	Right	Cover him up
6	38	+38	Field goal defense	Fake field goal defense	Fake	Middle	Option left
7	28	50	Kickoff receive	Kickoff receive	Middle return pooch kick	Left	Follows 15-yd. penalty on receiving team, look for pooch and fair catch or onside kick
8	41	+3	Extra point defense	Block left B, extra point defense	Block left B	Middle	Bad snap, fire right
9	29	−35	Kickoff receive	Kickoff receive	Right return	Middle	Kickoff into endzone, buddy turn and tell returner to kneel or bring it out
10	68	−48	Punt coverage	Spread	Rugby punt	Right	Must give up 0-yard return, get between ball and endzone
11	10	−35	Kickoff coverage	Muddle huddle	Left, left, left	Left	Be onside
12	27	50	Oskie	Muddle huddle	Onside kick	Middle	Follows 15-yd. penalty on receiving team
13	65	+19	Field goal	Field goal	Option left	Middle	4th and 4
14	67	−28	Punt coverage	Spread	Punt	Middle	Fumble punt, first man hit fumbles, second man recovers ball
15		+13	Field goal alert	Field goal	Kick	Middle	End of half, 12 seconds and counting
16	55	+21	Field goal	Field goal	Kick	Middle	Last play of the game

Figure 9.4b   Sample kicking game script.

This is followed by the entire team, without helmets and shoulder pads, jogging 400 meters, and then, in 10 rows, performing all stretching exercises in unison. As head coach, I lead this segment to impress on the team that this is a very important part of what we do to prepare for practice. We conclude the stretching with jumping jacks done in cadence to the spelling of the mascot's name. Players then put on their pads and helmets and come to the coach for any needed announcements. Impress on your players the theme of the day (e.g., consistency, in the sample shown in figure 9.2a). Players then break quickly to their stations and coaches for period 1.

For this practice schedule, period 1 consists of the offensive team practicing a special play, in this case a reverse. The team then moves into four periods of individual drills. The offensive line starts with a drill that stresses correct form: hands out in front as if driving a defensive man and finally turning him and finishing the block. Players move to the seven-man sled, exploding into the sled in unison, and driving it. The third period of individual drills is devoted to the slip block and is done against simulated linemen and linebackers. The horn block against simulated defensive personnel is next. Form and technique are carefully scrutinized in these full-speed drills.

Periods 6 and 7 are group work in which the offensive line polishes their assignments in all running plays against offensive second-teamers who play defensive positions. At the same time, receivers, backs, and quarterbacks are polishing their assignments in all pass plays. This is done against air, with no defensive players.

We then move into three periods of special teams. The first two are individual drills associated with the spread punt, and the final period puts it all together in the team punt. Given that most linemen are not part of a punt-coverage team, these players spend these three periods working on pass protection versus defensive pass rush, one period of one on one, and two periods of group work. At the same time, quarterbacks work on screens, basic mechanics, finding the screen receiver, and the proper reaction to a covered potential receiver. Period 11 consists of the offensive line as a unit working on screen pass protection, while receivers, backs, and quarterbacks practice four screens from various formations.

The team moves into nine-on-seven and seven-on-seven drills. Here, tight ends split their time between the two drills, and half the offensive backs are with the nine-on-seven drill and the other half with the seven on seven. The nine-on-seven drill includes all offensive positions except the two wide receivers against all defensive players except the defensive backs. This is largely a running game drill. In seven on seven, all offensive positions except guards and tackles are used, while the defense uses linebackers and secondary. This drill includes all aspects of the passing game, including draws and screens.

Periods 14 and 15 are devoted to rehearsing the two-minute offense versus the first-team defense. Practice the two-minute game every practice, but sometimes change the personnel, make it a team drill, do it against air without any defense, or, as in this practice, make it a seven-on-seven drill. Change the situation of the two-minute drill: starting yard line, opponent's time-outs remaining, and game clock. In this practice, because it's a seven-on-seven drill, the offensive line uses this time to practice play-action pass protection against defensive linemen and linebackers.

In period 16, the team is ready to put everything together in a team drill against a scout team defense. For seven on seven, nine on seven, team offense, and team goal-line offense, follow a prepared script to ensure you see certain plays against the defensive look you anticipate.

Use scout team cards so the group simulating the opponent's defenses can see exactly where they are expected to be and what to do when the ball is snapped. The scout team coach is there to instruct that group and answer questions about their assignments.

Periods 18 to 20 go back to special teams, this time punting from a double-tight, double–wide receiver, shotgun formation. Rehearse a rugby punt, boundary punt, and pooch punt, all from the shotgun. The first two periods are devoted to individual drills relative to the punt, and the final period puts it all together, including coverage. During periods 18 and 19, the quarterbacks are in a scramble drill with the receivers who are not involved in practicing the punt.

Period 21, the final period of practice, is a drill we call fourth quarter, as mentioned earlier. In this period, players execute drills designed to totally exhaust them and prepare them for the final minutes of a hard-fought game. The drills are usually football skill related, but sometimes they include sprinting, running in place, hitting the ground, doing push-ups, and so on.

A well-organized practice ensures that specific plays are run against specific defenses (see figure 9.3*a* for a sample defensive practice schedule), certain stunts and pass coverages are seen against particular offensive plays, and specific kicking game plays are practiced against what is expected on game day (see figure 9.4*a* for a sample kicking game practice schedule).

Late in the practice week, rehearse a prepared special-teams script (figure 9.5). One of the most important benefits of this drill is to ensure you always have the correct personnel coming on and off the field as needed. You don't ever want a situation in which too few, or too many, players are on the field.

Coaches use charts, one that shows an offensive drill against the scout team defense and one that shows a defensive drill against the scout team offense, to prepare their offensive and defensive teams for upcoming opponents. These forms are used in every single practice and during pregame preparation on game day. The charts are put on large and heavy cardboard stock. On the chart for the offensive drill against the scout team defense, the complete base defensive adjustment for the offensive formation employed is diagrammed at the bottom. The remaining diagrams show various stunts and coverages for the defensive scout team. On the chart for the defensive drill against the scout team offense, the complete formation, play, and blocking is diagrammed at the bottom against one of the defensive fronts. The remaining diagrams show expected blocking adjustments versus fronts being used.

If you have a great offensive player, you must get the ball in his hands 25 to 30 times a game. This means putting together a short list of plays during game week and rehearsing these plays during that week's practices. The list must have the exact formations, personnel packages, motion, passes with tag words, and so on that you want to run to exploit this player's abilities. This list shouldn't be something pulled out of a hat during the game; it must be prepared by the head coach earlier in the week. To be blessed with a highly skilled scoring threat and have him touch the ball only five or six times per game makes no sense. Let him win the game for you.

Figure 9.6 on page 178 shows sample lists if your great offensive player is a wide receiver, a running back, or a quarterback. Your superb athlete might play more than one position. He might also be on most of the special teams. In any case, make a plan to get the ball in his hands.

Scripts are prepared early in the week. They become the basis for practices throughout that week. The quarterback has the same information on his wristband that the coach has on his script. This allows the coach to signal a particular script number to the quarterback, who then calls that corresponding formation and play in the huddle.

Short lists are also important for practice so the team can practice automatics, red zone plays, third-and-long plays, and any other plays you feel are the best plays for specific situations against the defenses you expect to face.

---

1. Kickoff coverage, left corner
2. Punt return, wall right
3. Field goal, +14, left hash
4. Punt coverage, -27, middle
5. Oskie coverage, middle dribble kick
6. Kickoff return, middle
7. Pooch punt coverage, +48, right hash
8. Pooch kickoff receive, our left end
9. Regular kickoff receive, onside kick to our right
10. Field goal block, +12, middle
11. Punt receive, punt block right C gap
12. Hands team, onside kick to our right
13. Offense, 2-point conversion, 8A, 362
14. Offense, +22, second and 8, 1I, 162, left hash
15. Offense, field goal alert, +19, third and 5, middle, 15 seconds with clock running
16. Sudden change from offense to extra-point block
17. Sudden change from defense to extra-point kick
18. Punt return, middle
19. Offense, punt from shotgun, 1F
20. Offense, 9A, 852, +38, third and 4, right hash
21. Red punt, Red 1CI 111, +38, fourth and 4, right hash
22. Red punt, Red 9DI 316, +38, fourth and 4, right hash
23. Red punt, Green - 281, +38, fourth and 11, right hash

Figure 9.5 Friday special-teams play script.

Wide Receiver (premier player is at Z)

Run

Script number	Personnel package	Formation	Play
212	Regular	2I	918
213	Regular	2I	918 double reverse
216	Regular	2I	913 option reverse
218	Regular	1I	928 double reverse
220	Regular	2	938
222	Tiger	2-9	938 double reverse
225	Regular	1B	948 double reverse

Pass

Script number	Personnel package	Formation	Play
83	Tiger	2EI	404 (put him at X)
101	Regular	2C	251Z T and X change
104	Hawk	2 Flex EI	251Z R and X change
108	Empty	1 Flex EF Stack	252Z
111	Fox	2 Flex C	254Z
114	Hawk	2 Flex EI	254Z R and X change
171	Fox	1 Flex CI	281
177	Hawk	2 Flex FI	281 X and Z change
183	Fox	1 Flex C	282 T and Y change
190	Hawk	9 Flex EI Stack	285 Under
196	Hawk	2 Flex FI	285 X and Z change
197	Hawk	1 Flex EI	285 Y and Z change
210	Fox	1 Flex D	291 (put him at Y)
212	Fox	1 Flex D	293
213	Fox	1 Flex D	296 (put him at Y)

Figure 9.6a   Sample play list for a wide receiver.

Running Back

Run

Script number	Personnel package	Formation	Play
1	Regular	1I	111
6	Tiger	9FI R March	911
24	Tiger	1-8I Winter	122
21	Regular	9I	922
28	Tiger	8FI R March	131
40	Tiger	9FI R June	944
53	Regular	1I	162 counter sweep
60	Regular	2I	995
46	Regular	SG 1	152 cross
47	Fox	SG 9 Flex	952 cross

Pass

Script number	Personnel package	Formation	Play
77	Regular	8A	362 T flat
79	Tiger	9DI	401
87	Regular	2A	411
89	Regular	2D	422
90	Hawk	9 Flex FI	482 T
94	Fox	1 Flex C	692
112	Regular	2C	254T
113	Regular	8D	854T
116	Regular	9I	282
117	Regular	1I	882
189	Regular	1	285 under
193	Regular	9A	285
197	Regular	1D	285 T and X change
205	Fox	2 Flex C	285 T and X change
208	Tiger	8-1I	285 T and Y change

Figure 9.6b　Sample play list for running back.

Quarterback

Run

Script number	Personnel package	Formation	Play
45	Tiger	SG 1-8	152 QB trap
214	Regular	1I	113 Option
215	Regular	2I	113 Option—fake reverse
226	Regular	1	164 Option
227	Regular	2	164 Option—fake reverse
229	Tiger	9 EI	995 QB draw
230	Empty	9 Flex EC	195 QB draw

Pass

Script number	Personnel package	Formation	Play
239	Wolf	1EI	338 double reverse pass to QB

Run-pass option

Script number	Personnel package	Formation	Play
8	Regular	9I	316
27	Regular	8I	326
30	Regular	9	336
45	Regular	9A	346

Figure 9.6c　Sample play list for quarterback.

The chart shown in figure 9.7 should be in your hands during the game. This chart includes a number of offensive facts you need access to as the game progresses, including information on the game plan of your opponent and their reactions to what you are emphasizing. The next item listed is when to kick and when to go for two points after touchdowns. This needs to be considered during the week and should not be an emotional decision made in the heat of the game. List automatics for the game, things to emphasize, and a plan for substitutions, and, after scouting yourself, how to break the tendencies you developed. As head coach, I prepare at least three drive scripts to open the game, using formations I want to see the opponent defend. These drives provide an opportunity to break tendencies, such as pass in a normal running situation or run when the usual call would be a pass.

Observations

1. Fronts and coverages

   40   C3_____

   80   C2_____   C3_____   C4_____

   90   C2_____   C3_____   C4_____

   00   C2_____   C3_____   C4_____

   10   C2_____   C3_____

2. Tendencies to their fronts and coverages

   _____

   _____

3. How much they bring ILBs and OLBs and in what down-and-distance situations

   _____

   _____

4. Twist or fold stunts

   _____

   _____

5. Reaction to doubles and trips

   _____

   _____

6. Reaction to motion and shifting

   _____

   _____

7. Mismatch

   _____

   _____

8. Best patterns

   _____

   _____

Automatics

1. If automatic to different play, count is Bingo; if Railroad, count stays as called.
2. Versus 4-4, all DB passes are blocked 58, 88, or 88 Read; versus 10 with SS to SE side, use 48; if SS to TE side, 88.
3. Trap widest interior lineman and use Set.
4. On play-action pass, check backside numbers for potential unblocked rusher.
5. Draw to TE side versus 10 defense.

Tendency breakers

1. Pass more out of Wolf.
2. Run more out of Tiger.
3. Run more from the flexes.
4. From A, run 122 and 111.
5. Run 144, 141, 746, 141 FR, and 948 from 1B.

Extra-point strategy

Ahead by

10—kick
9—kick
8—kick
7—kick
6—kick
5—go for 2
4—go for 2
3—kick
2—kick
1—go for 2
0—kick

Behind by

1—kick
2—go for 2
3—kick
4—kick
5—go for 2
6—kick
7—kick

Figure 9.7   Game-day short list for the offense.

(continued)

8—kick

9—go for 2 (maybe kick, go for 2 on next TD)

10—kick

11—kick

12—go for 2

Substitutions

1. Maciel and Smith at OT; Patrick, Payne, and Rasnake at OG

2. Rotate Tester, Oliver, and Clark

3. Williams at right WR, Daniel at left WR; Jiggetts and Poitier are next at Fox and Wolf

Points to emphasize

1. Unbalanced

2. Misdirection

3. Shifting

4. Lots of 285 passes to delay receiver

5. Stack motion

6. Big horizontal splits

7. Big vertical splits in 280s and 250s to read stunts

8. Double moves in routes vs. Man

9. 250s from Twins and Trips change

10. Counter Trey to SE side

SCRIPTS

Script 1	Two-minute (Tiger unless clock is stopped)
1. 96 R 9I 316	1. 96 T 2E 995
2. 73 W Motion 1 Tight E 144	2. 106 T 9DI 401
3. 106 T 9DI 401	3. 108 T 8F Over 403
4. 96 T 2E 995	4. 115 T 2-9I Stack 251
5. 157 H motion 9 Flex EI 285 Y and Z change	5. 127 T 2 EI 254R X and Z change
6. 1 R 1I 111	6. 146 T 2-9I 282 T and Z change
7. 138 R 9A 282	7. 158 T 8-1I 285 R and T change
8. 89 R 9I 962	8. 64 T 8-1I Stack 131
9. 94 R 1B 995	9. 157 H motion 9 Flex EI 285 Y and Z Change
10. 25 R 2 B Fall 911	10. 160 F 1 Flex D 291
11. 126 F 1 Flex I Stack 254Y	11. 161 F 1 Flex D 293
12. 50 R 8I Stack 122	12. 162 F 1 Flex D 296
Script 2	**Red zone**
1. 160 F 1 Flex D 291	1. 90 R 9I 162 Counter
2. 9 F 1 Flex I Stack 111	2. 42 W 1 Tight C Over Str 113
3. 41 C 0 1 Tight PIL 113	3. 76 W Motion 9-1 944
4. 100 R 8I 326	4. 92 R 1 164
5. 168 T 9FI 931 db. rev. tossback	5. 123 F 2 Flex C 253X T and Z change
6. 54 R 2CI 922	6. 97 W 1 Tight C 311 Delay Drag
7. 123 F 2 Flex C 253X T and Z change	7. 101 R 9 336 08 Zig Out R Flat
8. 88 R 1I 162	8. 56 W 1 Tight E 922
9. 70 C1 9 Wing A 931	9. 26 W 9 Tight F 911
11. 112 R 9A 646	

Figure 9.7 *(continued).*

Script 3

1. 101 R 9 336 R Flat
2. 50 R 8I Stack 122
3. 134 W Motion 1-9 281
4. 15 H 1 Bunch I 111
5. 29 R 1CI 111 Cutback
6. 89 R 9I 962
7. 86 R SG 9 953
8. 64 T 8-1I Stack 131
9. 147 R 2A 282 Z Corner
10. 82 R Shotgun 9 952
11. 103 R Shotgun 9 352 805
12. 89 R 9I 962

Sudden change

1. 157 - H motion 9 Flex EI 285 Y and Z change
2. 42 W 1 Tight C Over Str 113
3. 109 T 9-2I 411
4. 158 T 8-1 285 R and T change
5. 152 F 1 Flex I Stack 285
6. 97 W 1 Tight C 311 Delay Drag
7. 168 T 9FI 931 db. rev. tossback

Red punt

1. 175 Green	Punt formation	Punt
2. 176 Green	Punt formation	281
3. 177 Red	Shift to 1-9	111
4. 178 Red	Shift to 1-9	316
5. 179 Red	Shift to 1-9	113
6. 180 Red	Shift to 1-9	162
7. 181 Red	Shift to 1 Tight C	311 Delay Drag

Opening drive of second half

1. 51 W Motion 1 Tight E 122
2. 108 T 8F Over 403
3. 114 E 1 Flex EF 251Y
4. 96 T 2E 962 Counter
5. 25 R 2B Fall 911
6. 128 R 1D 211
7. 69 T 8FI Strong 931
8. 143 E 9 Flex FE 882
9. 6 R 2D Strong 111
10. 159-E 1 Flex FC 285 X and T change, R and Z change
11. 133 R 1B 281 R and Y change
12. 140 R 9I 282

Two-point plays

1. 90 R 9I 162 Counter
2. 124 E 1 Flex EF 253Y R and Z change
3. 101 R 9 336 08 Zig Out R Flat
4. 164 C1 PIR 331T GL Pass Z Flat
5. 159 E 1 Flex FC285 X and T change, R and Z change

Goal line to −20

1. 73 W 1 Tight E 144
2. 119 H 1 Bunch I 251R Y and Z change
3. 89 R 9I 962
4. 10 W 1-9 111
5. 26 W 9 Tight F 911
6. 34 W 1 Bunch Right 111 Cutback
7. 56 W 1 Tight E 922
8. 76 W Motion 9-1 944
9. 100 R 8I 326
10. 101 R 9 336

Goal line

1. 19 C1 1 Wing A 111
2. 97 W 1 Tight C 311 Delay Drag
3. 41 C0 1 Tight PIL 113
4. 88 R 1I 162
5. 90 R 9I 162 Counter
6. 100 R 8I 326

Figure 9.7 *(continued).*

(continued)

Overtime	Second and 20 (don't have to have it all on this play)
1. 42 W 1 Tight C Over Str 113	**1.** 147 R 2A 282 Z Corner
2. 109 T 9-2I 411	**2.** 157 H motion 9 Flex EI 285 Y and Z change
3. 74 H motion 1 Bunch 144	**3.** 96 T 2E 995
4. 119 H 1 Bunch I 251R Y and Z change	**4.** 106 T 9DI 401
5. 34 W 1 Bunch Right 111 Cutback	**5.** 151 R 9A 285
6. 97 W 1 Tight C 311 Del Drag	**6.** 143 E 9 Flex FE 882
7. 131 R 2A Stack 281	**Third and 6**
8. 126 F 1 Flex I Stack 254Y	**1.** 144 F 9 Flex CI 282 R and T change
Last play	**2.** 90 R 9I 162 Counter
1. 160 F 1 Flex D 291	**3.** 109 T 9-2I 411
2. 161 F 1 Flex D 293	**4.** 142 R 1D 882
3. 162 F 1 Flex D 296	**5.** 120 R motion 4I 252
4. 136 R 2I 281 Z Comeback X Go	**6.** 141 H 1 Flex EI R Stack 282
5. 148 R 2B 282 X Shake	**7.** 157 H motion 9 Flex EI 285 Y and Z change
Four minutes (we're leading)	**Third and 10**
1. 96 T 2E 995	**1.** 147 R 2A 282 Z Corner
2. 6 R 2D Strong 111	**2.** 131 R 2A Stack 281
3. 30 R 9CI 111 Cutback	**3.** 107 F 1 Flex CI R Spring 402
4. 38 R 1 113	**4.** 108 T 8F Over 403
5. 48 R Motion 1B 122	**5.** 143 E 9 Flex FE 882
6. 23 R 9I 911	**6.** 128 R 1D 211
7. 122 R 9B 253	**7.** 138 R 9A 282
8. 97 W 1 Tight C 311 Delay Drag	**8.** 139 R 2I 282 X and Z change

Figure 9.7 *(continued).*

Include a script for the opening drive of the second half. Add a formation or two not used in the first half and maybe an unused play as well. Include a list of plays to choose from for two-minute, red zone, and sudden change situations. List plays you can run from your red punt formation. List plays you can choose from for specific situations, such as 2-point plays, goal line, bringing it out from the goal line to the minus 20, plays and formations for overtime, second and 20, third and 6, third and 10, four-minute offense when leading, and the last play of the game when you need a score.

Defensive coaches prepare similar charts (figure 9.8), providing them easy access to defensive calls for various situations, such as second and short, second and middle, second and long, third and middle, third and long, fourth and short, or third and short in three-down territory. Other situations include sudden change, goal line to -20, possession down and very long, two-minute, last play of the game, overtime, four-minute when behind, red zone, 2-point try, and opening drive of the second half.

Second and short	Third and middle (four-down territory)
1. 35 R 30 ***Slant 232, 432, 233, 433, 235, 435, 237, 437	**1.** 39 R 46 Sam C*** 242, 442, 243, 443
2. 36 R 30 Go B***Slant Weak 233, 433	**2.** 27 R 20 Go***Slant Weak Opp. B 223, 423
3. 27 R 20 Go***Slant Weak Opp. B 223, 423	**3.** 111 - R 00 Saber C Sam A*** 203, 403
4. 43 B 40 Go***Pinch Go 243, 443	**4.** 23 R 20 Opposite B***Near A 223, 423
5. 48 R 50 ***Pinch 252, 452, 233, 453, 255, 455, 257, 457	**5.** 70 R 70 Go Mike B*** 273, 473
6. 51 R 50 A***Slant Opposite B 252, 452	**6.** 89 R 90 Mike C Sam A*** 293, 493
7. 55 R 50 A***Opp. B Free B 253, 453	**7.** 90 R 90 Mike C Sam B*** 293, 493
8. 104 R 90 Go B***Twist Split 293, 493	**8.** 73 R 70 Sam B***Saber B 273, 473

Second and middle	Third and long (three-down territory)
1. 13 R 10 B***Slant Go 213, 413	**1.** 17 P 10 Fold Tight***Will Opposite B 212, 412, 213, 413, 215, 415, 217, 417
2. 18 R 26 Sam C*** 223, 423, 225, 425	**2.** 14 P 10 A Free B*** 213, 413
3. 25 R 20 ***A Saber B 225, 425	**3.** 37 P 30 Twist Giant Tight*** 232, 432, 233, 433, 235, 435, 237, 437
4. 80 R 80 B***Go Will A 283, 483	**4.** 104 P 90 Go B***Twist Split 293, 493
	5. 27 R 20 Go***Slant Weak Opp. B 223, 423

Second and long	Fourth down or third and short (three-down territory)
1. 16 P 10 Twist Tight***B 212, 412, 213, 413, 215, 415, 217, 417	**1.** 32 Li 30 B*** 233, 433
2. 17 P 10 Fold Tight***Will Opp. A 212, 412, 213, 413, 215, 415, 217, 417	**2.** 33 Li 30 Saber C***Near A 233, 433
3. 14 P 10 A Free B*** 213, 413	**3.** 45 Li 50 A***Opposite B 253, 453
4. 37 P 30 Twist Giant Tight*** 232, 432, 233, 433, 235, 435, 237, 437	**4.** 72 R 70 Will C Mike A*** 273, 473
5. 101 P 90 Fold Tight*** 292, 492, 293, 493, 295, 495, 297, 497	**5.** 27 R 20 Go***Slant Weak Opp. B 223, 423

Sudden change	Goal line to –20
1. 61 R 60 D***Opposite A 263, 463	**1.** 62 R 60 B***Saber B 263, 463
2. 33 B 30 Saber C***Near A 233, 433	**2.** 61 R 60 D***Opposite A 263, 463
3. 36 B 30 Go B***Slant Weak 233, 433	**3.** 106 R 00 Mike C Sam A*** 203, 403
4. 44 B 40 ***Will Opp. A Saber B 243, 443	**4.** 110 R 00 Saber C*** 203, 403
	5. 43 R 40 Go***Pinch Go 243, 443

Figure 9.8 Game-day short list for the defense.

(continued)

Possession down and very long	Two-minute
1. 20 P 20 Near A*** 222, 422, 223, 423, 225, 425, 227, 427	**1.** 16 P 10 Twist Tight***B 212, 412, 213, 413, 215, 415, 217, 417
2. 48 G 50 ***Pinch 258, 458	**2.** 28 P 20 B***Free B 223, 423
3. 49 G 50 ***Slant 258, 458	**3.** 51 G 50 A***Slant Opp. B 253, 453
4. 50 G 50 ***Slant Weak 258, 458	**4.** 82 P 80 ***Corner B 283, 483, 282, 482
5. 51 G 50 A***Slant Opp. B 253, 453, 255, 455	**5.** 83 P 80 Saber B*** 283, 483
6. 91 P 90 ***B 292, 492, 293, 493, 295, 495, 297, 497	**6.** 103 P 90 Sam Opp. B***Fold Split 292, 492, 293, 493, 294, 494
7. 103 P 90 Sam Opp. B***Fold Split 292, 492, 293, 493, 294, 494	**7.** 112 P 00 ***Corner C 203, 403, 202, 402
8. 17 P 10 Fold Tight***Will Opposite B 212, 412, 213, 413, 215, 415, 217, 417	

Overtime	Red zone
1. 32 B 30 B*** 232, 432, 233, 433, 235, 435	**1.** 39 R 46 Sam C*** 242, 442, 243, 443, 245, 445
2. 33 B 30 Saber C***Near A 233, 433	**2.** 43 R 40 Go***Pinch Go 243, 443
3. 34 B 30 Go*** 233, 433	**3.** 44 R 40 ***Will Opp. A Saber B 243, 443
4. 36 B 30 Go B***Slant Weak 292, 492, 293, 493, 295, 495	**4.** 61 R 60 D***Opposite A 263, 463
5. 38 B 30 Fold Giant Tight*** 232, 432, 233, 433, 235, 435, 237, 437	**5.** 62 R 60 B***Saber B 263, 463
6. 68 B 70 B Mike Opp. A*** 273, 473	**6.** 65 R 70 ***Saber Opp. A Will Delay A 273, 473
7. 70 B 70 Go Mike B*** 273, 473	**7.** 69 R 70 A***Free B 273, 473
8. 72 R 70 Will C Mike A*** 272, 472, 273, 473	
9. 73 R 70 Sam B***Saber B 273, 473	

Last play	Two-point plays
1. 56 Ch 50 Opp. B Saber C***A 253, 453	**1.** 39 R 46 Sam C*** 242, 442, 243, 443
2. 49 Ch 50 ***Slant 256, 456, 258, 458	**2.** 111 R 00 Saber C Sam A*** 203, 443
3. 46 G 50 ***A 256, 456	**3.** 47 Le 50 Near A***Opp. B 252, 452, 253, 453
4. 102 P 90 ***Fold Split 233, 433	

Figure 9.8 *(continued)*.

Four minutes (they're leading)	Opening drive of second half
1. 43 R 40 Go***Pinch Go 243,443	**1.** 33 B 30 Saber C***Near A 233, 433
2. 35 B 30 ***Slant 232, 432, 235, 435, 237, 437	**2.** 36 B 30 Go B***Slant Weak 233, 433
3. 36 B 30 Go B***Slant Weak 233, 433	**3.** 38 B 30 Fold Giant Tight*** 232, 432, 233, 433, 235, 435, 237, 437
4. 27 R 20 Go***Slant Weak Opp. B 223, 423	**4.** 73 R 70 Sam B***Saber B 273, 473
5. 59 Li 60 CB*** 263, 463	**5.** 65 R 70 ***Saber Opp. A Will Delay A 273, 473
6. 60 Li 60 DB*** 263, 463	**6.** 72 R 70 Will C Mike A*** 272, 472, 273, 473
7. 65 R 70 ***Saber Opp. A Will Delay A 273, 473	

Figure 9.8 *(continued).*

Each game week I prepare an offensive short list that contains every play we might possibly run that week, along with the personnel package and formation for each play as it was practiced that particular week. Some runs have blocking variations, and the pass plays contain all of the route variations and tag words for that week. Each listing is numbered sequentially. This same information is on the quarterback's wristband.

In the script, the first column is the script number, followed by the play call and the personnel package. R is for regular, F for fox, W for wolf, H for hawk, C2, 1, or 0 for crow, and E for empty. The formation is in the next column. The final column notes the passing pattern variations of the play-action passes.

Getting the play call to the quarterback is not difficult. Start with the personnel package. When the personnel package is called, the proper personnel go on and off the field. If there's no call, the quarterback knows the personnel package is the same as for the previous play. The quarterback has all the informa-

tion he needs on his wristband. I can signal him the script number, and he then finds that number on his wristband, which gives him all the information to call the play in the huddle. All players on the field have similar wristbands in case we want to go no-huddle. The quarterback calls out the script number and a code word for the snap count. Each player finds that script number on his wristband. We change the code for the script number if we feel it's necessary to avoid having the defense pick up what we're running.

We have similar defensive short lists and wristbands with the script number, personnel package, defense, stunt, and coverage. If we're playing an option team, we also have wristbands that tell the wearer of that particular wristband his responsibility for every phase of the option for every defensive call. There's no guesswork. The wristbands help prevent a defensive player forgetting who has the dive, who has the quarterback, and who has the pitch for each defense and stunt that might be called. All these responsibilities are included on the wristband. Each position player has different information on his wristband from his teammates at other positions.

In the defensive short list, the first column lists the script number, followed by the base defense and the stunt that might be called. The basic defensive call is a three-digit number. The first digit indicates the orientation—right or left, tight or split, open or closed field, multiple or single receivers. The second digit indicates the front to be used. The third digit indicates the pass coverage. When three asterisks are used in place of the three-digit number, it means that for a particular call we could choose from several orientations and pass coverages. Those options would be listed with the call. If the stunt is called after the three-digit number, the stunt is to the side away from the orientation. For example, if the call were twist in 243, a twist in stunt would be run to the tight side. If the call were 243 twist in, the twist in stunt would be run to the split side.

When the personnel package is called, the proper personnel go on and off the field. If there's no call, the signal caller knows the per-sonnel package is the same as for the previous play. The coach signals the three-digit call for the orientation, defense, and coverage. The signal caller checks his wristband and calls the play and stunt, if necessary.

Every member of special teams has a wristband listing each phase of the kicking game, including fakes, pooch kicks or punts, sideline punts, rugby punts, and so on. In this way there's no need for a special huddle or call when we want to run a fake. There's simply a script number call for every special-teams play.

The kicking-game script has three columns: the script number, the special-teams unit required, and instructions for that unit. The special-teams captain has the kicking game script on his wristband. The coach signals the script number to the special-teams captain, who checks his wristband and calls the play.

These wristbands can be as simple or complicated as needed. Using them eliminates misunderstanding and miscommunication. Essential ingredients of the play call for offense, defense, and the kicking game are right there in written form.

10

Game Day

During the final 48 hours before the first game, coaches review a number of points with the squad. Many of these points should have been discussed previously, but it is important to emphasize them again.

Important points deal with football issues, relationships, game-day procedures, and other keys to success. For example, advise players to stay away from people and situations that will distract them. They should get to bed early and get plenty of sleep. Remind players they must treat everyone with respect and always portray a positive image for the program.

To prevent any surprises, players should rehearse everything that happens on the field or in the locker room. When the time comes, players must be ready to explode through the locker room door and take the field. Leave nothing to chance. A disciplined, confident team knows exactly what to do and where and when to do it.

On game day, everyone dresses exactly the same, with jerseys tucked in. There should be no tape on game pants. Wristbands are on the wrists only. No player should wear anything that draws attention to him and away from the team.

Football is an emotional game, and those who excel at the game play with emotion, but these emotions must be regulated and under control. Players run on and off the field throughout the game, consistently displaying aggressiveness. They create breaks and opportunities, force turnovers and take advantage of them. Players display consistency and acquire and maintain momentum throughout the game. How players respond to adversity and prosperity during the game is a mark of their maturity.

When each unit (offense, defense, or special teams) comes off the field, they first come to the bench and huddle with the appropriate coach.

Each player understands not to throw a block if the teammate is gone. Each player knows to be on the field when he's supposed to be and is always mentally in the game. There are no wasted time-outs. Time-outs are used for the exchange of information only. They should never need to be used for resting, for getting personnel on the field, or for avoiding a delay-of-game penalty.

The backup quarterback is by the coach's side and records play by play. When the team is on offense, all offensive personnel package players (second and third tight ends; third, fourth, and fifth wide receivers; third running back) stay by the coach's side. When the team is on defense, all defensive personnel package players (fourth interior lineman, third defensive end, third and fourth linebackers, fifth and sixth defensive backs) stay by the coach's side. If a player goes down, the assumed replacement is by the coach's side. A player who is hurt gets off the field. Whether an injured player returns to the game is a decision the trainer and medical staff make, not any coach. If an injury is severe enough to require a stop in play, the player is probably not going back into the game.

Players learn to anticipate the next situation. The appropriate special team gathers on the 50-yard line box next to the special-teams coach prior to third down. The special-teams captains fulfill their duties every time their unit is on the field. Special-teams players know to block only in front and above the waist. On a punt rush or field goal rush, players aim for 2 feet in front of the kicker's foot.

There is no retaliation. Each player's commitment is to his team. A player cannot help his team if the team is penalized and the player thrown out of the game. A player doesn't have to land a punch to get tossed. Merely winding up can lead to a player being removed from a game. Retaliation is not a sign of manliness or courage; restraint is a sign of courage and teamwork.

The captain is the only player who speaks to the officials. A player who feels he's being held should tell the captain, and the captain will speak to the appropriate official. The officials will watch that player the next couple of plays. If the player is not holding, the accusing team loses credibility.

The head coach—not a player or other coach—is the only one who says anything to the officials about penalties. Each player's mission is to concentrate on his job. He must not become distracted.

Discuss postgame procedure. Players shake hands with their opponents and then huddle on the 20-yard line in a semicircle. Players do not remove any equipment or tape until they are in the locker room.

In interviews with the media, players compliment their opponents and teammates. Each player should draw attention away from himself and to the team and program. Nothing said or implied should provide locker room poster material for an opponent.

There are many ways to select team captains. The squad can vote for captains for the season. For the last 15 or 20 years, I have told upperclassmen that I want all of them to be leaders and to lead with their individual personalities. During those seasons, I rotate through the seniors, each senior assuming the captain's game-day responsibilities for a game. However captains are chosen, the head coach reviews the captain's options relative to the coin toss in great detail and then repeats them.

Ever have a player forget to take an article of equipment to an away game? It's distracting and, depending on what has been forgotten, it might mean a starter will wear something that doesn't fit or a different-numbered jersey. Taping an equipment checklist (figure 10.1) inside each player's locker doesn't guarantee that some players won't forget something now and then, but it should reduce the possibility.

Many articles have been written and suggestions made about how to do things on game day to ensure your team is emotionally and mentally ready to perform at its highest level. But no matter how hard you try to control events, some are uncontrollable. Obviously, it's easier to have control when you're playing at home, but even then unexpected incidents can cause disruptions. Maybe the game officials or the visiting team arrive late (or not at all), something delays the pregame meal, or the home crowd is minimal because of weather conditions. When on the road, the bus might arrive late, the bus might break down en route to the game, or a player might forget his equipment.

Equipment Checklist for Away Games

Check off each item as you put it in your equipment bag.

Helmet	_ _ _ _ _	_ _ _ _ _	_ _ _ _ _	_ _ _ _ _	_ _ _ _ _
Jersey	_ _ _ _ _	_ _ _ _ _	_ _ _ _ _	_ _ _ _ _	_ _ _ _ _
Pants	_ _ _ _ _	_ _ _ _ _	_ _ _ _ _	_ _ _ _ _	_ _ _ _ _
Laundry bag	_ _ _ _ _	_ _ _ _ _	_ _ _ _ _	_ _ _ _ _	_ _ _ _ _
Towel	_ _ _ _ _	_ _ _ _ _	_ _ _ _ _	_ _ _ _ _	_ _ _ _ _
Shoulder pads	_ _ _ _ _	_ _ _ _ _	_ _ _ _ _	_ _ _ _ _	_ _ _ _ _
Girdle and pads	_ _ _ _ _	_ _ _ _ _	_ _ _ _ _	_ _ _ _ _	_ _ _ _ _
Forearm pads	_ _ _ _ _	_ _ _ _ _	_ _ _ _ _	_ _ _ _ _	_ _ _ _ _
Hand pads	_ _ _ _ _	_ _ _ _ _	_ _ _ _ _	_ _ _ _ _	_ _ _ _ _
Shoes	_ _ _ _ _	_ _ _ _ _	_ _ _ _ _	_ _ _ _ _	_ _ _ _ _
Knee pads	_ _ _ _ _	_ _ _ _ _	_ _ _ _ _	_ _ _ _ _	_ _ _ _ _
Thigh pads	_ _ _ _ _	_ _ _ _ _	_ _ _ _ _	_ _ _ _ _	_ _ _ _ _
Mouth guard	_ _ _ _ _	_ _ _ _ _	_ _ _ _ _	_ _ _ _ _	_ _ _ _ _
Rib pads	_ _ _ _ _	_ _ _ _ _	_ _ _ _ _	_ _ _ _ _	_ _ _ _ _
Glasses	_ _ _ _ _	_ _ _ _ _	_ _ _ _ _	_ _ _ _ _	_ _ _ _ _
Wristband and script	_ _ _ _ _	_ _ _ _ _	_ _ _ _ _	_ _ _ _ _	_ _ _ _ _
_____	_ _ _ _ _	_ _ _ _ _	_ _ _ _ _	_ _ _ _ _	_ _ _ _ _
_____	_ _ _ _ _	_ _ _ _ _	_ _ _ _ _	_ _ _ _ _	_ _ _ _ _

Examine these items two days before every game.

Helmet
- Chin strap
- Face bar bolts

Shoes
- Shoestrings
- Cleats

Examine all straps and laces on all pads.

Figure 10.1 Equipment checklist for away games.

Players can easily read their coach's face and tell when he's mad or frustrated. If you're the coach, never show the effects that uncontrollable situations are having on you, even if you're burning up inside. If something is bothering you, it will bother your players, and that's the last thing you want to have happen as you approach kickoff. Control what you can control, and don't worry about what you can't. Concentrate on keeping your players razor sharp and ready to compete at their highest level. To keep them loose, you might sometimes need to interject some humor into a situation that really isn't funny. Uncontrollable disruptions might require coaches to be psychologists. As much as possible, keep all things the same, whether you're playing at home or on the road. The taping schedule can be adjusted on the road if the travel squad is smaller than the home squad. If game time on the road is different from at home—different time zone, late afternoon or night game—then the entire schedule (figure 10.2) will change. Make sure all players and coaches are familiar with everything that's going to happen on game day and that they know where to be and when. Rehearse every detail.

Figure 10.3 shows the areas on the field for pregame specialty. In pregame specialty, quarterbacks take the center snap, both regular and shotgun, and take their three- and five-step drops as they throw to receivers running each of the normal routes. Running backs also run routes with either a quarterback or coach throwing passes to them. At the same time, centers snap to punters as punt receivers catch and return those kicks. Kickers practice kickoffs, and receivers return those kicks. Kickers practice regular, onside, and pooch kicks. Punters perform regular punts for distance, pooch punts, directional punts, and rugby punts. Centers snap to holders for extra points and field goals. The extra point and field goal kickers should be on the field before the opponent so they can kick on the end of the field the opponents will have for their warm-up,

thus kicking both with and against the wind.

Devote 15 minutes to pregame warm-up and then 15 minutes in the locker room. This does not include the time for stretching. Specialty personnel stretch for 15 minutes before taking the field, and the remainder of the squad stretches while specialty is executing their skill.

Game-day schedule for a 1:30 game

9:30	Pregame meal
10:15	Pro highlight film
11:10	Group I tape (specialty) (11:40 on road)
11:30	Group II tape (nonspecialty starters) (11:55 on road)
11:50	Group III tape (nonstarters) (12:10 on road)
12:00	Quarterback, centers, and receivers warm-up
12:15	Specialty stretch
12:35	Specialty, nonspecialty stretch
12:55	Pregame warm-up
1:10	Locker room
1:25	Return to field
1:30	Kickoff

Game-day schedule for a 7:30 game

3:30	Pregame meal
4:15	Pro highlight film
5:10	Group I tape (specialty) (5:40 on road)
5:30	Group II tape (nonspecialty starters) (5:55 on road)
5:50	Group III tape (nonstarters) (6:10 on road)
6:00	Quarterbacks, centers, and receivers warm-up
6:15	Specialty stretch
6:35	Specialty, nonspecialty stretch
6:55	Pregame warm-up
7:10	Locker room
7:25	Return to field
7:30	Kickoff

Figure 10.2 Sample game-day schedules.

Players do all their normal stretching exercises in unison, with a coach conducting that exercise. Conclude the stretching with some running drills so players break a good sweat and get totally loose.

Team warm-up begins with the squad in lines, 5 yards apart, doing jumping jacks as they chant the spelling of the team mascot. That's how we do it. This takes only a minute or two. Afterward, break into position drills for four minutes, followed by three minutes in group drills, and five minutes of team work.

Each position coach has his players execute two individual drills:

Offensive lineman

1. Run block with perfect stance and explosion into a simulated defensive lineman catching his block.
2. Pocket pass protection steps and jam.

Receiver

1. Stalk and block. One-on-one block versus the defender. Break down, hands on breast plate, and move with him as he moves toward the ball carrier.
2. Tap-tap drill. Receiver must get one foot down in bounds after the catch.

Running back

1. Form the pocket and receive the handoff from the coach or quarterback.
2. Over-the-head drill. The coach or quarterback lofts the ball over the running back's head as he runs downfield. The running back finds the ball, adjusts to it, and brings it in.

Defensive lineman

1. Explosion drill with perfect stance and explosion into a simulated offensive lineman.
2. Loop and slant drill. Align head-up on a simulated offensive lineman. Loop outside into the adjacent hole or slant inside through the adjacent hole.

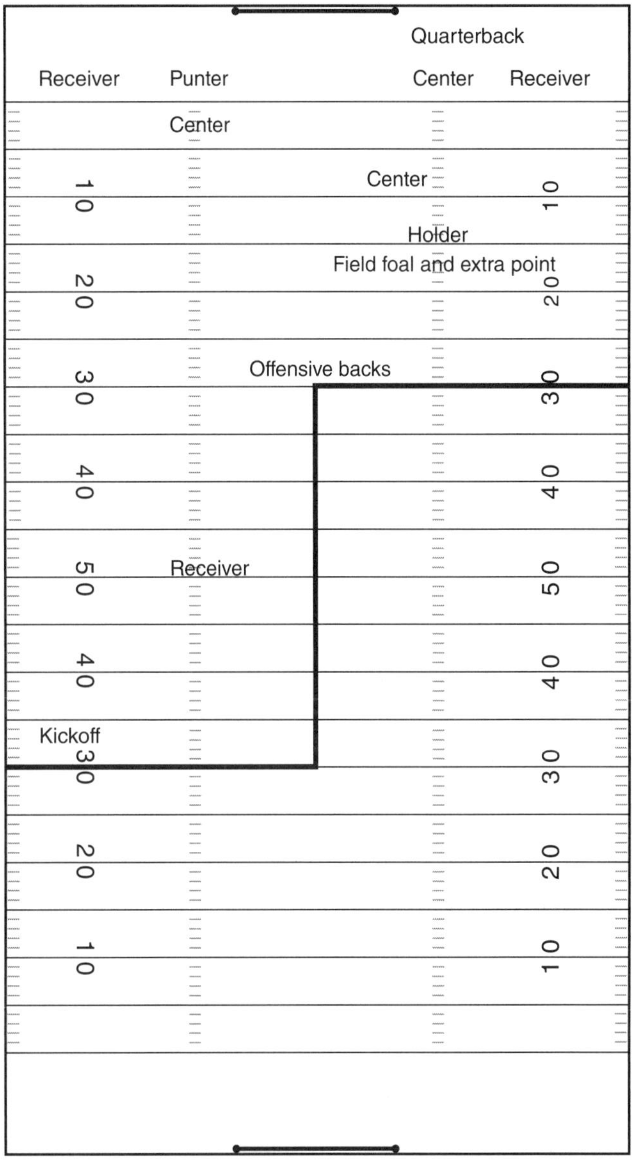

Figure 10.3 Pregame specialty.

Inside linebacker

1. Form tackle drill. Using proper body alignment and technique, walk into the tackle with head on the ball and arms wrapped around the ballcarrier.
2. Interception drill with player coming toward the coach, who is throwing the pass. Catch the ball at the highest possible point

Outside linebacker

1. Perfect tackle drill. Similar to the form tackle drill, except approach the ballcarrier from the side and drive your head across the front of his body.

2. Interception drill with player sprinting toward the sideline.

Secondary

1. Open-the-hips drill. A player sprints backward. On signal, he opens his hips and makes a 45-degree turn as he continues moving straight back with his eyes on the coach. He makes several turns back and forth. End the drill with the coach throwing the ball and the player making the interception. This drill may also be run using a receiver who makes several cuts with the defender opening the hips and maintaining proper position relative to the receiver.

2. Pass drop, then leverage tackling drill into sideline.

Group work drills follow:

- Offensive line: at full speed, execute run and pass blocking adjustments versus anticipated defensive fronts.
- Backs: review all running plays.
- Receivers: review all pass plays.
- Defensive line: review alignments, stems, and stunts versus anticipated formations.
- Linebackers: review alignments, stunts, and coverages versus anticipated formations, shifts, and motion.
- Secondary: review alignments, stunts, and coverages versus anticipated formations, shifts, and motion.
- Team drills: at full speed, offense versus scout team defense, then defense versus scout team offense.

In the final 15 minutes in the locker room, players meet with their position coaches to review every detail. Coaches answer any questions players have and emphasize the things that were practiced all week. Now is the time to put those adjustments to work. Review all special-teams assignments and personnel for each team, including key backups. Stress that personnel for each special team must always be mentally in the game, anticipating the next play and determining whether the next play might involve a special team of which they are a part.

For the last 5 minutes, the head coach addresses the squad. Now he must be a psychologist, knowing the mental and emotional state of the players and determining what words the squad needs to hear. Leave time for traditional rituals done before every game. Stay on schedule so you don't have to hurry to get to the field on time. Meet with captains and review their options relative to the coin toss. State your instructions in great detail, and have players repeat the instructions back to you. Never assume that because something sounds like a formality to you, it's received in the same way by a player.

After the coin toss, again address the assignments and personnel for the game-opening kicking or receiving unit. Remind the quarterback and the defensive captain to face you when discussing a penalty with the referee. They must make sure that you're fully aware of the options. Signal your decision to them before the referee is told whether your team accepts or declines the penalty.

If you're the head coach, there's no substitute for remaining positive and displaying poise throughout the game. Players will react as they see their leader react. If you show confidence and belief in them, they'll play with confidence and poise. If they see you out of control and unable to handle adversity, they'll react similarly. Stay in touch with your coaches and let them know what offensive play, or defensive alignment, stunt, and coverage is being employed. By being aware of the plan, they'll have their eyes focused on the appropriate location to give the other coaches on the sideline the best advice possible.

Time-outs are best used when there's a swing in momentum, a need to exchange essential information to the unit on the field, or a two-minute drill. Time-outs should not be used to give players a rest or to avoid a penalty because the play clock has been allowed to wind down.

When an injury occurs, the presumed replacement for the injured player must be by the coach's side, ready to enter the game. This is the backup's responsibility.

The head coach sets the tone and schedule at halftime (figure 10.4). The tone must be set immediately and followed by the entire coaching staff. Halftime is for sharing information, not for displaying negative emotion. Use the dry-erase board to show what the opponent did to cause problems in the first half. If the team dominated the opponent in the first half, caution them that to have success they must continue to play with fierce determination for the remainder of the game.

With rare exceptions, the limited time you have at halftime must be for constructive review of the first half (what worked well and what didn't), followed by what adjustments must be made to be more effective in the second half. Let players know why these adjustments will be successful. Again the dry-erase board is helpful for illustrating the second-half adjustments and why these changes will bring success. The changes must be minimal, not wholesale. Too many changes will leave the squad doubtful of the system they have been practicing and skeptical of trying to do things they have not practiced. Remind them which things they have practiced but have purposely held out and not yet shown that will be used in the second half. Reinforce that you have total confidence in the squad's ability to be successful in the second half. Maintain eye contact with players as you address them. Remember that they can see in your eyes whether you believe unconditionally in their ability to succeed. Stay on schedule; get them back on the field in time to stretch fully, drill with their groups, and drill as a team.

Halftime Schedule

20:00 to 18:00	Set tempo in locker room.
18:00 to 15:00	Coaches meetings; squad may take off shoulder pads; squad sits in position groups; drink for squad.
15:00 to 7:00	Coaches talk with players to recap first half, correct mistakes, explain second-half adjustments, explain second-half game plan; players put on shoulder pads.
7:00 to 6:00	Head coach's final statements to squad.
6:00 to 5:00	Players return to field.
5:00 to 3:00	Stretch.
3:00 to 1:30	Individual groups.
1:30 to 0:30	Team.
0:30 to 0:00	Family together.

Figure 10.4 Halftime schedule.

After the game, regardless of the outcome, go through the traditional handshakes with the opponents and then gather in a semicircle. Look everyone in the eye and say a few words about the game. If things didn't go well, lift players back up with words of encouragement. If things did go well, bring them back to reality with reminders of things they need to work on. But don't go into depth at this point. Keep your comments very general. You can go into specifics later during video review.

I again want to emphasize that whether it's during the game, after the game, during practice, or at any other time, there is no good time for sarcasm or cynicism, no matter what has happened. A positive attitude is much more powerful, not only in football, but in life. Sometimes I may get upset or angry if mistakes have been made or if I see a lack of effort on a play, but I leave each player with a positive statement and remove any doubt about my belief in him and my belief in the team and what we're capable of accomplishing.

Remind players of the schedule for the next few days, including the training room hours over the weekend. Sunday afternoon and evening are important times for coaches, but, other than keeping training room appointments to treat injuries, players are off for the day. Remind them to represent their teammates and the program in a positive way in every decision they make. Make sure your final words are positive about where the team is, where you are headed, and what you have to do to get there. Close the huddle by bringing every member of the football family, including cheerleaders, student trainers, and managers, close together. Players raise their helmets as one and sing the fight song after every win and, regardless of the outcome, chant in unison. Players do not start tearing off tape or removing any of their uniform until all this is completed. Then they are free to visit with friends and family.

About the Author

Bill Ramseyer's coaching experience spans both the high school and college ranks. He began his coaching career with 8 years at the high school level, which included guiding Firelands High School in Ohio—a school that had not had a single winning season until Ramseyer's arrival—to a 24-2 record during his tenure.

Bill then turned to the college level, where he was an assistant coach and head scout for the University of Missouri for the 1969 Big 8 Championship team. From there he moved on to coach the Wilmington College squad, which had accumulated only 28 wins over the previous 15 years. Bill amassed a record of 114-58-4 during his tenure, which included qualifying for the national championship game in 1980. He also earned 5 conference or district coach of the year honors while at Wilmington. Ramseyer completed his career as the first-ever coach at the University of Virginia's College at Wise, which included back-to-back 10-win seasons in 1995 and 1996, the first program ever to accomplish this feat in its first 6 years of existence.

Bill holds a PhD from the University of Missouri and has been inducted into seven halls of fame.